THE RISE OF
AMERICA

REMAKING THE WORLD ORDER

MARIN KATUSA

THE RISE OF AMERICA

Remaking the World Order

ISBN   978-1-5445-2144-2 *Hardcover*
      978-1-5445-2143-5 *Paperback*
      978-1-5445-2142-8 *Ebook*

To Maia, Sofia, and Leo, you are unique, precious, and much loved. Never forget who you are on this amazing journey of life.

And for my wife, Marina, who makes everything possible.

CONNECT WITH MARIN

THE RISE OF AMERICA WILL BE A POLITICAL AND INVEST-ment framework that will be with us for many years. Adjuncts and updates to the book will be provided at www.katusaresearch.com for all readers of this book at no cost.

Scan this QR code for an
exclusive offer from Marin Katusa.

CONTENTS

ACKNOWLEDGMENTS 11

FOREWORD 13

INTRODUCTION 21

1. THE NEW NORMAL 25

2. UNDERSTANDING THE US DOLLAR 57

3. A BRAVE NEW MONETARY WORLD 99

4. A SHORT HISTORY OF MONEY 157

5. WHY GOLD MATTERS 177

6. ENERGY TO FUEL THE RISE OF AMERICA........................... 195

7. CRITICAL METALS FOR THE RISE OF AMERICA.................... 227

8. THE RISE OF AMERICA WILL RAISE THE REST OF THE WORLD .. 241

APPENDIX I 271

APPENDIX II 323

APPENDIX III 329

APPENDIX IV 347

APPENDIX V 407

ACKNOWLEDGMENTS

I HAVE BEEN FORTUNATE TO HAVE BEEN SURROUNDED BY incredible people in my career and personal life. This book is not just my own thoughts backed by strong analytical data points, but an accumulation of thoughts from my network of friends within the industry who have challenged and pushed me to question all my convictions.

I want to thank Robert Quartermain, Worth Wray, and Brent Johnson, who spent an incredible amount of time going through my draft and questioning and challenging my thesis. Thank you; this book is better for it.

Marina, my wife, who is brilliant professionally and is an incredible life partner who supports my chaotic work schedule and all my financial ventures. I could not ask for a more loving and loyal wife.

Marin Svorinic, Rob Fuhrman, Doug Hornig, Mike Chang, Steen Rasmussen, Simon Hua, Maria Zurbito, Jim O'Rourke, Roman Shklanka, and the rest of the Katusa Research team that works incredibly hard to facilitate the platform for me to do what I do; I cannot thank you enough.

To all my subscribers, this book is for you. My goal with this book is to put together the geopolitical and economic headwinds we will all face to best position our portfolios.

Marin Katusa, January 21, 2021.
Vancouver, Canada.

FOREWORD

BY ROBERT KIYOSAKI

MARIN KATUSA AND I GREW UP IN THE SAME TOWN... thirty years apart.

The town we grew up in is in Canada—Vancouver, British Columbia—and is one of the world's most beautiful cities. Marin is Canadian, the son of Croatian immigrants. His phenomenal success and reputation in the world's financial markets reflect his humble roots and work ethic.

I am a fourth-generation Japanese American, born in Honolulu, Hawaii. I am best known for my book *Rich Dad Poor Dad*, published in 1997. In 2020, *Rich Dad Poor Dad*'s sales went through the roof when the world economy shut down. And that begs the question...why?

If you have not read *Rich Dad Poor Dad,* it is a book on financial education. My poor dad, who studied at Stanford University, University of Chicago, and Northwestern University, had a PhD in Education. In the 1960s, when I was in high school, my poor dad was the superintendent of education for Hawaii. In other words, he was much like Marin Katusa, a math and academic genius.

I was not. I flunked out of high school twice because I could not read, write, or spell. Ironically, I am best known today as a writer.

In my defense, it was not that I could not read. I simply did not like what I was required to read. It was true; I could not spell. I even tried this line on my teachers: "It is a creative person who can spell a word many different ways." Not surprisingly, that excuse did not work. Today I'm thankful for spell-check on my computer. I should point out that it was not that I could not write; my teachers just did not like what I was writing. In my essays, I kept writing, saying, and asking the same things: "Why am I in school?" "When can I study what I want to learn?" "I want to be rich." I wanted to know, "When will we learn about money?"

I wanted to learn about money and business because I wanted to be an entrepreneur. I did not want to be an employee like my poor dad. At the age of nine, my poor dad, an excellent teacher, suggested I study with my rich "dad," my best friend's father. That is when the story of *Rich Dad Poor Dad* began.

Rich dad did not graduate from school. At the age of thirteen, his father died, so he took over the family business. He ultimately became an extremely wealthy man. If you look at the Hyatt Regency Hotel on Waikiki Beach, rich dad owned the land on which the Hyatt Regency Hotel on Waikiki Beach sits, as well as hotels on four of the outer islands of Hawaii.

After school, rich dad was my teacher. His son and I would go to his place of business and work for about an hour, for free. He refused to pay us, saying, "If I pay you, I will train you to think like an employee. Entrepreneurs work for free."

After an hour of working for free, rich dad brought out his Monopoly game, and, as agreed, our financial education began.

I am a rich man today, not from my poor dad's academic education, but my rich dad's business and financial education.

Both my dads were geniuses. Simply put, my poor dad was a genius in academics and my rich dad a genius in business. I was fortunate to have them both as teachers.

And although my grades were horrible, I received congressional nominations to the US Naval Academy at Annapolis, Maryland, and the US Merchant Marine Academy at Kings Point, New York. Both are extremely tough schools to get into, and it is even tougher to graduate from them.

I chose Kings Point because I wanted to sail the seven seas—not on a Navy ship but on board a merchant ship—since I was eleven years old. As a young boy, I read books about great explorers like Columbus, Cook, Magellan, Pizarro, Cortez, and da Gama. I saw *Mutiny on the Bounty* starring Marlon Brando, who sailed to Tahiti and was greeted by beautiful Tahitian maidens. I couldn't get enough.

When I was fourteen years old, rather than carve salad bowls for my mom in woodshop as other boys did, I built an eight-foot El Toro-class sailboat. Woodshop was the only A I ever received in school.

I also chose the Merchant Marine Academy because Kings Pointers were the world's highest-paid graduates. In 1969, the year I graduated, my classmates were earning up to $120,000 a year. Not bad for a twenty-one-year-old in 1969.

Unfortunately, the Vietnam War was still raging in 1969. Rather than sail for the Merchant Marines and make a lot of money, I chose to join the US Marine Corps. I was selected for pilot training and went to Navy flight school in Pensacola, Florida. In 1972, I was flying helicopter gunships in Vietnam.

In 1994, I retired at forty-seven, having never had a job or pension. I retired because I began playing Monopoly in real life.

In 1997, I wrote *Rich Dad Poor Dad*.

In 2000, Oprah Winfrey invited me to be a guest on her show and tell the story of my rich dad and poor dad. The book went international in the blink of an eye.

In 2006, Donald Trump and I published the first of two books together. We were planning to write a third book in 2015, but, as you know, he applied for another job.

In 2020, I met Marin Katusa, not in person yet, but via his reputation. Marin is known for restructuring an existing hedge fund, turning it into one of the most successful funds in the sector and raising over $2 billion in financing for some of the largest mining companies in Canada.

As I learned more about Marin, I was not at all surprised to find that some of the wealthiest and most powerful players in the resource sector have been personally advised by Marin on complex technical matters, often in their own fields.

I then checked Marin out—watching him first on YouTube. Then I interviewed him for *The Rich Dad Radio Show*, a financial education podcast.

When I found out Marin was a former calculus teacher, the pieces of the puzzle began fitting together. I realized Marin has a combination of the genius of my poor dad and the genius of my rich dad.

I say Marin and I grew up in Vancouver thirty years apart because I was bitten by the gold bug in 1972 while flying for the Marines in Vietnam.

As you probably know, President Richard Nixon took the US

dollar off the gold standard on August 15, 1971. The price of gold began climbing from $35 an ounce to approximately $50 an ounce in 1972. Since it had been illegal for Americans to own gold since 1933, most Americans did not know much about gold.

In 1972, the NVA, the North Vietnamese Army, was rolling south. America was losing the war, just as the gold bug bit me. Looking at a map of South Vietnam, my copilot and I found a symbol for a gold mine. The problem was the mine was now behind enemy lines. Despite that fact, my copilot and I formed a business partnership and flew behind enemy lines looking for gold.

The Vietnamese gold dealer we found—a tiny woman—refused to sell us gold at a discount. My copilot and I failed to make a deal that day, and my first gold-mining venture failed.

Thank God we only failed to buy gold that day. We were lucky not to have been killed or captured and were able to return to our carrier alive.

As I've said, I was bitten by the gold bug—and gold mining. That is why I was in Vancouver, British Columbia, in the 1990s, putting gold- and silver-mining deals together.

In Vancouver, I met more cowboys, conmen, BS artists, and promoters—as well as a few real gold miners with real gold mines. I loved it. It was exciting. It was a real-life financial education. Doing my best to put mining deals together with this cast of characters was an education that was impossible to get in a classroom, study in a book, or learn from a teacher like my poor dad.

On March 4, 2004, my partners and I took a gold mine public on the Toronto Stock Exchange. I was in heaven. It was like receiving a PhD in entrepreneurial business and finance. Little did I know at the time that my real education had just begun.

The problem was that the gold mine was in China, not Canada.

After raising $27 million via an IPO, the Chinese government took the mine. Some tried to warn us that the Chinese steal IP, intellectual property. We learned that they also steal physical property. I now had a PhD in international business.

You cannot receive that kind of high-level, high-quality, real-life education from college professors or in graduate school. Real life can be the hardest, harshest, yet best teacher if you survive.

After my Vietnam experience in 1972 and witnessing the price of gold rise from $35 to over $800 an ounce on January 14, 1980, then watching it crash, I knew gold was about to become the hot new investment.

In 2000, the price of gold was depressed. In 2000, my partners and I believed gold was about to become the world's best investment opportunity.

In 2004 we launched our gold-mining IPO.

In 2007, the Chinese government granted me a PhD in real-life international business.

Financial guru Jim Rickards, author of *Currency Wars* and *The Road to Ruin*, expects gold to hit $15,000 an ounce by 2025.

What is the next biggest investment in the world? Marin has a better investment than gold.

The next best investment is the socialists' Green New Deal. It is both funny and ironic that socialists will gain popularity pushing the environmental agenda while *"Capitalists will save the environment...and get very rich."*

In 2021, Marin is in an enviable position. He is the right person, in the right place, at the right time. His years of experience, first as a calculus teacher and then a leader in the world of resource hedge funds, give him an edge, give him insights into the next new Boom: an investment much bigger than gold.

The Rise of America is about just that. As you turn the pages of this book, you will enter a world only a person with Marin Katusa's genius, vision, and years of real-world experience can see.

If you want to be early, to be a part of the world's biggest investment opportunity—an opportunity bigger than gold, bigger than oil, and bigger than technology—read this book.

You will see the world the way socialists see the world—and the future.

The problem is that socialists won't get rich because socialists do not know how to make money.

Marin's book is about an opportunity for:

"Capitalists to save the environment...and get very rich."

INTRODUCTION

THESE DAYS, THERE IS NO ESCAPING THE NEW DOOM-AND-gloom sentiment in America. From the mainstream media to the most partisan of internet blogs, the message is the same. And it's everywhere:

- The sun is setting on the great American experiment.
- The US economy is in a state of terminal decline.
- The dollar will soon become as disposable as toilet paper.
- If the twentieth century was America's, the twenty-first would be China's.
- Blah, blah, blah.

To all of which I say: not so fast.

The reality is quite the opposite.

To be sure, *disruption* is the watchword of the day. Turmoil engulfs us—political, economic, social—and a worldwide, virus-induced recession only highlights it. There will be major economic dislocations, changes in the patterns of international trade, new political alignments and tensions, deep social adjustments, and a reshuffling of the global monetary system.

But the big winner is going to be America.

I know you don't believe me. And I don't blame you. The opposite view bombards you with the idea that the US is fading as a world power. Day in, day out, with no end in sight. No surprise, because that's what it looks like to the naked eye: the American economy is in tatters, propped up only by stimulus money from Washington; unemployment is at levels not seen since the Great Depression; proponents of differing political points of view can no longer talk to one another; government is floundering; the Federal Reserve is "printing" too much money, and the dollar is falling in value; racial tensions that have been simmering for decades are boiling over; and internationally, China is eating our lunch.

And so on. You know the drill.

It doesn't matter what TV channel you watch or whose blog you read. The only difference is whom the messenger chooses to blame for the received belief that everything is going to hell.

You're probably wondering how I can confidently predict the Rise of America amidst all this negativity. It's simple. I don't listen to it. It's just a boiling cauldron of opinion, signifying nothing.

Instead, I look carefully at what's happening in the world. I have to. I'm an investor. As one of the largest independent financiers in the natural resource sector globally, my personal money is at stake along with the assets of those who invest along with me.

Unlike most commentators who freely offer their unsolicited opinions, I have skin in the game.

I can't afford to be wrong.

Thus, I look at the world the same way I plan my investments—according to what's out there, not what I agree with or not what I would *like* to be out there. What *is*.

I pay no attention to pontifications such as "We've never been here before," or "The country has never been so divided." Nonsense. America, as a nation, has been down this road before. America has suffered much, much worse.

How have people forgotten that the US once had a civil war that nearly tore the country in two? That the early twentieth century featured labor/management strife so bad that blood ran rivers in the streets? That a ten-year depression caused near-intolerable stress that often exploded into violence? That the civil rights and anti-war movements of the 1960s generated reactions that ranged from attack dogs to police riots?

It doesn't take an Einstein-level intellect to realize that there has never been much of a period in the US when different groups of people *weren't* at one another's throats.

Even COVID-19 is nothing new. The Spanish flu pandemic of 1918–19 sprang from a virus that was both more easily transmitted and far more lethal than COVID-19. It is estimated to have infected 500 million people, almost one-third of the world's population at the time. The global death toll was at least 50 million. About 675,000 Americans died. (If COVID-19 achieves the same mortality rate as the 1918 Spanish flu, well over 2 million will have to die in the US alone to be comparable on a population-percentage basis.)

The point is that bad stuff happens, and when it does, the United States of America gets through it. Americans are an amazingly resilient lot and are especially at their best when their backs are to the wall. At the time the country entered World War II, it was woefully unprepared. Yet, in an astonishing turnaround, within four years, it had fashioned the most powerful military in the history of the planet and is the main reason German is not now the spoken language in London nor Japanese in San Francisco.

In fact, the US military is still present in over 600 bases in over seventy nations as of late 2020. Do not forget the United States' geography provides an advantage over every other nation in the world. A friendly neighbor in the north (Canada), oceans on its boundaries, and the Rocky Mountains and Mississippi River locations provide the US a geographical barrier from invasion that no other nation on the planet has. The United States has an incredible mineral endowment for the elements required in the twenty-first century. Not only does the United States have incredible hydrocarbon reserves (both onshore and off), but it has the unique position to be a global leader in wind, solar, hydro (including geothermal), and nuclear energy.

The United States is in another rough patch, no question—economically, politically, socially, you name it.

But America is ***made*** for this. The nation will come out the other side, stronger than ever. Count on it. Recovery won't happen overnight, but of one thing I am certain: deep within the soil of the current discontent, the seeds of a brighter future have been planted and are sprouting the Rise of America.

In this book, I will show you why you should ignore the naysayers, as I do. The world is changing, by forces that you are probably unaware of at the moment. But you won't be in the dark for long. You will very shortly become aware of the planetary makeover that is underway right now.

You will be a part of it and will benefit from it financially and socially.

Because the Rise of America is at stage center.

CHAPTER ONE

THE NEW NORMAL

THE NEW NORMAL IS NOT "NORMAL," NOT BY ANY DEFI-
nition you can think of. And I'm not talking about the dislocations
caused by COVID-19. Those have been painful, but they are not
permanent. Though it'll take time, the dark days wrought by the
virus will pass. The economy will recover.

No, I'm talking about more basic changes that will be enduring. Economics, politics, debt, credit, even money itself—all are
being redefined. Radically. Yet much of what is happening is
entirely out of the public view.

More than that, the voices of discord are so loud that they are
drowning out the voices of reason.

In titling this book *The Rise of America*, I realize that I may
well become an object of scorn. A lot of people don't believe that
things are going to get better. Many probably don't even *want*
things to get better if that doesn't fit their agenda.

Ignore them. They're wrong.

The Rise of America will happen. In fact, it has already begun,
right in the faces of those who'd rather it didn't.

Much of what you will read in the following pages will be news to you. But I want to emphasize that this is not because I have access to documents that bear the government's TOP SECRET stamp. There is not some evil conspiracy dedicated to keeping you out of the loop. There's nothing here that isn't publicly available. It's all sitting there in plain sight.

The reason much of it will come as a surprise is that we depend on the mainstream media or the internet—or both—to keep us informed about the world, and those outlets have fallen down on the job. Making sense of the larger issues of the day is hard work. You first have to dig out the relevant information and then you have to connect some dots.

Few people these days—politicians, journalists, economists, whatever—are inclined to put in the time. And in my experience, fewer still manage to connect the dots in the proper sequence. So, while there are certainly those who wish to mislead us deliberately, there are many, many more who do not themselves understand what's going on.

Small wonder that so many citizens are angry, alienated, or merely confused.

I want to show you how and why the Rise of America will proceed, regardless of the naysayers' nonsense that often seems like the only thing we hear.

That's what this book covers.

To begin: historically, under capitalism, businesses and individuals who need capital are prepared to offer a reasonable return rate to individuals or institutions who have capital to lend. Sometimes one or the other party gets the upper hand—but the free market tends to sort things out.

That system hardly exists anymore.

Like it or not, governments now play a major role in determining who has access to and who can use capital. In a sense, they have positioned themselves in the center of the capital allocation chessboard. Let's take a closer look.

A nation must have a workable monetary system to remain stable.

Note that I didn't say a *sound* monetary system. There are plenty of very smart people who will argue that we haven't had a sound monetary system since Nixon took us off the gold standard in 1971. I'm not going to argue with them. As I said, it's immaterial what I (or anyone else, for that matter) think *should* be. We have what *is*. That's our reality. I neither deny it nor pray for something better. Remember my first principle: **I am an investor by trade, and I always play the hand I'm dealt, not the one I wish I had.**

> Though I come at this book's themes from an investor's perspective, it is not an investment guide. But for those interested, I lay out my personal investment framework and specific strategies in Appendix IV.

THE FED DEALS, WE PLAY OUR CARDS

Right now, the Federal Reserve of the United States is doing the monetary dealing. And that will be the case for the foreseeable future. It makes no difference if Fed policy is *sound* or *unsound*. Only the long run will tell us that. But at least for the moment, it appears workable (despite all the voices of objection). We play these cards because there is no alternate universe in which we get different ones.

I don't want to get too far ahead of myself at this point, but it does behoove us to take a thumbnail look at some of the ways the Fed's new normal is affecting—and will affect—our lives.

The global economy is addicted to fiscal stimulus and low

interest rates. I will explain Modern Monetary Theory (MMT) in detail in Chapter 3, but first, I want to discuss the Federal Reserve framework under Jerome Powell and Janet Yellen, President Biden's pick for US Treasury Secretary. The plan will be a "looser" version of fiscal-monetary coordination, much like what occurred from 1942 to 1951 but not MMT quite yet.

A REPLAY OF 1942–1951 FEDERAL RESERVE FRAMEWORK?

As I will cover in detail later in the book, many writings exist about the Federal Reserve during the timeframe between 1906 and the end of FDR's New Deal in 1939. However, very little exists about the critical 1939–1951 timeframe that laid the groundwork for a long-term debt cycle that funded the build-out of America's vast western infrastructure expansion after WWII. Also, something few talk about today is that the Federal Reserve was successful in the 1940s with its yield curve control, which is a very important aspect of its framework. America would not have undergone the incredible expansion to the western frontier of the United States—building the largest dams for energy utilities, steel mills, and other manufacturing facilities to establish a wider supply chain—without the collaborative work between Congress and the Federal Reserve. This period was the first in America's history when there was extended fiscal and monetary coordination between the Federal Reserve and Congress. This period was the first of fiscal-monetary coordination.

Let us jump to the present: In 2021 infrastructure in the United States needs a major upgrade. Infrastructure doesn't refer to just roads, bridges, and schools. It refers to manufacturing an electrical grid to supply chains to technology training. And if the United States isn't able to upgrade its workforce, workplace, and infrastructure, it will find itself in much the same place England found itself in post-WWI. England did not invest in keeping up with Germany's growth and, as a result, ended up trading its vast global empire for survival after WWII. But America's equivalent to Germany is China, with assistance from Russia, and we have time to prevent suffering the same fate as England.

China is investing heavily in its infrastructure, technology, and weapons. Will America invest in its future? It has no choice but to do so, and I will explain why and how investors can benefit from such a move.

A major clue was what happened on Thursday, August 27, 2020. On that day, Jerome Powell—chair of the Open Market Committee—outlined the new playbook for the US Federal Reserve, setting policy for many years into the future.

He did this at the end of summer to give the markets—regardless of which party won the election—a framework for stimulating a sluggish economy moving forward. The guidelines are essentially an official US modern version of fiscal-monetary coordination. Many are saying the Federal Reserve will fail at yield curve control. That may happen, but as I mentioned before, it succeeded in the 1940s and nothing new is being applied on that front this time around.

That said, many argue that it was the confirmation of Modern Monetary Theory, the current successor to the Keynesianism that preceded it. If this is the case, this is a revolutionary change, and I do mean *revolutionary*. All investors need to understand what MMT is, what it portends, and how fiscal-monetary coordination and Modern Monetary Theory are integral to the Rise of America. That is not a simple subject. For me to fully explain, it will require a chapter unto itself. See Chapter 3. Suppose Congress fails to coordinate with the US Federal Reserve in making the long-term investments now needed to compete with China. In that case, FMC will fail, and MMT will be the framework that will be relied upon to move forward.

MMT is a modern take on FMC except for one significant difference. With FMC, deficits, and national debt matter, and within the theory of MMT, deficits and national debt don't matter.

For now, suffice it to say that the Fed's focus is two-fold:

· Create inflation and prevent deflation from ever taking hold.
· Do whatever it takes to create maximum employment.

Powell admits that while the US is in recession, it is teetering on the edge of something worse, a deflationary depression.

Now, many of you will remember the 1970s, when the country experienced double-digit inflation. The fear was that it would continue at a high level or even get worse. Inflation erodes the purchasing power of a currency and is disastrous for workers whose wages aren't keeping pace with prices. The country needed help, and Paul Volcker turned out to be the man to do it.

Volcker, appointed to chair the Federal Reserve, was the last inflation fighter to hold the position. He raised interest rates to nosebleed levels, decreased the money supply, and put the brakes on the flow of capital. With thirty-year mortgages pushing past 16 percent interest rates, it was full-bore shock therapy—extremely painful, but it worked. Slowly, inflation subsided, and the economy found a productive equilibrium.

(It is worth reminding ourselves that there are always good investment opportunities, no matter what the economy is doing. Those who took advantage of late-'70s CDs paying 18 percent in interest were very happy campers.)

You who remember those gloomy years might think that the

specter of excessive or even hyperinflation would always be the paramount worry on the Fed's collective mind. But you would be wrong.

Since Volcker, every chair—Greenspan, Bernanke, Yellen, and Powell—has presided over a 180-degree turn. The Fed no longer acts as an inflation foe. On the contrary, it actively *promotes* inflation, albeit at a level that it determines is both controllable and "benign," defined as a net positive for economic growth. The Federal Reserve considers 2 percent inflation to be the magic number. In a later chapter, I will explain why 2 percent inflation is the target by the Federal Reserve. Its primary role now is as a deflation preventer, and its primary message is to say "never again" to the 1930s. Or, as Jerome Powell might put it, "Not on *my* watch."

Deflation is deemed the planet's nastiest *bête noire*. Yet, with a mighty shove from the pandemic lockdown, that's where the economy is headed.

To counter the deflation and attempt to foster inflation, the Fed will use the two primary tools in its box.

First, Powell has signaled the Fed's willingness to keep interest rates near zero for the foreseeable future—even for five years. He stated that the Fed will also tolerate the economy running above the 2 percent inflation rate that is its long-term target—at least for some time *if* inflation can rise that much. Using the Fed's metric of inflation, we are not there yet.

How did the 2 percent inflation rate become the target for all central bankers?

The first central bank to publicly announce an inflation target was the Reserve Bank of New Zealand in 1989. The Reserve Bank of New Zealand was dealing with 7.6 percent inflation when Don Brash, the head of the central bank, announced a 2 percent inflation target. Two years later, New Zealand succeeded, and the inflation rate was 2 percent. Central bank after central bank around the world adopted the 2 percent inflation target.

So why was it 2 percent?

Believe it or not, there was no serious math or economics behind the decision. The powers to be debated between 0 percent and 2 percent targets and decided 2 percent could be achievable.

However, I have a different take. Between 1834 and 1971 (when the gold standard began and ended), the average annual growth rate of gold production was 2 percent. Coincidence? I think not.

Powell gave no indication how far beyond 2 percent inflation the Fed would tolerate, nor for how long. But they'll do what they feel they have to do, including not only zero interest rates and higher inflation, but also yield curve control and possibly even Negative Interest Rate Policy (NIRP), both of which I explore in detail later.

Second, as you might expect, they will create boatloads of money.

And from where is all this "money" coming? It, of course, comes from thin air. Or, as Chairman Powell said in a *60 Minutes* interview in 2020: "We print it digitally. So, we—you know, we—as a central bank, we can create money digitally, and we do that by buying Treasury Bills or bonds or other government-guaranteed securities. And that actually increases the money supply. We also print actual currency, and we distribute that through the Federal Reserve banks."

"FREE" MONEY

Free money. Hey, what's not to like? As Glenn Frey sang in his classic, *Smuggler's Blues*:

> *It's the lure of easy money*
> *It has a very strong appeal*

Indeed, it does for bankers and politicians, every bit as much as for smugglers. And "money" is especially easy when you can print your own. But here is the cold, hard truth: the global economic markets need the leadership and support of the central bankers and without their actions, the economy would be much worse off than it currently is.

So, if staving off deflation requires the creation of trillions of digital dollars, well, that's what it takes. In so doing, the Fed may eventually embrace MMT and decide to let the chips fall where they may.

As you will see in Chapter 3, MMT proponents believe that our traditional concept of "money" is passé. Money used to be tangible, i.e., bits of precious metal or the paper exchangeable for that metal. But today's paper currency and coins are little more than vestigial remnants of times past. Most of what is now called money are just entries in a giant logbook that doesn't even have a physical existence. The Federal Reserve has a digital "cloud" that serves as a credit/debit ledger, which logs an increase in the "money supply" when issuing credit and a decrease when receiving debt repayments (i.e., when taxes are collected).

In a sense, the credit/debit ledger doesn't even record real transactions. Money creation doesn't run up debt; instead, it is government investment in the economy, and enhanced economic strength is itself the repayment. Or so they say.

I hope they're right because the truth is that no one knows if MMT will work and for how long. Fiscal-monetary coordination worked after WWII for America, and that would be the logical framework for the current administration. Still, MMT will be the fallback if it doesn't work, and that's why I want to discuss it in this book. But proponents point to Japan as the poster child. Over there, the government has been fighting a major deflation for twenty-five years through money creation that, as a percentage of GDP, exceeds that of the US. Its economy, while hardly robust, has nevertheless been kept afloat. And the terrible inflation that should have happened? It hasn't yet put in an appearance.

I don't try to fight the Fed. Its policies are working for the moment. The stock market and bond market have not only accepted that MMT policy is "the way" moving forward but more importantly, have become totally dependent on the expected stimulus of MMT. The current fiscal and monetary policy is like a gray area between FMC and MMT. I also believe this policy will be in place for years, if not decades, and is integral to the Rise of America.

I make my plans accordingly. So should you.

The only thing that's likely to bring down the Fed and MMT is a crisis of faith, which I will explain in Chapter 3. It will occur when the greedy politicians who control Congress attempt to control and influence the Federal Reserve's monetary policy.

All money, even the physical kind, has its ultimate existence only in the human mind. A unit of currency is valuable to the extent that people value it. As long as people accept it in trade, it's sound; once they don't, it goes to currency heaven. It's all about faith. Zimbabwe-style monetary catastrophes happen when a nation's citizens collectively lose faith in their money.

So, ask yourself: have Americans, or even the world, lost faith in the US dollar? Hardly. Unless they are currency traders, investors need to focus on the longer-term trend of currencies.

There has been selling pressure on the US dollar since the stock market crash of late March 2020. According to the Bloomberg Dollar Spot Index, the buck dropped about 10 percent against a basket of ten other currencies between late March and mid-September of 2020. However, if you go back just a few months earlier to January 1, 2020, the US dollar is up during 2020 compared to the same basket of currencies.

The same can be said when you look back five years. And ten years.

However, many commentators use a small-time frame of the US dollar's decrease to that basket of ten currencies in mid-2020 to push their narrative that the dollar is collapsing.

It isn't.

Think about it. When investors get nervous, when whole countries battle insolvency, where do they run? To the world's reserve currency, the one where international trade occurs, and the only one everybody trusts more than any other fiat currency—the US dollar.

What's going to challenge it? The euro? Europe's in worse economic straits than the US. The British pound is not going to stage an epic comeback. The yuan? Seriously? Despite China's burning desire to become an economic superpower, you have to ask the obvious question: Who's going to switch their allegiance to a currency controlled by a communist government? I am not trying to downplay the power China currently yields. The yuan, the currency of China, is becoming more viable quickly. And China and many nations within Europe are moving forward on trade deals.

Many nations will continue to complain about dollar dependence. So be it. But in reality, what has any central bank anywhere done over the last three to five years to replace the US dollar as the global reserve currency? **Nothing** is the only honest answer. The US dollar will remain the reserve currency of the world, and throughout this book, I will explain why.

WHO GETS THE DOUGH?

The Fed creates all this digital dough. Now, who gets to knead it and turn it into bread? You will probably not be shocked to learn that, when released, higher-ups in the banking world and the ultra-rich will get access first. The Federal Reserve's major goal is to achieve minimum unemployment while reducing middle- and lower-class inequality. However, suppose Congress stalls the president's stimulative tools. In that case, the Federal Reserve will have no alternative but to print more over a long time, eventually leading to Modern Monetary Theory.

MMT guarantees increased income inequality.

I know, that's not what you wanted to hear. But MMT will be the result of a divided Congress that does not support the president and the Federal Reserve. FMC's current framework should work as it did in the 1940s, subject to whether Congress makes the right decisions, however, it is a big risk relying on politicians to do the right things.

But why is income inequality a guaranteed outcome in MMT? Because the average Joe will not get access to these new digits that those at the top will use to enrich themselves, yet, at the same time, Joe will suffer from the everyday price inflation that this flood of printed digits will eventually lead to, as I'll explain in Chapter 3.

You'd think that the banks, given access to this printed

"money" would be incentivized to make loans to those who need help buying homes or starting businesses. That's the way it "oughta" be in any "fair" system. But in the real world, banks would much rather either invest it for their own benefit or loan it out to the ultra-rich and well-connected for them to invest. That represents a lower risk for the banks. They do love how this capital flows into the stock market, pushing it ever higher and swelling their profits—far beyond what individuals or small business borrowers could deliver through their modest interest payments.

It will take a long time before banks are comfortable loaning to average citizens again unless it becomes mandated by law. Even if that were the case, it would take some time before the money starts trickling down to the people who need it unless Congress approves direct stimulus payments, which happened in 2020 during COVID-19. Either way, the money will first flow to those who will benefit from higher prices in the markets for stocks, bonds, real estate, and fine art. Why? Banks do not want to take the risk of funding the "average person," as the memory of the housing crisis of 2008 is still fresh enough to make banks' risk departments ultra-cautious. Even at higher interest rates than we currently have, loans would still be a dribble.

Thus, despite the unprecedented money creation that has happened and will continue, those new digits are not provoking the economic stimulation that is supposedly their primary purpose. We remain in a deflationary environment.

The new currency is not working its way through the system and until it does, there will be no serious price inflation on everyday goods. To be clear, however, I have to point out that the money has to go somewhere. So, even though we are in a generally *de*flationary environment—with sectors like restaurants, airlines, hotels, mom-and-pop storefronts, low-end services, office buildings, and much more taking a hit—there will be *infla-*tion in the form of rising prices for certain assets, like stocks, gold, silver, Bitcoin, art, and property and estates outside cities, as well as for some staples like high-quality food.

This policy will hurt working folks. Not only will they have to wait while the money shoveled to the banks finally makes its way down to them—if it ever does. But they will also have to bear the burden of the CPI level increase. It's important to keep in mind that inflation has a negative impact on people trying to save, as it erodes the value of their money. However much you have, it buys less.

And the response to that will be more direct payments to people and more digits with which to do it. New stimulus packages are going to become as much a part of the landscape as belt tightening.

Additional consequences:

Stores of value, such as gold, and certain cryptocurrencies, such as Bitcoin, will benefit from MMT, with rising prices, as will silver. Copper and rare earth metals will benefit from the massive stimulus packages that will keep on coming, regardless of whether Democrats or Republicans control Congress or the White House in the years to come, which will be necessary to upgrade America during the Rise of America. I will get to this in Chapter 7.

It's also possible that the Fed will not be able to provoke inflation like it wants to. Japan has been trying for a quarter-century to no avail. But the dollar will strengthen due to the trends in motion that I'm covering in this chapter.

And that's the silver lining—both to individuals who hold the currency and to the government that issues it.

DE-GLOBALIZATION

We are in the process of de-globalization—replacing globalization. America will benefit the most from this shift because of its current situation involving the US dollar, the US economy, Fiscal-Monetary Coordination, demographics, and most likely Modern Monetary Theory. I will get into details later in the book.

But as you're already well aware, the coronavirus has laid bare the globalized economy's hidden weaknesses.

Now, no one can deny the benefits of the past half-century of globalization. Huge advances in transportation and communications sped up the movements and exchanges—of people, goods, services, capital, ideas, and technologies—across the planet. Regions and populations that had barely spoken to one another found themselves knit together in the fabric of international trade. Money moved freely. Former enemies became friends. Dictatorships collapsed as the notions of capitalism and liberal democracy spread.

The demise of the Soviet Union in 1991 not only removed the tensions of the Cold War, but also left the world with just one great superpower. Jumping to today, and although nobody wants to talk about it, the "Coldest War" is underway in 2021. It is between the United States of America and China. Their allies will be caught in the middle and will eventually have to choose sides.

In the US, companies prospered by offshoring production, and consumers benefited from the bargain prices of imported goods. At the same time, in the developing world, the infusion of American dollars and technology lifted hundreds of millions out of poverty.

Americans luxuriated in their triumph. No one noticed the structural problems of a globalized economy, or if they did, they didn't care. America's middle class steadily eroded. Despair eventually drove the rise of populism. Using social media and other hi-tech online techniques, China and Russia have exploited the current rift within American populism.

Then the virus shut down the domestic economy, and people finally realized how vulnerable the country had become. With the production of just about everything offshored, the US depended on other nations for goods for which there was a sudden, critical need, from medical-grade masks to pharmaceuticals. The global supply chain began to fracture.

As a result, Americans found that they could, in fact, still respond to a crisis. Manufacturers of unrelated items quickly retooled to mass-produce masks and ventilators. Drug companies plunged into a concerted effort to develop vaccines at warp speed.

What is now a crisis response is just a part of a trend in which the US revitalizes its domestic economy. It was going to happen regardless because the benefits of offshoring were becoming questionable.

There were a lot of factors at work.

The cost of production in the developing world was rising because of increases in workers' wages. Concurrently, the US became energy independent with the development of its own oil and gas fields. The increase in natural gas byproduct production via the shale oil wells, combined with significant investment in economically viable, renewable energy production, has been a significant catalyst to lower electricity costs compared to the past. Energy and electricity prices will stay low in the US relative to the rest of the developed world for years to come due to domestic energy sector success. All this will result in lower energy costs for manufacturers that set up shop within the US.

Advances in technology have also kicked in. Such things as 3D printing, just-in-time delivery systems, automated inventory control, robot-dominated factories, artificial intelligence, high-speed internet connections, and much more have contributed to the streamlining of American productive capacity. Domestically based businesses are increasingly cost-competitive.

And, of course, "America First" became a popular political slogan.

De-globalization is bad news for the developing nations in the short run, as their primary market turns inward. But in the long run, they will themselves retool and use these new technologies to create economies of their own that are less dependent on the export market. And it's good news for American workers who were laid off during the pandemic. Jobs are coming back, and there will be a creation of new ones. There will be regulatory changes, and universal income will eventually start becoming the norm globally. FMC will finance all of this; if that fails, the magic of MMT will finance it eventually. Again, as you will see, America will benefit from this trend in motion.

DEBT

If Modern Monetary Theory is the new playbook for the most powerful central bankers in the world, we need to understand what MMT is. Under this policy, debt as we know it will not matter to governments as it once did. I know this will be a difficult concept for readers to accept, especially those who still see the world within a hard-currency framework. But as I will explain in Chapter 3, this new monetary regime will not be a short-term solution. It will be with us for many years, and politicians will push it to the brink.

American investment spurred much of the economic progress being made in the developing world over the past quarter-century.

Many companies outside the US have to fund their debts with US dollars, even in the developed world. The capital expended to build the plants, manufacturing facilities, etc., was mainly denominated in US dollars. Even today, the US dollar makes up over 60 percent of all currencies held globally.

Thus, there are mountains of debt around the world, denominated in dollars. All of it has to be paid back, much of it on a continuing basis.

For sure, there will be still-impoverished countries that will say, *screw it*, default on their debt, and commit to expropriation and/or nationalization of their resources. (Expropriation is the taking of private property by a government acting in its sovereign capacity; nationalization generally refers to a government takeover of an entire industry.)

My expertise is in natural resources, and I see this sort of thing as a real threat to that sector, especially in those places that feel they haven't gotten a fair shake from foreign investors doing business in their countries.

Those who go that route will pay a heavy price. For one thing, they will likely mismanage the expropriated businesses, meaning less productivity, which means less free cash flow. More importantly, actions taken due to a lack of US dollars mean that fewer US dollars will be invested in the country in the future because of the higher risk. It is a vicious, ugly cycle created by a global demand that exceeds US dollar supply.

The more prudent countries will find compromises with foreign investors so that those investors don't hang out to dry while these countries retain access to dollars that will remain strong into the foreseeable future.

SWAP LINES

The US has gained unprecedented geopolitical leverage. The dollar is being *weaponized*; there's no other word for it. And there are just no challengers to the new American hegemony yet.

SWAP Lines are another expression of US dollar indebtedness. Countries with liquidity problems in a deflationary environment—i.e., just about everyone—are begging for dollars.

I talk with top investment industry pros and business executives all the time. Almost all of them are totally unfamiliar with SWAP Lines, which I examine in detail in Chapter 2. That's pretty amazing because these lines of credit will play a huge role in the world's financial restructuring.

Consider that in 2020, the Federal Reserve pushed almost $500 billion in fresh US dollar digits out the door without any congressional or presidential approval over twenty days. That is not chump change, by any measure. But the thing is, those particular funds didn't go where you might expect them to, into the domestic economy. Instead, they went to foreign central banks, via SWAP Lines, to alleviate the emergency short-term shortage of US dollars in the foreign markets.

If the SWAP Lines didn't exist, there would have been an incredible squeeze on central banks that would have had huge adverse effects on global financial markets. The US came to the rescue without any media attention whatsoever. It was not the first SWAP Line lifeline. It is far from the last.

US dollars dominate the international credit market. Who is going to challenge that dominance, China? It may have great geopolitical ambitions and it may have the fastest-growing economy. But as long as it remains communist, and as long as it continues to steal intellectual property from the West, it isn't going to be allowed in the club. It could conceivably try to open competing

SWAP Lines in yuan. It will be many years before the demand matches anywhere near that of the US dollar. At the same time, do not under-estimate China's will to pull as many countries as possible into its orbit, creating a demand for the Chinese currency, the Yuan. During this time frame America must upgrade its internal infrastructure and re-establish its relationships with its allies.

Russia? Forget about it. Europe? Already addicted to dollars. The developing world? As noted, some of those countries may get dollar help provided that they strongly align with US interests; others will team up with China, and the others will go back decades.

This is another facet of the new normal, and it will be with us for a long time to come.

"You're either with us or against us" is going to become a truism. Those who ally "with" the US will get a SWAP Line lifeline, meaning generous support for their economies. Those identified as "enemies" will be left to sink or swim on their own.

Could this result in a shooting war or a more insidious cyberwar? Yes, it could. We certainly have to hope that doesn't happen, and I don't think it will because of technology. The tech sector is the new battlefield and will be for the next few decades.

TECH

Technological advances are proceeding at an exponential pace, and America will continue to lead the way. Things are happening so fast that normal human minds cannot keep up. Most people have no idea how far we've already come, much less how many monumental changes to our way of life will arrive over the next decade or two.

Humanity is at the dawn of an age of real-world abundance that previously has only been the stuff of dreams. Abundance not only raises standards of living but it eliminates a major cause of war: covetousness of what someone else has. Of course, wars are fought over political, religious, ethnic, and/or cultural differences too. Abundance won't solve those problems right away, but I think they will also fade over time. Contented people are more likely to develop a live-and-let-live attitude.

It would take a whole book to cover the subject of modern technology, and this is not that book. Besides, it's impossible to keep up with tomorrow's technology and future vision. There will be lots of surprises. Remember that before Steve Jobs took the stage just a short time ago, in 2007, the smartphone didn't exist.

Fossil fuel usage will still be part of the energy matrix, but it's incredible dominance over the last hundred years is coming to an end. Within a hundred years, the world will be powered by cheap, universally available electricity generated from renewable clean energy sources funded by FMC and then MMT, as I will explain in Chapter 6. Nikola Tesla stated this exact thing more than a century ago. Technology and funding from MMT will coalesce to make his dream a reality.

In no particular order, here are just a few of the other places tech is taking us:

- *Food*—There will be plenty to feed the whole planet, and it will be produced in more environmentally friendly ways than it is now.
- *Medicine*—We are cracking the genetic code of disease and will soon be able to treat anything and prevent most ailments from ever getting a foothold in our bodies. Pandemics will be

a thing of the past. We'll live longer and, more importantly, our senior years will be far healthier.

- *Communications*—The internet is already wiring up the planet. Connectivity will get better and faster, and everyone will have it. 5G is here. We have just started to see the coming explosive growth of the "Internet of Things," or as some are calling it: Internet 2.0.

- *Natural resources*—We'll still need them, as many elements and metals will be absolutely critical to locking in a green, clean future. But we'll get better at extracting them while doing less harm to the environment.

- *Labor*—Advances in software and robotics are making most repetitive, manual labor jobs obsolete. Marginally productive white-collar jobs are going too.

- *Transportation*—Private cars will disappear from cities, replaced by always-on-call electric vehicles. Our children's teenagers may never know what a driver's license is.

- *Nanotech*—Nanotechnology will impact almost every aspect of our lives. To take just one example, building materials made of carbon nanotubes have a tensile strength approximately one hundred times greater than that of steel, at about one-sixth the weight.

The list goes on and on. Look at it again. What do all these things have in common? Or, to put it a little differently, who will lead the way with these technological innovations, just as it always has?

Right.

America will.

THE RISE OF AMERICA: THREATS AND PROMISE

We all suffer, to some extent, from what is known as *recency bias*. We tend to think that the present and the immediate past are how things always were and always will be. When times are good, we believe they will never end. When times turn bad, we believe they'll never get better again. It's a pretty big blind spot.

Not that we aren't undergoing massive changes in society, economics, politics, and especially in business. We are. Even optimistic economists estimate that the US economy won't return to pre-pandemic levels until the end of 2021, at best. In other words, we're going to be in turmoil for a while.

In the broadest sense, this is a book about *money*, albeit from a unique perspective you may not have seen before.

In these pages, I'll be presenting you with the global financial situation the way that I perceive it. I'll cover money itself; currencies; credit; debt; the banking system; markets, including stocks, bonds, and especially natural resources and energy—my specialty; inflation and deflation; recession and depression; the role of government; the Federal Reserve; Fiscal Monetary Coordination; Modern Monetary Theory; interest rates; and, most importantly, the future of the US economy and America's place in the world to come.

A lot of this stuff initially seems hard to understand, given how the media most often presents it. That's not entirely unintentional. Financial "experts" have a big stake in keeping you in the dark—by cloaking all of their pronouncements in a language only other "experts" can penetrate. It's what they do. It's the way they maintain their exalted positions in society. It gives them the power they crave (or at least the illusion of it).

But the truth is that matters of finance and monetary policy are not that difficult to understand once you strip away the jargon and revert to plain English. That's my goal here, to present the material in a way that's accessible to anyone of reasonable intelligence.

Along the way, you'll find plenty of disagreements with the talking heads of TV business channels and the chattering scribes of the print media. You'll also see where I beg to differ with the "specialists" in the Treasury Department, at the Federal Reserve, in the C-suites of corporate America, and among the mega-investment banks on Wall Street.

As a contrarian, I question every "fact" or opinion that comes out of the financial sector and prosper because of it. Right now—with the American economy seemingly coming apart at the seams—I'm probably as contrarian as I've ever been.

You know the grim facts. We all do: the novel coronavirus pandemic and the government-mandated shutdowns, have plunged the US into recession, if not worse:

- Unemployment is nearing Great Depression levels. Nearly 50 million Americans filed for unemployment benefits over the three-month period from April through June of 2020. According to official data from the US Bureau of Labor Statistics, more than 23 million jobs have been lost, with the reported U-3 unemployment rate at a record-high 14.7 percent in April of 2020. (And some believe that even that number is an understatement of reality by 7 percent or more—when you factor in those who only work part time when they want full-time employment and those who have stopped looking.) Despite a pickup in hiring over the summer and fall of 2020, dropping official unemployment to 6.7 percent as of November, that number is not expected to improve much, as a fresh surge in COVID infections threatens business reopenings.

- GDP growth has fallen into a chasm. The Bureau of Economic Analysis estimates that US GDP for the second quarter likely fell by 31.7 percent—a decline that's "off the charts"...four times worse than any recession since 1960. While GDP picked up in the third quarter, most of that was likely due to federal stimulus money rather than real growth.
- Bankruptcies are soaring.
- Defaults: According to Fitch Ratings, the monthly tally of defaults in the US leveraged loan market has hit a six-year high. Fitch forecasts that US leveraged loan defaults will reach $80 billion in 2020, surpassing the previous high of $78 billion in 2009.
- State and local governments face catastrophic revenue short-falls, ranging from 11–15 percent in Illinois and New York to greater than 20 percent in California for the current fiscal year (ending June 30, 2021). For the fiscal year 2021, experts predict average budget shortfalls of 25 percent. Unlike the federal government, states have to balance their budgets, which will require some fancy footwork, including spending cuts, increased taxes, and probably massive subsidies from Washington.
- Small businesses face daunting difficulties in reopening, and many have thrown in the towel. It is possible that over 5 million small businesses will be closing permanently due to the virus shutdown.
- Many state pension plans are in deep trouble. The crunch point of a plan running out of assets is known as the "depletion date." After this point, a plan must move to a so-called "pay-as-you-go" arrangement where retirement benefits are paid solely by employers and by current employees' contributions. Reaching that point will severely impact a state's finances, as

contributions fail to fund promised benefits. According to The Pew Charitable Trusts data, the fiscal year 2017 (the most recent available) saw a combined $1.28 trillion in state pension plan funding deficits. Twenty states had pension plans that were less than two-thirds funded, and five states had pension plans that were less than 50 percent funded.

- Corporate insolvencies are on the rise to an unprecedented level. By June 2020, bankruptcies had already surpassed those of 2008. The US economy hasn't seen this level of insolvency in over seventy-five years.
- The fragility of the globalized supply chain has been exposed, with many companies scrambling to procure raw materials and products after sources in virus-affected overseas areas dried up.

How's that for a witch's brew of toil and trouble? Sounds pretty hopeless, doesn't it?

And, of course, Washington has responded in the only way it knows how. It is throwing money and credit at our problems by the *trillions*.

So, you see the extent of the problem, and you probably know the "consensus" of what it all means from the conventional point of view. Our self-appointed "expert" pundits (remember, just because the pundits say the below doesn't mean it is true) tell us that:

- There is an "everything bubble" that has been building in the markets since the end of the 2008–2009 financial crisis, with investors reaping outsized returns in the real estate, stock, bond, and collectibles markets, among others—even as average Americans have struggled to make ends meet.

- A monetary policy that kept interest rates near zero, encouraging reckless borrowing and speculating, inflated the bubble. Massive government deficit spending and trillions in new currency created by the Federal Reserve and funneled to its friends in the banking industry helped to maintain the bubble.
- Now the bubble has popped. The novel coronavirus merely supplied the pin to an inherently unstable bubble.
- We have fallen into recession. The prospect of declining even further into an outright depression has caused panic in Washington. Government and the Federal Reserve will do whatever it takes to prevent a return of the 1930s, but the only real tools in their box are to push interest rates ever lower and issue ever more new currency units.
- The chosen monetary policy will either fail to prevent a prolonged recession, or will foster large-scale inflation, or will result in ugly stagflation—depending upon whom you ask.
- The US dollar is ready for a historic decline and the potential loss of its position as the world's reserve currency.
- We face a massive blow to our standard of living. The American economy is about to descend into a long night from which it will take years to recover. By that time, China may be the world's premier economic superpower.

And so on.

The naysayers are in the ascendant, with hardly a positive voice raised anywhere.

I'm not saying I disagree with every bullet point on these lists. I don't. In fact, many of them are self-evident. However, the current "everything bubble" results from years of monetary policy without proper long-term fiscal investment by Congress. Thus, to all those who hate fate and call for the #ENDTHEFED, you need to study your facts a bit better as the everything bubble is a result of Congress' failure, not the Fed's.

Our bodies will take time to recover from COVID-19 itself. But the economic fallout resulting from the everything bubble's pop is likely to be much more serious and require a much longer recovery period. Complicating things is the government's response. The consequences of creating trillions of units of new fiat currency, and the massive new debt that goes along with it, are not easily anticipated. Congress must focus on productive fiscal long-term debt that will rebuild the infrastructure and supply chains of America.

This is truly virgin ground for any politician or central banker today, as none were in the workforce the last time this challenge presented itself to America. You can find eminent economists who predict a 1930s-style Depression ahead and probably an equal number who predict hyperinflation. Some have even staked out a middle ground (if that's what it is) by saying that we could end up with '70s-era stagflation. And that, they say, is if we're *lucky*.

Eventually, we were going to be in a world of hurt, pandemic, or no pandemic. There are systemic problems to address and, as the 2020s unfold, you're going to see politicians of all stripes grapple with how to do that. Or, to put it another way, the inner economic circles in DC will be inhabited by those academics who most closely tell the political class what it wants to hear.

There will be many really stupid ideas advanced, and, in truth, there already have been.

I'm not optimistic about the wisdom of policymakers. Most of them—mainly from Congress to all the president's most-learned advisors—don't have the foggiest notion of what's going on. (Remember that these are largely the same group who told us in

'07 that the housing market couldn't be stronger and who insisted in '08 that the financial crisis was going to be no big deal.) In my opinion, and I speak as a math nerd, few could pass a basic Math 101 course.

They have made and will continue to make, incredibly poor decisions. They will create bad outcomes and then make them worse. But the good news is that many of the forces at loose in the world economy today can't be manipulated by the self-serving politicos and bureaucrats in the nation's capital. I expect a new generation of leaders to rise upon the middle and unite the majority in the middle. This is required and will most likely come from the new generation of self-made entrepreneurs with large social followings.

No matter what, though, the whole international system of money, credit, banking, and markets will change and change profoundly in the decades to come. China will spearhead a new version of Bretton Woods that will use a basket of central bank digital currencies (CBDC), including many of its allies, to reduce and eventually illuminate the United States' dependency SWIFT system, which is a core part of the US dollar dominance internationally. Eventually, this system will eliminate the need for cash and create complete government control of the flow of funds and maximize tax payments. These are all challenges the US dollar will face moving forward as the king of currencies.

There are tough times ahead. But (*properly*) forewarned is forearmed.

I will present here a reasoned alternative to the cacophony of voices that overwhelm our attention on a near-daily basis. I will try to provide a clear-eyed vision of what's happening behind the scenes in our globalized economy and where the trends in place are likely to lead us. I don't believe in sugarcoating anything, but neither do I believe in indulging in the kind of thoughtless fear-mongering that's all too familiar to you.

I'll say it again: we're in for tough times. But in adversity also lies opportunity. If you're content to let crowd sentiment carry you along, then you're going to pay a high price for that. But if you educate yourself on what's actually going on behind the scenes and act upon your knowledge, you will do more than survive. You'll fully participate in the Rise of America, and you will prosper.

Since this is a book about money, we will have to learn how modern governments define and manage money. What they do affects every aspect of your life.

Here, as in so many things, the past is prologue. But if you're American and are like the vast majority of your compatriots, you don't have a clue about your nation's monetary history. You can have no real idea where we're going until you know where we've been.

To understand what money really is, how it functions in a modern society such as ours, and what its future might be, it's important to have an overview of money's long and colorful history. Where, how, and why did the ideas of money and banking originate, and how have they changed over time? That is a tale that's fascinating in its own right; in a very real sense, the story of money is the story of civilization itself. I'll cover that subject in Chapter 4.

The restart process around the world will be challenging—and perhaps the most challenging in the US. The coronavirus pandemic will pass, as pandemics will. The present recession will burn itself out, as recessions always do. The civil unrest we are currently experiencing will die down as people grow increasingly wary of violence in their streets.

I would submit that these are the times for which America was made.

Champagne socialists will bitch and whine about how things are (as they always do). Ignore them. Even though higher taxes and backward regulations will be pushed through by this crowd, they won't be able to stifle innovation. The next generation of Elon Musks, Bill Gates, and Steve Jobs are right now working one-hundred-hour weeks for their own companies. They will come up with the applications and solutions that will enable the Rise of America. Capitalists will solve the environmental problems.

I believe you should ignore the negativists calling for the collapse of the US dollar, if not for the entire country coming apart at the seams. It's almost as if they're *hoping* for that. But in my view, the exact opposite will happen. There will be strong and ongoing dollar demand, culminating with a SWAP Line system that holds the whole structure together. If this sounds like the Fed is on its way to becoming the central bank of the world, well, in a sense, maybe it is.

At the least, I believe a very powerful new international monetary alliance is forming, anchored by the dollar. Maybe not today, and maybe not by 2021—but soon, and for the rest of your life, **America will rise.**

For many reading this, I am sure I come off as a naïve and unrealistic optimist out of touch with the current state of affairs. Nothing could be further from the truth. I have traveled the world, financed projects around the globe, and come to see and accept the world for what it is—and that is: whatever we make it to be.

In this book, I will use the hard facts to prove the next era of financial dominance will, in fact, be America's. The Rise of America is upon us, but not for any political moves either Democrats or Republicans will make. Its foundation will be money and American innovation.

To understand why we are verging upon the Rise of America, we first have to understand modern notions of money and the current state of global finance. The following two chapters deal with these subjects in terms of MMT and SWAP Lines. They are not going to be easy reading. But hang in there. They are essential. Think carefully about them.

CHAPTER TWO

UNDERSTANDING THE US DOLLAR

ONE OF THE MAJOR DETERRENTS TO THE RISE OF AMERICA would be a cratering US dollar, something that many of the self-appointed "experts" in the field of economics predicted. I couldn't disagree more. In this chapter, I will discuss some new financial concepts and their effects on the global economy: *cross-flation* in certain sectors of the economy; positive SWAP Line Nations (+SWAP) vs. negative SWAP Line Nations (–SWAP); and the deflationary pressure most of the emerging markets will experience.

At the same time, let me carefully build a solid case for what I see as sustained global support for the US dollar.

FISCAL VERSUS MONETARY POLICY

Here's the way it's supposed to work in America: each fiscal year, the Executive Branch draws up a proposed budget for the federal government. Members of Congress tweak it to make sure none of their pet projects go unfunded; then they send it back to the president, who signs it. Then it goes to the Treasury Department, which allocates tax money to pay for the various items in the bill.

Today's government is huge, and it reaches into virtually every aspect of American life. It must pay for the day-to-day operation of its own functions, the various departments like Defense, Interior, Energy, Homeland Security, etc.; it must pay for the obligations incurred by its entitlement programs, like Social Security and Medicare; it must fund its wars; and it can engage, to whatever extent it can get away with, in discretionary spending, funneling money into the private sector through an exhaustive list of programs designed to support this or that industry. As we've learned through the stimulus efforts during the 2020 pandemic response, it can also just give free money away to whomever it chooses.

It's a complex undertaking, and the result is called *fiscal policy*. Simply put, it uses government revenue collection (taxes) and expenditures (spending) to influence a country's macroeconomic variables.

Macroeconomics is the really *BIG* picture: it's a view of the entire economy, including the roles of and relationships between corporations, central banks, governments, consumers, the different types of markets (such as bonds and stocks), labor, commodities, and so on. Macroeconomists examine the finest details of every conceivable economic topic, including (but not limited to): GDP, production, unemployment, national income, price indices, output, consumption, inflation, saving, investment, energy, trade, and international finance.

As they say, it's a big job, but somebody has to do it.

Or so we're told.

It's true that it is important because a lot of government activity is based upon what these economists tell the politicians and lifelong government bureaucrats. Clearly, no one person can get any kind of handle on all of these factors. So, the government employs thousands of economists, and academia many more, each of them examining some piece of the whole and hoping that their collective output will lead to doing what's best for the country. As opposed to the undesired result: the indecipherable noise generated by thousands of people with different opinions and sometimes working at cross purposes.

I'll leave it up to you to decide how well they're doing.

Macroeconomic thinking as the basis for fiscal policy came into its own after the Great Depression. Before that, the government took more or less a hands-off approach to economic management. In fact, the word depression didn't even exist in the sense of a severe economic contraction. Such events were called *panics*.

Herbert Hoover introduced *depression* in its modern sense during his campaign against Franklin D. Roosevelt. Hoover presided over the Crash of 1929 and the recession that followed—for which FDR blamed his opponent. Hoover, trying to save himself, wanted an economic term that would comfort people rather than remind them of the Panic of 1907, and he and his team thought *depression* sounded less nasty than *panic*.

That worked for a while, as the public accepted the notion of a depression as being a short-lived phenomenon from which the economy would quickly recover. By mid-1930, though, it was clear that that was not the case. In 1932 Franklin D. Roosevelt ran against Hoover, with his team appropriating the term *Great Depression* to attack the president.

FDR got himself elected in a rout. His landslide victory defined the beginning of a new era in American politics that many believe included a vast intrusion of government into the nation's social and economic life.

The onrushing "Capital D" Depression, the worst economic calamity ever to hit the country, made anxious citizens clamor for change. They wanted their representatives in government to *do something. Anything. Please, just make it all better*. Though they might not have put it this way, they were demanding a new fiscal policy. And that required a new monetary policy because the Treasury Department was very nervous about the bond market impact of so much fiscal expansion. That was the beginning of what morphed into Fiscal-Monetary Coordination in 1942 and was the primary framework until 1951. Without the successful implementation of FMC, I would argue that the vast development of dams, electrical grids, and other infrastructure to the American West and the rise of the middle class wouldn't have happened.

That traumatic moment also marked an important psychological shift among its citizens, one that I see strongly echoed in what's going on today. I'll have much more to say about that and about monetary policy shortly.

Before I go into that, though, a few quick last words about fiscal policy.

If the two government figures—taxes and expenditures—add up, you have a balanced budget.

Of course, the US hasn't had one of those since the Clinton administration. Subsequently, the US government has been running deficits of ever-increasing magnitude year after year. There have been trillion-dollar wars to finance, recessions to deal with, and public pushing of the *do something* mantra ever further into our lives.

It's all extraordinarily expensive, necessitating outlays way beyond what the government collects in taxes. So, to make up the shortfall, the Treasury manufactures Treasury bonds, goes to the Federal Reserve, asks it to "print" the necessary money, and uses it to buy the bonds.

This is not, strictly speaking, a borrowing operation analogous to your home mortgage. It's a shuffling of electronic digits in a ledger that exists only in cyberspace, according to the policy of Modern Monetary Theory, which I analyze in detail in Chapter 3.

This brings us to *monetary policy*.

This shouldn't be, but often is, confused with fiscal policy, which is the government dispersal of tax receipts, as I've just explained. Monetary policy, on the other hand, is the method used by the monetary authority of a nation—generally speaking, its central bank, and in the USA, the Federal Reserve—to construct its financial backbone.

In general, the goals of a central bank are to:

- control interest rates and the money supply,
- ensure the liquidity of the banking system,
- avoid extremes of either inflation or deflation (promote price stability),
- provide an environment that fosters maximum employment, and
- generate a general trust in the value and solidity of the nation's currency.

Some job description, isn't it? That anyone ever conceived that a single entity could efficiently do all of those things in a market economy may seem crazy. Perhaps it was. But that was the best idea the financial experts of their time could devise.

In the US, it's a relatively modern invention. Historically, the country had no central bank for well over the first hundred years of its existence (save for two short-lived and failed early experiments). The whole of the nineteenth century was characterized by laissez-faire economics and a monetary policy based on a gold, silver, or bimetallic standards. It was an era of enormous expansion and prosperity and a bumpy business cycle that featured many ups and downs.

After the Panic of 1907, there was a push to restructure monetary policy so that the business cycle might be smoothed out a bit. A central bank—the Federal Reserve, or Fed—was created with that in mind, along with the introduction of an income tax. [**Note**: the story of how the Fed came to be and how it has evolved over the years is too involved to go into here. But for those interested, I cover the subject at some length in Appendix I.]

But the real sea change came after the Great Depression. The federal government, and the Fed, were determined never to let anything like that happen again.

Enter John Maynard Keynes.

Keynes—the influential, early-twentieth-century British economist—was adamant that the Great Depression was worse than it had to be and lasted longer than it should have because of faulty monetary policy. He argued that the key to fighting depressions is to cut taxes, increase the money supply, and inflate your way out of the downturn. Pump money into the system—people will start spending, and employment will pick up. Controlled inflation is a good thing.

FDR did make some inflationary moves, such as confiscating private gold and re-valuing the metal relative to the dollar. But he also raised taxes to nosebleed levels. Overall, it added up to the wrong response, at least in Keynesian terms.

Keynesians theorized that the proper government changes in the levels of taxation, government spending, and the money supply would influence aggregate demand and the level of economic activity. It was the way out. Once equilibrium was reached, then Keynesian monetary policy would stabilize the business cycle and maintain:

- a "healthy" inflation rate of 2 percent,
- a "natural" unemployment level of no more than 4–5 percent,
- and an ideal, sustainable annual GDP growth in the 2–3 percent range.

The problem is that the classical Keynesian approach didn't work as advertised. It failed to prevent the runaway inflation of the '70s or the recessions of the early '80s and early '00s. Thus, monetary authorities have opted for the updated version known as MMT (analyzed in Chapter 3)—in which the creation of currency digits represents an investment in the economy, not debt.

THE 'FLATIONS

So where are we now, and what happens next?

We are in familiar territory in terms of a recessionary reaction to the financial malinvestments of the prior decade. But we are in uncharted waters in terms of the effects of a global pandemic unlike any other. And we see "money" creation on a scale previously unimaginable.

The Fed controls the money supply. Over the past forty years, the US money supply (according to M2, the most commonly used measure) has fluctuated within a fairly narrow range, only reaching as high as a 10 percent increase (year over year) four times. That has changed dramatically. In May 2020, for example, it jumped 23 percent, compared with May 2019. In merely two months, between March and May of 2020, it surged by 12 percent.

For comparison purposes, there were only two other times during the twentieth century when M2 growth rose above 15 percent year over year—when the country hit peak levels of military spending during World Wars I and II. That growth was predictable. What's happening now was not (although some might argue that we are indeed at war again, this time against a virus). Add in the China-Russia (and their allies) axis against America, and one can easily argue that another, more discrete war is being fought at the same.

And it's not as if the Fed is alone in its actions. It's happening abroad too, as both the European Central Bank and Bank of Japan have seen a major swelling of their balance sheets (the more entries on a central bank balance sheet grow, the more money that is being put into circulation).

Many are predicting that this massive money creation will inevitably result in a debasing of the US dollar. But will it?

At the outset, let's get some definitions straight. *Inflation*. As I noted earlier, the term originally related to increases in the money supply or monetary inflation. Historically, price inflation has generally been held to be the *consequence* of monetary inflation. It makes sense. Provided that you have more money chasing the same supply of goods and services—or if production hasn't kept pace—prices will rise.

A little inflation can be a good thing. An increasing money supply makes people feel good. It encourages them to spend, resulting in expanding prosperity (like what happened in the 1940s). But if inflation gets out of control—i.e., if governments try to help a country's economy by printing more money willy-nilly—then you can get inflation's evil stepchild, *hyperinflation*. This is the most ruinous economic situation imaginable, as a national currency careens toward utter worthlessness, as people use it to start fires or for wallpaper—Weimar, Germany, Zimbabwe, Yugoslavia, and so on.

The flip side of inflation is *deflation*, where the money supply is shrinking. The money supply shrinks for many different reasons but think of it as fewer dollars chasing the same supply of goods and services. A little deflation can be a good thing. It rewards the financially prudent and those on fixed incomes because their money becomes more valuable and goes further. As I've said, the nineteenth century was one of modest deflation overall, and the country prospered enormously. But it was also an era peppered with frequent panics and recessions. This, as noted, led to the creation of our central bank, the Federal Reserve, as a hoped-for antidote to these fluctuations.

Deflations, especially sharp and sudden ones, are disastrous for debtors. They still have to service their debt, even though the value of the underlying asset has dropped. This is what happened in 2008. As real estate prices fell, those who had taken on mortgages at the limit of their means—and many of those with adjustable-rate mortgages (ARMs) that were resetting substantially higher—could no longer make their payments. And the value of their properties, in many instances, was sinking far below what they owed. Thus, the market crashed, and many were forced just to walk away from their homes, leaving banks loaded with repossessed assets they didn't want and couldn't resell. It was a mess, and only an emergency re-liquefication of the Fed's banking system kept the financial system from collapsing.

Then there is *stagflation*, which is when the money supply is being inflated and prices are in an upward trend, but wages are lagging. People are increasingly unable to afford to buy the things they want. It's inflation in a stagnant economy, hence the name. This is what happened in the 1970s when OPEC drove the price of oil up fourfold and, since economies run on oil, the price of everything else followed. Price inflation hit double digits. Hard-working, lower-income people couldn't keep up and were going broke.

It was an ugly time. The remedy was some really difficult medicine, but it had to be taken. And Paul Volcker, appointed to chair the Fed in late 1979, was the doctor to administer it. The money supply had to be reduced, so Volcker raised the key interest rate and then did it again and again to as high as 20 percent in 1981. The deflation hurt debtors, but it was a saver's heyday. You could take out a simple CD and earn 15 percent on your money and increasingly valuable dollars as icing on the cake.

Inflation was slowly brought under control, with the recession of the early '80s as a necessary byproduct. After that, the economy really caught fire for nearly twenty years. And Volcker was the last Fed chair to pursue a deflationary monetary policy. All his successors have been monetary inflationists to their core, culminating in the perceived triumph of MMT, which I'll get to shortly.

Today, we have a growing deflation and are moving toward a new state of affairs, which I call *crossflation*. By that, I mean that we will have broad deflation areas with concentrated pockets of inflation popping up here and there. Understanding that is central to the way I see the status of the US dollar going forward.

THE VELOCITY OF MONEY

First, I want to talk briefly about another variable that reinforces my deflationary view: the *velocity of money*.

The velocity of money is the frequency at which one unit of currency is used to purchase domestically produced goods and services within a given time period. In other words, it is the number of times one dollar is spent to buy things per unit of time. Or, if you want to use street lingo, the velocity of money is how fast dollars are moving through the economy. In the years since 1960, the US dollar velocity rose rapidly. During the Boom years of the 1990s, it hit its peak in the third quarter of 1997 when the average dollar was spent 2.198 times. It declined after the market crash of 2000 and has been in a slow but steady downtrend ever since.

Typically, the velocity of money slows during a recession, as you'd expect. (A corollary of this is that a slowing velocity of money is a very good indicator that recession is on the way.) When times are tight, people are naturally more cautious with their spending. Times are tight right now, with tens of millions unemployed in the US.

In the first quarter of 2020, the average dollar was spent 1.374 times. That confirms the two-decade-long trend. The second quarter of 2020 had the lowest velocity ever recorded at 1.104. This confirms a continued slowing of the velocity of money. 'When there's a rising flood of new currency pouring into the system, it may seem counterintuitive that the cash wouldn't be moving much. But it isn't.

Partly, this is due to the greatly increased savings rate brought on by the virus. People are sobering up, and they have fewer places actually open in which to socialize and spend because of the forced closures due to the virus. They're doing their best to set funds aside to help them ride out the pandemic and to be a little better prepared when subsequent emergencies strike. Thus, the national savings rate, which had been low for decades, has nearly tripled—from 7 to 20 percent—post-COVID-19.

To my mind, that's a change that's here to stay for a while. And since saving slows the velocity of money, it will continue finding new lows well into the future.

[**NOTE:** As I write in mid-November 2020, the velocity of money for 3Q20 has just gone up a tick, to 1.146, for the first time in nearly two years. What, if anything, this means remains to be seen, but I stand by my assertion.]

As I've stressed, we are in a deflation. The savings rate and velocity of money are just further indicators.

Banks aren't lending at the same rates that they have in the past. And the banks are not lending at a pace that comes anywhere near the level of the dollars that are being digitally printed. Thus, the average person is not getting access to the new digital dollars from the increased money supply. Yes, the money supply is increasing, but not its velocity. The money is not getting to the middle and lower classes. Until this changes, you won't have to worry about broad inflation.

MORE ON 'FLATIONS

Now back to my discussion of the various *'flations*.

While inflation and deflation are terms more properly used to denote increases and decreases in the money supply, they are more commonly used today to denote changes in the prices of goods and services, usually measured by the government's consumer price index (CPI). That's the sense in which I'll be using them here.

Though there is generally a direct connection between monetary and price inflation, that's not always the case.

Not today, for instance. As I've said, the increases in the money supply have been unprecedented. That should quickly lead to a rise in the CPI, but it hasn't. The CPI fell 0.4 percent in

March, 0.8 percent in April, and 0.1 percent in May, before notching a 0.6 percent gain in June 2020. The twelve-month inflation rate was 0.2 percent in August 2020.

Don't be misled by thinking that the "modest" CPI inflation the Fed has tried to engineer for the past two decades hasn't been destructive. Remember the flip side. The true way to gauge inflation is in the buying power of the currency. Higher prices mean currency devaluation. Thus, since 2000, in a "low" inflation environment, the USD has nevertheless lost 44.2 percent of its purchasing power! Nearly half.

This is no small matter, especially to those on fixed incomes. According to a poll of 2,000 workers conducted by the Transamerica Center for Retirement Studies in 2015, the No. 1 fear of retirees is not loneliness, boredom, declining health, or even death. It is, by a wide margin, **running out of money**.

GDP for the second quarter of 2020 was down 31.4 percent, and consumer spending was down 35 percent—far and away the worst performance since the 1930s. The US real GDP for the third quarter of 2020 increased at an annual rate of 33.1 percent ($1.64 trillion), partly due to the reopening of businesses and resumption of activities at least equal to the government's fiscal stimulus. The scary part is the rate of insolvencies that will catch up with the decrease in GDP.

Also, the rate of change in the number of people working part time is now four times higher than pre-coronavirus.

Make no mistake about it; we are in a recession, a very serious and deflationary one—possibly the first stages of a depression. People have lost jobs, businesses have closed, disposable income is scarce, belts are being tightened around middles that had grown complacently large. In this environment, the consumer spending that drives 70 percent of the American economy is shriveling up. And it isn't coming back in the near term. There is just no easy way out.

But remember, the Federal Reserve has branded itself as, first and foremost, a deflation fighter. Its members right now are very afraid. The economy seemed to be humming along so well, and all of a sudden, the music stopped. You can blame it all on the coronavirus if you want. But the truth is, that was only one factor. An important one, for sure, but just one.

The hard reality is that, from 2010 to 2019, we were in an inflationary asset bubble where certain assets—like stocks and real estate—were on a tear. That bubble was bound to pop at some point. The virus turned out to be the pin to pop the bubble. (I know, a lot of that asset inflation has reignited, and I'll explain why a little later.)

The past ten years have been good times in a lot of ways. Low unemployment, rising stock prices, and a bond market propped up by an easy and cheap money policy, maintained by the Fed to ensure that the bad old days of the financial crisis never came back.

DEBT

Unfortunately, we as a society were building a magnificent structure whose foundation was debt. And lots and lots of it.

From 1948 to 1976, productivity and hourly wages in the US rose in lockstep. But then they diverged. And how. Inflation-adjusted wages are barely higher than they were forty years ago, while productivity has steadily continued to climb, rising about 150 percent. This has caused a significant gap between what workers earn and what they want to buy. In other words, all except the wealthy cannot afford the lifestyle they desire.

When you're caught in that kind of divergence, there's not much you can do. Either you can rein in your desires and live within your budget. Or you can fill the gap with debt. Americans *en masse* chose the latter. They maxed out their credit cards, and when that wasn't enough, they borrowed. The numbers are staggering.

Mortgage debt in the US is currently at its highest rate ever, sitting at $16.1 trillion. The current mortgage debt is 8.8 percent higher than at the height of the 2008 mortgage crisis.

US household debt balances are also on the rise and have now exceeded $14.3 trillion. Consider that that's $1.6 *trillion* above the previous nominal high of $12.7 trillion in the third quarter of 2008—a response to the financial crisis. The trend is going the wrong way here.

I expect US credit card debt, which stood at over $1 trillion in late 2020, to fall as COVID is factored in. People who celebrated their spouses' birthday or their anniversary by booking a table for two at their local fancy restaurant—who started with a $100 bottle of wine and got there via a cab or Uber—are going to downsize their celebration with a cheaper bottle of wine or will stay at home to celebrate. Those who dropped $100 in one night to take a family of four to the movies are going to spend twenty bucks a month on Netflix and Disney+. This has hurt the economy (well, except for Disney and Netflix).

On the other hand, people will be forced to use their credit cards for life necessities as the direct government payments—in the form of unemployment and stimulus money—run out. These are countervailing forces, and which one will be the more powerful remains to be seen.

But overall, just how much debt is $14.3 trillion, anyway?

This much: there are about 197 million adults (over the age of twenty-one) in the US. Each of them, on average, owes about $72,600. Obviously, that debt is not spread evenly across the population, so some exist happily debt-free, while others stumble around with enormous weights on their shoulders, simply trying not to go under. To put this debt into perspective, currently in America, there is over $100 trillion in total wealth.

It isn't just individuals, either. The government has piled up the debt, as well. But it can create more money as its backstop. As I've noted, with MMT, government borrowing isn't really borrowing; it's just the migration of digits across a ledger. It's investing in the economy for a return later through taxes and productivity. (This is a difficult notion for anyone to comprehend, I understand, but hang on, and I'll do my best to explain it in Chapter 3.)

Beyond individuals and government, the corporate sector has also gone berserk with debt—albeit with central bank help. Here are some eye-popping numbers:

Globally, corporate debt rose from 84 percent of gross world product in 2009 to 92 percent in 2019, about $72 trillion. In the world's eight largest economies—the United States, China, Japan, the United Kingdom, France, Spain, Italy, and Germany—total corporate debt was about $51 trillion in 2019, compared to $34 trillion in 2009, a 50 percent increase in a decade. Over $1 trillion of corporate debt was added in the first half of 2020. As crazy as this will sound, the corporations used billions of dollars of this debt to buy back the shares of the company from the open stock market (in many cases buying the stock from management), which resulted in higher share prices. Thus, as the price of the shares rose, the perception was that all was well with a company, even though the balance sheet was rotting from within from higher debt ratios.

US companies owe more than $10 trillion, nearly half of the country's 2019 GDP of $21.5 trillion. If you add other forms of business debt, including partnerships and small businesses, that figure stands at a nosebleed-level $17 trillion, the *Financial Times* reported in July of 2020.

Since the most recent Wall St. debt party began in 2008, corporate debt held by non-financial companies has increased 92 percent, to nearly $6.8 trillion. (Financial firms often aren't included because they borrow money with at least an alleged intent to lend it again. This could result in a kind of double counting, although in the real world a lot of that money disappears instead into the black hole of corporate buybacks, M&A, and stock dividends.)

The recession, a bit counterintuitively, hasn't restrained corporations from taking on further debt. Far from it. According to financial markets analysts at Dealogic, issuance of investment-grade corporate bonds took a moon shot in 2020, rising to over $1 trillion from less than $400 billion in 2019 and less than $175 billion during its most recent low at the tail end of the financial crisis in 2010.

And the big banks have been hustling these deals through like there's no tomorrow. They couldn't care less where the economy is. They just keep pushing corporate bonds to market because of the enormous fees they collect. As of July 2020, investment banking revenue was up 91 percent at JPMorgan Chase. Citigroup's underwriting business for investment-grade bonds shot up 131 percent, year over year. Goldman Sachs also reported record numbers for debt underwriting, "reflecting a significant increase in industry-wide volumes."

I mentioned earlier how new Fed money does not make its way through to the common worker very quickly. This could change very quickly with direct deposits or other forms of government-mandated stimulus or investments. But as it is now stands, the banks would rather lend at a lower profit to their high-net-worth clients knowing the loans are backed by assets. Thus, a deflationary event. Even though the money supply is increasing, the velocity is not.

This, too, will happen in the corporate bond market. Currently, rating agencies "rank" the company's risk, and its debt is priced relative to its business outlook. The best ranking a corporation can get is AAA. The higher the ranking, the lower the interest rate the company pays out.

The lowest ranking bonds are known as junk bonds, which have to pay the highest interest rates because the company is at great risk of failing.

The global economy is not doing well. We are now entering the corporate bond market's insolvency phase, where many corporations that once held a AAA rating have fallen to BBB, the lowest ranking before junk. General Electric (GE) is a perfect example of this. GE was once the most dominant company globally (GE at its height made up 1 percent of America's GDP) but has already been demoted to BBB and is most likely going to end up getting re-rated to the bottom of the barrel. This means their bonds will have to pay a higher interest rate. Unless the company sells noncore assets to reduce its debt load and does an incredible turnaround, GE is on its way to junk bond status.

There are hundreds of companies that have already descended from BBB to junk bond status. Over 90 percent of all corporate bonds are expected to be in the high-risk and junk category eventually. So, the question becomes: Who is nuts enough to invest in this massive influx of junky new corporate debt?

The Federal Reserve to the rescue. The Fed has become the buyer of last resort. It has already begun to step up, to print new digital cash, and to start buying high-risk and junk bonds in volume to support the economy. All this new debt will be deflationary, although the government will frame it as supporting and creating jobs.

This all seems out of control, like the loons in charge of the madhouse. So, what's going on? Low, low interest rates are a factor, of course. Companies take on more debt because it's cheap and they can. But that doesn't address their primary motivation. It's simple. Hundreds of billions of existing debt in the bond market for these companies was due over the next year. Because of COVID and the economy, there would be no market to refinance the existing debt.

When investors realized that, it tripped the panic button. Fear that companies wouldn't pay their debts led to a big bond selloff in the first weeks after the virus landed. Then the Fed stepped in, stating that it stood prepared to buy corporate bonds for the first time in its history, to whatever extent it deemed necessary. There were going to be bankruptcies aplenty no matter what; the Fed just didn't want them to decimate the corporate sector completely.

That reassured investors. The panic ebbed, and the corporate bond market was open for business as usual.

It wasn't so much a matter of running up new debt. Think of it as a massive rolling over and refinancing of existing debt. When a company has a lot of debt on its balance sheet that needs to be refinanced, I call it the *wall of worry*. Somehow that debt will have to be paid back.

A company caught in this bind usually doesn't like to devalue itself by selling assets to come up with the cash to pay it off. It normally can't pay the debt down from free cash flow, which may be declining in the current deflation. It usually doesn't want to issue new equities, which means dilution for shareholders (many of whom may be company executives themselves). So, the solution of choice tends to be to just refinance the debt. That was a problem when interest rates were higher than the borrower's original rate. But in a zero-interest-rate environment, it's a no-brainer to roll over. And now, even if the market turns thumbs down on the company's bonds, the Fed will step in and buy. A double no-brainer.

This strategy is what I call *amend, extend,* and *pretend,* i.e., what the company does is *amend* the terms of the debt, *extend* the length to pay the debt as cheaply as it can for as long as it can, and *pretend* that everything is going to work out just fine.

Of course, there are some obvious flaws here. One consequence of this Fed-backed borrowing's low cost is that it will inevitably keep some corporations alive that would otherwise have gone bankrupt. Thus, we have a whole class of so-called *zombie companies* that stagger around like their namesake, too weak to invest and grow but kept alive by cheap cash that might be put to better use elsewhere. In this way, the US is beginning to mirror Japan, the poster child for the zombie phenomenon. The Japanese government and their central bank have been propping up weak companies for over twenty-five years, contributing to the country's economic stagnation over that period. Another good example is how the UK lost its mantle as the most powerful nation after WWII. Why? Its government and central bank failed to provide a framework for the expansion and upgrade of its infrastructure and keep up with America.

CONVEXITY OF BONDS

Where bonds are concerned, we live in what some call a "yield grab" trading environment. For a long while now, investors have cared not a whit about bonds as interest-bearing instruments;

all they wanted was to bask in the big returns from increases in premiums as interest rates plummeted. (The value of a bond increases as its rate decreases.) Investors are now playing the bond market as if it were the NASDAQ, seeking equity-style gains. This is called *convexity*. With the backing of the Fed, the corporate bond market is becoming just like the stock market. A casino.

There's a lot of risk here, as increasing amounts of corporate debt sit on the borderline of investment grade and are in danger of sliding to junk status. Goldman Sachs estimates that $765 billion worth of investment-grade and high-yield bonds experienced rating downgrades during just the first three months of 2020. And rating agency Moody's notes ominously that some $169 billion of debt will come due in 2020 along with another $300 billion in 2021—and that rolling over that debt will be difficult "under these trying conditions."

Accordingly, Moody's cut its outlook for US corporate debt from stable to negative. Fitch, another ratings agency, is likewise gloomy, forecasting a doubling in defaults in 2020 on US-leveraged loans, meaning bank loans to businesses considered riskier. The agency expects a default rate of 5 to 6 percent for all of 2020, compared to 3 percent in 2019. Fitch predicts defaults of between 8 and 9 percent in 2021 for a nominal value of $200 billion in bad debt over two years. Among retail and energy companies, the default rate could approach 20 percent. Other hard-hit sectors are likely to be airlines, hotels, restaurants, casinos, and cinemas.

Yet with the Fed backing this debt, you might ask: Who needs Moody's? And bond investors would certainly agree with you.

To me, the bond mania is plenty ill-advised. The new normal will include extensive bankruptcies and consolidations, all of which will contribute to what I see as a widespread, deepening deflation.

Now let's step back and contemplate where we are.

For many reasons, the US has fallen into a deflationary recession that could turn into a depression—although the distinction between the two is rather fuzzy. Harry Truman's definitions are probably as apt as any. "It's a recession when your neighbor loses his job; it's a depression when you lose yours," Truman famously said.

In addition to the indicators I've already detailed, there is also a change in consumer spending. Seventy percent of GDP in the US goes toward household items, and people's attitude toward consumer goods is rapidly shifting from *what I want* to *what I need*. I believe this will hold true for at least the next few years. Lowered personal spending is deflationary.

Moreover, people are making different, thriftier choices within their entertainment budget. Excursions to the cinema are replaced by streaming, with cheap homemade popcorn instead of expensive bucketfuls. A night at the ballpark has yielded to watching games on TV, played in empty stadiums. Flying someplace on vacation gives way to driving someplace less glamorous. Air travel itself has taken a huge hit and will be a long time in recovering. **Lowered discretionary spending is deflationary.**

Though we haven't seen it yet—if the explosion of corporate debt in 2020 is any indicator—I think that ultimately there will be a shift toward prudence in the corporate world too. The pandemic has demonstrated how fragile even the most successful businesses can be, and businesses' bankruptcies unable to access the Fed's largesse are soaring. I believe the appetite for risk, and thus for reckless spending, will decline. Capital will be deployed into safer investments. A new mentality will take hold in time, and it'll be here for some time to come. **Lowered corporate spending, as well as bankruptcies, are deflationary.**

The workspace has changed dramatically. With some 40 percent of the workforce now toiling at home, many people and companies have realized that downtown offices are not nearly as necessary as previously thought. Large numbers of at-home workers mean less driving, lower gasoline consumption, less money spent on parking lots, decreased usage of taxis and Ubers, fewer restaurant lunches, and a rise in empty office buildings, among other things. **All deflationary.**

Furthermore, senior management teams have realized that within their organizations, Pareto's law—the 80/20 rule, where 20 percent of the employees can be expected to carry 80 percent of the workload and generate 80 percent of the gains—is truer than ever. Thus, cuts will be made, and the focus will be placed on efficiency and reducing costs, **both deflationary.**

I think I've made my point.

Deflation is everywhere.

If a full-on resource race occurs between America and China (with its allies) accelerates and leads to fast-tracked remobilization of the US economy over the next few years, that would be inflationary and help tackle the deflationary forces in play. Thus, crossflation would still be the end result.

TECTONIC SHIFTS

Of course, in response to deflation, the Fed is doing whatever it can to encourage spending and, hopefully, kick the economy back into a higher gear: keep interest rates artificially low, print trillions in new currency units, and hand them out to individuals and businesses.

It worked well enough during the financial crisis, they proclaim. Therefore, it is bound to work this time, just like it did before.

But I disagree. In my view, we have entered an entirely new era, one that involves tectonic shifts, including new realignment of the allies. It is characterized by major changes in behavior and demographics, both personal and corporate, and has implications across the economy. I detailed many of them in the previous pages, as I ticked off the deflationary forces at work in the US. But underpinning all of those is a **radical shift in the psychology of the citizenry.**

We had a great reset before, back in the 1930s, and there are some similarities to the present that are worth noting:

- Back then, monetary policy was radically revised, from the gold standard to a mostly fiat currency. Today, Keynesian monetary policy has been supplanted by MMT.
- Back then, the government began to play a much larger role in the economic life of the country through such things as FDR's make-work programs. Will President Biden be the modern-day version of FDR and put in place the framework for the retooling and upgrading of the existing American infrastructure and supply chains?
- Back then, there was the new national policy of turning inward, an enhanced engagement with domestic affairs, an imperative to fix a broken country. President Trump's *America First* policy resonated with large numbers of people (much like Hoover and Benedict Arnold did during their times in power). Then, the pandemic forced even larger numbers to turn a more internationalist outlook into one that is closely focused on preserving the health of the nation. Trillions of dollars will be created by the Fed. Congress must use them to modernize infrastructure across America, which will lead to the Rise of America.

- Back then, despite unprecedented levels of government economic intervention, people still had to fall back on their own self-reliance to a large degree, just like today.

The latter two of the above reveal the psychological transformation that comes with a great reset. In normal recessions, people don't change; in times of great crisis, such as we face today, they do. I can't stress enough how important this is, nor how long-lived I expect it to be. The coronavirus and the economic contraction it triggered, have changed the way Americans will be looking at themselves, their families, their government, and the world.

We have all been attending a grand party that went on for decades. We ran up debt and lived beyond our means, both as individuals and businesses, as well as the government. Globalization made it possible for us to access low-cost producers and run up trade deficits that exported dollars to import cheap consumer goods.

Now reality has set in. As I said, both the people and the nation will be turning inward. *Satisfying needs instead of wants will be the watchword.* The economy will be more dependent on the government to function. At the same time, people will have to become more dependent on themselves after the initial stimuli fade away. Saving will be embraced. Mountains of debt will start to be paid down. If national politics shift to the left under the Democrats, expect the government to intervene more often in personal finance, helping out with student debt, healthcare, rent subsidies, maybe even a guaranteed basic income for all citizens. If Republicans bounce back and the country moves to the right, expect the government to focus more on bailing out corporate debt and reflating the business sector.

Here are some more aspects of life after the great reset:

- The civil unrest we are currently experiencing will pass, as people grow increasingly wary of violence in their streets. They will demand that authorities respond to put it down, and they will do so. There may be some positive changes that come out of it, but the negatives will be severe.
- The government will become even more heavy-handed.
- Surveillance will follow the Chinese model, where everyone is tracked all the time.
- Your basic freedoms will be eroded.
- The model of individual liberty that was forged in the 1960s will be replaced by a more supportive model of the collective good. The notion of "doing your own thing" will be frowned upon and will fade away (much like it was during the 1940s and 1950s).
- People will come to accept that "money" is electronic digits. Paper currency will shrink, if not disappear entirely. Coins will become history. Eventually, everything will be paid for (and tracked) digitally via your smartphone, smartwatch, and even your smart clothing. Humans could even be implanted with smart technology to regulate their internal bodily functions better, track their purchases, etc.
- Cryptocurrencies will continue to proliferate as blockchain technology becomes integrated into our lives. Bitcoin today is promoted as a cheap call option in the future; I am not so sure about that. The government will have its own crypto. So will the big banks and private corporations like Google and Facebook.
- The movement of money around the world will be simplified. It'll almost be like the nineteenth century when private banks sprang up all over the place.

- De-globalization and the restructuring of supply chains of critical items will be important new watchwords. Companies that shipped their businesses offshore will find it more advantageous to return home. The US will develop domestic supply lines for its most important needs, like pharmaceuticals and manufacturing.
- But despite a deflated economy, technological advances will proceed by leaps and bounds. I'll go into some of them in a later chapter. Prosperity during the Rise of America will be more widespread than it is today. There will still be extremes of wealth inequality, but poorer Americans will generally improve.
- Unemployment will be a persistent problem for a long time. The economy will struggle to recover, and automation/robotics/artificial intelligence will displace more millions of workers. But whole new fields will emerge, most of the hard physical labor that still exists will be taken over by machines, and the government will have to step in to support workers whose jobs disappear. There will be great difficulties, no doubt about it. But time will continue to improve overall living standards that have been rising since the Industrial Revolution.

Obviously, I don't have space to go into these topics at any length here; that's a whole book in itself. However, I will have more to say about some of them in the chapters ahead. In summary, all things taken into account, I am optimistic about the future. But it will be a very different future than what people are used to today. We will be forced to adapt, and we will. We are in for a period of mixed blessings. A time of great challenges but also great opportunities lie just ahead.

We are headed into the state I call *crossflation*. Crossflation will be the direct result of the implementation of MMT as the eventual guiding monetary policy. Certain sectors of the economy, those that are primary recipients of MMT's generosity, will experience significant inflation. On the other side, there will be significant deflation in sectors that are in direct competition with the ones that have most benefited from the government's easy money.

Here is a concrete example of the crossflation I see coming: As "going green" gains traction, expect trillions of MMT digits (dollars) to find their way into East Coast offshore wind electricity generation. That will cause significant inflationary costs in the labor, materials, and other items required to build out wind farms because such a large amount of capital is forcefully injected into a small sector. The direct crossflationary results would be deflation in the East Coast natural gas and coal sectors and utilities that are fossil-fuel dependent. Eventually, as I'll explain in Chapter 6, the green energy companies will have a lower cost of capital (partly as a result of federal support). They will eventually buy out the oil companies, benefit from the cash flows (which will fund green energy production), and then phase out the fossil-fuel energy sector.

My point is that the crossflationary effects of the present monetary policy will be large. There will be significant pockets of inflation in some spaces and directly correlated deflationary pressures in others.

DEMAND FOR THE DOLLAR

It may seem that I have wandered far from the promised topic of this chapter. But I wanted to present, in detail, some of the challenges faced by the US dollar going forward. These are formidable. Many powerful forces are running loose. Inflation, deflation, stagflation, crossflation, recession, depression, economic collapse—all of these things are in play. And no one can say with certainty what the eventual outcome will be as they interact.

Many, if not most, of the mainstream economic talking heads predict a devaluation of the USD, if not the outright end of the USD's reign as the reserve currency of the world. Some are calling for ruinous inflation that will savage the currency, if not destroy it.

I have a different view. I don't like baseless speculation. As I've said over and over, I prefer to deal with what lies right in front of me. And what I see is a world that is currently in desperate need of US dollars and will be for a long time to come. It's within the full power and authority of the US Fed, via the tools of FMC and then MMT, to "print" the digits necessary to satisfy the global dollar addiction. If you take nothing else away from these writings, take this: **the USD will remain the strongest global fiat currency going forward**.

To understand why, let me go back seventy-five years to World War II. It has been the benchmark for government spending, by far the most expensive war ever fought. The total cost of WWII for all countries, inflation-adjusted, was a combined USD 6 trillion.

The current war against the COVID-19 virus is going to dwarf that number. Already, the stimulus money committed to the current crisis by global governments and central bankers—just in 2020, mind you—exceeds the total cost of WWII, at more than USD 7 trillion. And more will be coming. By the end of 2020, it's estimated that in something excess of $10 trillion will have been spent.

Domestically, we are currently experiencing a trifecta: our monetary, healthcare, and financial systems are all failing. The coronavirus was simply the catalyst that popped the leverage bubble and caused massive asset liquidation and the need to settle or at least roll over debt. As a consequence, there was a mad rush to obtain US dollars.

But that demand was not only domestic. It extends way beyond the country's shores.

For one thing, there is the waning of the *petrodollar*.

The petrodollar originated in the 1970s as a result of the US going off the gold standard, and it served to solidify the buck's status as the world reserve currency for forty years. First, Saudi Arabia, then all of OPEC shortly after, and then other oil producers were compelled to do their trading in US dollars. World trade—based on oil dependency—followed suit.

This meant an unshakeable demand for the USD for anyone who wasn't an oil producer or merely wanted to participate in the global trading boom. It led to not only demand for dollars for the product itself, but also the creation of derivatives priced in USD. Oil powered the world, and the dollar was the system's universal lubricant.

The shale revolution changed that. Within a decade, the US went from the world's biggest oil importer to its biggest producer. Suddenly, the outflow of USD to pay for oil dramatically slowed. Ripple effect: Countries formerly awash in dollars now faced a shortage. Shortages lead to increasing demand, leading to currency strength.

Here's another factor: debt. Other countries are deeply indebted to the US. They have borrowed to build out their infrastructures, modernize their industries, develop their natural resources, and so on. Those debts must be paid back in US dollars, not the local currency. True, that will be impossible for some; there will be bankruptcies and defaults along the way. There will also be places where the nationalization of resources takes place.

But in general, countries with access to capital in the form of USD will not want to jeopardize that access. It's a self-fulfilling loop: Continuing indebtedness that must be paid off in USD naturally creates a continuing demand for USD.

Let me put it a different way. The rest of the world (RoW) is in a predicament I call **DIC**.

D—Debt in USD is continuing or rising.

I—Income is down in USD as the US purchases fewer imports.

C—Capital outflows are increasing, meaning foreigners are selling assets to acquire USD.

This means that the central banks, corporations, states, and provinces of the RoW will be in a perpetual shortage of USD. This is especially true during the pandemic and its associated crisis, as people everywhere are engaged in a flight to safety, which always means dollars. And high demand strengthens the market value of any commodity, including money.

The RoW is in deflation (then eventually stagflation and then inflation) when the US markets are having their great reset. Yes, the RoW will experience deflation while the US markets keep attracting money and remain on an inflationary trajectory.

In a sense, it's global crossflation.

The dollar will remain dominant through it all, and the Fed's implementation of international **SWAP Lines will continue.**

THE ENORMOUS IMPORTANCE OF SWAP LINES

The US Federal Reserve has adopted a cunning strategy to satisfy the global demand for dollars while maintaining the buck's title as the planet-wide currency king. It has divided the world up into allies of the US and non-allies.

- Now this may be a hard thing for most of you to swallow, but the fact is that the United States has become more important to its allies than at any point in history.

I know this may sound crazy—and it *is* crazy—because as bad as the current crisis is, it's nowhere near as bad as World War II, humanity's bloodiest conflict. But I am strictly speaking monetarily here, not about the allies' dependence on the US military to win that war (with the help of the Soviets, of course).

And monetarily, to the politicians and central bankers around the world, the current crisis *is* worse than WWII. Why? Because nobody working at any central bank or any politician in any government was an adult during WWII. They don't remember it. They never experienced ration books and soaring debt/GDP ratios and shattered credit and unstable currencies—none of it.

The current crisis is *the* financial crisis of their lifetime. And they will have to deal with it.

In the 1940s, there was a massive need for dollars to combat the threat of totalitarianism. Today, everyone needs the stability of the USD in a world turned upside down with economic turmoil. Granted, that stability may be only relative to other countries' own currencies. But our allies have to deal with that reality. They know it; the Fed knows it. That's why the Fed has created unprecedented access to the US dollar for government-identified friends of America and denied access to those identified as unfriendly.

It's crucially important that you understand this (and when you do, you'll be miles ahead of almost everyone else). The US has put in place a system where all but the most die-hard anti-American nations will want to be included among the friendlies. In fact, many will do *anything* to make the list.

The Fed has accomplished this through *SWAP Lines*.

If you have access to a US SWAP Line, you are what I call a **+SWAP Line Nation (positive SWAP Line Nation)**, and if you don't have access to a SWAP Line, you are a **−SWAP Line Nation (negative SWAP Line Nation)**.

For the most part, when I bring it up SWAP Lines, I have found myself speaking into a vacuum. I haven't come across one person in a hundred—including business executives, politicians, or even bigshots in the financial industry itself—who is even cognizant of the program's existence, much less aware of its significance.

It's not like it's some big secret. Here's how the Fed explains SWAP Lines on its own website:

> When a foreign central bank draws on its SWAP Line with the Federal Reserve, the foreign central bank sells a specified amount of its currency to the Federal Reserve in exchange for dollars at the prevailing market exchange rate. The Federal Reserve holds the foreign currency in an account at the foreign central bank. The dollars that the Federal Reserve provides are deposited in an account that the foreign central bank maintains at the Federal Reserve Bank of New York. At the same time, the Federal Reserve and the foreign central bank enter into a binding agreement for a second transaction that obligates the foreign central bank to buy back its currency on a specified future date at the same exchange rate. The second transaction unwinds the first. At the conclusion of the second transaction, the foreign central bank pays interest, at a market-based rate, to the Federal Reserve. Dollar liquidity swaps have maturities ranging from overnight to three months.

That's some very dry prose that somewhat conceals the grim reality beneath. The economic contraction brought on by the pandemic is global, and it's worse in many places than it is in America. For instance, the GDP drop of the UK in Q2 of 2020 was twice what it was in the US. Spain was even worse.

To put it mildly, financial authorities in these countries have freaked out.

In the wake of the panic, many central banks quickly requested that America provide financial assistance to at least alleviate the stress caused by a lack of US dollar supply. SWAP Lines have provided that relief and will continue to do so. They are, literally, lifelines. But they are also in debt. All those dollars borrowed must be paid back in dollars, with interest, also requiring dollars. A clear illustration of demand breeding further demand.

It will be paramount for nations grappling with deflation to gain entry into the favored group capable of exercising SWAP Lines—those that I call the positive SWAP Line Nations (+SWAP Line Nation). Countries outside the group—the negative SWAP Line Nations (–SWAP Line Nations)—will struggle to access US dollars. Countries receiving SWAP Lines will follow any stipulations they are asked to follow. Suppose you want to be blessed with a SWAP Line from the US. In that case, you must be careful not to antagonize the hand that feeds you (which means not aligning in any way with nations designated as non-friendly and agreeing to follow any restrictions, such as sanctions, that the US government puts on).

The struggling nations that require emergency access to US dollars and can't get them may and probably will engage in the expropriation of foreign-owned assets as the world recession deepens. They may have no choice. It could be either that or face crippling depressions or revolutionary uprisings of their citizens, or both. So, American businesses with operations in these places had better beware. You have been warned.

Nations that do have existing SWAP Lines, on the other hand, won't screw around with foreign-operated entities (American companies). They won't nationalize their gold mines, copper mines, whatever. They also won't put foreign exchange restrictions on the foreign (American) companies operating there. There will be no prevention of the fruits of those invested US dollars being sent back home as dividends to the company's owners. Again, the dollar outflow demands that you procure the dollars to flow.

So, who made the cut? Here's the original list:

1. Bank of Canada
2. Bank of England
3. European Central Bank
4. Bank of Japan
5. Swiss National Bank

On March 19, 2020, the Fed added SWAP arrangements with these guys:

6. Reserve Bank of Australia
7. Banco Central do Brasil
8. Danmarks Nationalbank (Denmark)
9. Bank of Korea
10. Banco de México
11. Reserve Bank of New Zealand
12. Norges Bank (Norway)
13. Monetary Authority of Singapore
14. Sveriges Riksbank (Sweden)

As global deflation progresses, there will be more nations that will be granted SWAP Lines. But do not forget, SWAP Lines will always come in defense of American interests. Many other nations that do not have direct access to them will set up "sub SWAP Lines" with the fourteen nations that do have access to US SWAP Lines (but all of those would have to be preapproved by the US).

But that's it at this point—those fourteen are America's friends (read: allies) in the world.

And just so you know, this is BIG business. By April 2020, the drawdown of USD SWAP Lines was just under half a trillion dollars. The last time that foreign central banks took down that amount from US SWAP Lines was at the height of the 2008 global financial crisis. The SWAP Lines worked back then to prevent a complete worldwide financial meltdown, as the shortage of US dollars in the foreign markets was filled by the US Federal Reserve. Same thing now. But this is just the tip of the iceberg.

Few want to be shut out, and around eighty-five countries have applied for US SWAP Lines. In fact, Indian Prime Minister Narendra Modi has publicly confessed to having "SWAP Line envy." I'm pretty confident that India will get its SWAP Line at some point, not least because major American companies like Facebook and Google are itching to move into the planet's second-most populous country, big time. But India first has to solidify its ally status by lining up behind American foreign policy. And it will. Is it just a coincidence that Indian military tension is at all-time highs with China currently? I think not.

Over time, I expect these critically important SWAP Lines to be increased and more nations to be slowly added. They'll be subject to the terms set by the US government—both financially and geopolitically. But they'll accede. As monetary and fiscal policy are blending into one under MMT, it's just a matter of time before the president uses SWAP Lines as a big geopolitical leverage hammer.

BACKSTOPPING THE OFFSHORE US-DOLLAR SYSTEM

SWAP Lines had their origin in the 1960s, were briefly re-established in the wake of 9/11, but only became of global importance with the onset of the great financial crisis (GFC) of 2007–09.

They came to the fore at that time because the GFC threatened to take down the Offshore US-Dollar System, a financial infrastructure that is the linchpin of the international monetary system.

How the international monetary system is set up is of essential importance for the global political economy. It impacts everything from nations' internal financial stability to the global distribution of power.

The system developed after the collapse of the Bretton Woods agreement that was cobbled together as World War II was winding down. Bretton Woods acknowledged that the world's countries would have to have some kind of monetary system that would foster the re-establishment of international trade in the aftermath of history's most ruinous war. The agreement was based on the forty-three signatory nations' acceptance of the US dollar as the world's reserve currency. It established a gold exchange standard whereby each of these nations' currencies had a fixed parity to the dollar, which itself was pegged to, and could be exchanged for, gold at $35 per ounce.

It was the first attempt at financial globalization. It worked pretty well until, as noted earlier, Nixon took the US off of the gold exchange standard in 1971 and negotiated the subsequent creation of the petrodollar.

Outside of the petrodollar, the structural replacement for Bretton Woods that evolved over the next thirty-five years was notable in that it wasn't the result of any kind of purposeful design, no central planning or formal agreement. It just sort of happened, as private, profit-oriented financial institutions shifted the activities of credit money creation offshore.

Definitions: "Onshore" money creation occurs within a monetary jurisdiction, such as when the Fed creates legal tender dollars within the US. "Offshore" money creation occurs when an institution creates USD-denominated deposits that are legally situated in a different monetary jurisdiction, one that allows offshore money creation and where the issuing institution is domiciled.

The advent of the Eurodollar characterized the new system. It's not how it sounds. A Eurodollar is simply a US dollar created and deposited in an account outside of its country of origin. That could be anywhere in the world, not necessarily Europe. (Petrodollars, for example, are Eurodollars.) The US central bank, the Federal Reserve, facilitated the process and serves as a backstop but did not originate or drive it. Commercial banks create Eurodollar deposits (credit money) and what is known as the "shadow banking" system—shadow banks being non-bank financial institutions that have a legally different status than traditional banks but which in the realm of money creation perform functionally equivalent operations.

Eurodollars are attractive to the issuing institutions because they are not subject to domestic bank regulators' oversight. Commercial and shadow banks who employ them can offer higher interest rates on deposits, offer loans at lower interest rates, and enjoy greater profit margins.

At the same time, Eurodollars are attractive to their recipients. Offshore USD creation makes it possible to use a single unit of account for cross-border real and financial transactions. This reduces the need for currency conversion and foreigners' exposure to exchange rate risk. Exchange rates between different units of account are replaced by a par exchange rate between onshore and offshore USD.

The keyword here is *par*. The Offshore US-Dollar System will work as long as Eurodollars trade at par with domestically created dollars. That's the defining feature that makes them acceptable as "money." If the par relationship between domestic and Eurodollars breaks down, then holders of Eurodollars will get screwed. And then the system could collapse.

Which it almost did during the GFC.

As the effects of the US real estate market meltdown rippled outward, investors holding Eurodollars began to doubt whether those instruments could keep up the promised par exchange rate with onshore deposits. So, they hastened to convert their offshore and shadow money balances into onshore deposits protected by the Federal Deposit Insurance Corporation (Eurodollars are not).

It became a self-fulfilling prophecy. Out of fear that par might break, enough investors bailed on the system that they caused the par exchange rate to break down.

The situation was dire enough for the Fed to step in and take the "temporary" emergency measure of extending SWAP Lines to its partnering central banks. This fostered the liquidity that allowed the partner banks to create offshore USD as public money on their own balance sheets and then lend it on to banks domiciled in their own jurisdictions, thereby protecting financial globalization structures. It saved the system.

Many years ago, economist Milton Friedman commented

that "Nothing is so permanent as a temporary government program." I'm sure he would have agreed to apply that sentiment to the Federal Reserve as well. The Fed maintained its "temporary" SWAP Lines as the GFC abated—and had them ready to go when the coronavirus crisis hit.

The deeper meaning here should have received widespread attention. Still, it hasn't: By making other central banks dependent on its largesse, the Fed has effectively turned them into branches of itself. It is now firmly established as a central banker to the world and is recognized as the lender of last resort far beyond the United States' borders.

As you can see, I have made the case that you should ignore the negativists calling for the USD's collapse. In my view, the exact opposite is happening. I've already detailed several reasons for why there will be strong and ongoing dollar demand, culminating with a SWAP Line system that holds the whole structure together. As I wrote earlier, the Fed may be on its way to becoming the *de facto* central bank of the world.

But at the very least, I believe a very powerful international alliance is forming—a monetary alliance anchored by the dollar.

Poor countries will continue to attempt to renegotiate their loans with the IMF and use everything at hand to do so, whether it's natural and critical resources, livestock, access ways, and rights to pipelines, dams, rivers, and ports.

Many may ask for a debt jubilee, but we are still far off from jubilee time, as their bankers will first try to inflate their debts away.

Also, there is still lots of wealth for the champagne socialists to go after as they try to redistribute money to those who are less fortunate by their own definitions. Expect some or all: transactional taxes in equities and bond trading, taxes on cash and savings, a tax on net assets, new taxes on capital gains, and carbon taxes that will be levied against the old industries.

What does this have to do with the Rise of America? Everything.

Even with all of these daunting negative changes on the horizon, America will still be *the* place to create wealth, and the US dollar will remain in short supply in the RoW for years to come. Its strength will endure way beyond the easing of the current recession.

And now that I've already spoken so much about MMT, it's time for a deep dive into that revolution in monetary policy.

CHAPTER THREE

A BRAVE NEW MONETARY WORLD

THE POLICIES OF KEYNESIAN ECONOMICS COMBINED WITH shifting demographics helped fuel the global economy. With that came the rise of globalization, meaning that nations' economies became more intertwined than ever before. You can think of this as the "butterfly effect." Something that would happen in one nation's economy would have ripple effects across numerous other nations' economies.

Because of this increased economic interdependence, the policies of the US Federal Reserve had to evolve. Traditional Keynesianism had foundered on a monetary reef. It was no longer a viable policy, as it became starkly evident during the 2008 GFC.

Key components of the necessary change were the repo market (see below) and SWAP Line mechanisms (see Chapter 2).

Much of the current framework Jerome Powell, the current chair of the US Federal Reserve, has currently laid out is very similar to the FMC framework first used by Marriner Eccles, chairman of the US Federal Reserve from 1934–1948.

However, for FMC to work as it did under Eccles, Congress

must be fully in line to execute large fiscal plans and be united in its deployment. Sadly, the current rift in American politics and Congress is a major concern. Besides, if President Biden cannot unite the nation, the planned stimulus could fail. If either fails, MMT will become the go-to framework,

This would set the stage for a brave, new world, which will be completely realized by the full-on acceptance by most in the markets (bond, equity, and political) of **Modern Monetary Theory** by the Fed (and by central banks everywhere).

Now, it's not a foregone conclusion that MMT will be fully implemented by the US Federal Reserve. As I have stated before, there is a strong argument that framework will echo the same framework used by the US Federal Reserve from 1942–1951. The Federal Reserve and Congress worked in coordination to fund the war effort and develop the major infrastructure across America. This is an example of fiscal-monetary coordination. It worked then, and there is a strong possibility it could work today.

The major difference obviously between now and then is the actual dollar amount of stimulus printed and the direct-to-the-individual stimulus cheques. Either way, the central bank will do whatever it has to do and expect trillions and trillions of dollars of further stimulus.

Many in finance today argue that Modern Monetary Theory is just a modern version of fiscal-monetary coordination. The biggest difference between fiscal-monetary coordination and Modern Monetary Theory is that in FMC, debts and deficits matter, whereas in MMT, they do not. I do believe the current framework the Fed will apply under President Biden is FMC.

The biggest challenge President Biden's administration will have over the next four years is to usher in large enough long-term stimulus plans for the US economy to rebuild its infrastructure (from electrical grids to medical facilities to schools, bridges, roads, etc.) and supply chains. This will lay down the groundwork for the Rise of America while ushering in a new golden era for the US economy that will raise all Americans' living standards (including minorities, which the golden era of 1940s to the 1960s did not).

These are critically important topics that strengthen my view of the Rise of America. The country is poised to prosper, perhaps as never before, and monetary policy is at the center of it all. Thus, what's going on—largely out of the media and its pet economists' sight—demands a detailed and close examination.

So, let's dig into how we are eventually going to get to MMT. Spoiler alert: You are about to learn why the MMT experiment is the most radical redefinition of money since...well, probably since the invention of money itself.

Skeptical?

Read on.

REPO

What is the repo market, and why is it important?

In a way, the repo (short for *repurchase*) market is the linchpin that holds our financial structure together. It is hugely important, yet not one in a hundred citizens knows what it is. When they think of the word repo (if they ever do), most people will only tell you it is what happens to your car if you stop making your loan payments to the bank.

I'm talking, instead, about the financial repo market. When things break down there, that's bad. In fact, repo can serve as the canary in the coal mine.

Let me explain.

The repo market is a credit market, a source of funding. In today's financial world, the big banks often need liquidity—because of immediate demands on their assets—that they can't meet at the moment. So, they have an arrangement that allows them to privately borrow from each other or the Federal Reserve. The lending institution makes a collateralized loan, short term, typically at a low interest rate. Repo loans are intended to turn over quickly. Many are settled overnight, though they can be longer.

Think of them as the grease that keeps the wheels of finance turning, meaning the banks can use repo to avoid shortfalls and a freeze in the "flow" of capital. Once capital flow seizes up, you have the disaster known as a liquidity crisis. This can result in a loss of trust in the system, an eventual collapse of the bank, and the loss of assets of its customers.

Repo can be summarized essentially as the bank putting up collateral of assets for a short-term loan that the bank will repurchase later at an agreed-upon price. The percentage earned by the investor is called the "repo rate."

The repo rate is based on other securitized bonds and is analogous to the interest rate on a bank deposit.

So that you know, we're not exactly talking chump change here. On average, $2 to $4 *trillion* in repurchase agreements are traded each business day. (You may also see the term *reverse repo*. It's not really different. A repo is when a buyer initiates the agreement; a reverse repo is when the seller initiates it.)

A Brookings Institution paper explains that "the repo market is important for at least two reasons:

1. The repo market allows financial institutions that own lots of securities (e.g., banks, broker-dealers, hedge funds) to

borrow cheaply. It allows parties with lots of spare cash (e.g., money market mutual funds) to earn a small return on that cash without much risk because securities, often US Treasury securities, serve as collateral. Financial institutions do not want to hold cash because it is expensive—it doesn't pay interest. For example, hedge funds hold many assets but may need money to finance day-to-day trades, so they borrow from money market funds with lots of cash, which can earn a return without taking much risk.

2. The Federal Reserve uses repos and reverse repos to conduct monetary policy. When the Fed buys securities from a seller who agrees to repurchase them, it injects reserves into the financial system. Conversely, when the Fed sells securities with an agreement to repurchase, it drains the system's reserves. Since the ['08] crisis, reverse repos have taken on new importance as a monetary policy tool. Reserves are the amount of cash banks hold—either currency in their vaults or on deposit at the Fed. The Fed sets a minimum level of reserves; anything over the minimum are called "excess reserves." Banks can and often do lend excess reserves in the repo market.

Naturally enough, the repo market is built on trust. Lenders must be reasonably assured that they're going to get their money back or if worse comes to worst and the borrower defaults, that the collateral they hold will cover the money lost.

So, you can see why these loans can be the canary in the coal mine. A dead canary signals the onset of a liquidity crisis.

That's what happened in the panic of '07–'08. Banks were largely using mortgage-backed securities (MBS) as collateral in the repo market, an MBS being a bundle of mortgages treated as a single security. But as MBS's were increasingly *hypothecated* and *re-hypothecated*—which means that they could be sold and re-sold, including being split apart and bundled many times over—the system reached a dizzying level of complexity. An MBS that started out containing only blue-chip mortgages could wind up stuffed with junk instead—a situation of which buyers were seldom aware.

MBS's became hot potatoes, with no one wanting to be the one caught with burnt hands. The industry even invented a whole new instrument, the credit default swap (CDS), to deal with the situation. A CDS was a kind of insurance policy that buyers of an MBS would take out to protect themselves if the value of the MBS went into meltdown.

Too late.

CDS's were themselves traded, over and over, until it was difficult to say who owed what to whom.

As bad subprime mortgages increasingly went into default, there was less and less trust in the value of the MBS's used as collateral until it reached the point where, basically, no one knew what anything was worth anymore. When defaults happened, lenders found no buyers for the collateral they were holding, leaving them to take some nasty haircuts. Pretty soon, interbank lending dried up because all trust in collateralized banking was gone.

Liquidity evaporated. The system was on the verge of a fatal seizure—think empty ATMs and money market accounts with nothing in them—when the government stepped in at the last moment with its Troubled Asset Relief Program (TARP). Under TARP, the distressed banks got a $700 billion injection of capital and were allowed to divest themselves of large amounts of toxic assets at par, i. e., the government would take crap off the banks' hands, paying more than the junk was worth on the open market.

The system was saved, for the moment. But in actuality, the can was kicked down the road. Most of the systemic market mal-practices were not only not fixed, but they were also encouraged to keep going. The Fed maintained its low-interest-rate, easy-money policy, and capital continued to migrate into assets like the stock and bond markets, which rocketed to new highs.

Fast-forward to mid-September 2019. Though the media barely took notice, and the average person not at all, the canary passed out in the coal mine: the repo rate suddenly and inexplicably shot up, spiking as high as 10 percent intra-day on September 17, 2019.

Trust me, the financial world noticed. So did the Fed. It meant that the banking system's liquidity was on shaky legs. No one was certain what had caused the spike. Brookings offers this theory: *"Banks wanted (or felt compelled) to hold more reserves than the Fed anticipated and were unwilling to lend those reserves in the repo market, where there were a lot of people with Treasuries who wanted to use them as collateral for cash. As demand exceeded supply, the repo rate rose sharply."*

Other observers have speculated that a major (Too Big to Fail) bank was in deep financial distress, perhaps on the verge of insolvency, and needed some quick cash to right the ship, at least temporarily.

Whatever the cause, this was a genuine crisis. The Fed recognized it as such and immediately acted to pump liquidity into the system. It offered at least $75 billion in daily repos and $35 billion in long-term repo twice per week. Subsequently, it increased its daily lending to $120 billion and lowered its long-term lending. That's a major freak-out. It means short-term solvency was particularly imperiled.

The crisis passed.

Until the COVID-19 pandemic struck in full force, shutting down the global economy in March 2020.

At the onset of the pandemic, there was a run on money market funds as people panicked and fled to cash. These funds sold securities to meet outflows, but turmoil in the financial markets made it difficult to dispose of even high-quality securities. The Fed reassured markets by saying that its repo facility "will assist money market funds in meeting demands for redemptions by households and other investors, enhancing overall market functioning and credit provision to the broader economy."

The Fed's involvement in the repo market has continued to be extensive since the September '19 crisis, offering $100 billion in overnight repo and $20 billion in two-week repo. That's a lot. But the virus has blown the program wide open, both in the amounts offered and loan length. At this writing, in late 2020, the Fed is offering $1 trillion in daily overnight repo, $500 billion in one-month repo, and $500 billion in three-month repo.

In other words, there is one hell of a lot of currency sloshing around in a system that has come to depend on the Fed to keep it afloat. What the consequences are, we will find out only over time.

Meanwhile, Keynesianism got the boot.

An absolute turning point came when US Federal Reserve Chair Jerome Powell stated publicly in a May 2020 *60 Minutes* interview that the Fed has many bullets left in its arsenal. And the absolute key line was:

"We print digits."

With that interview and those words, Powell's announcement sounded to many like the US Federal Reserve is totally committed to **Modern Monetary Theory**.

I believe that the politicians will eventually push the limits of central banking, and fiscal-monetary cooperation will be pushed to the limit where the politicians do push on with MMT. If so, we'd all better get very familiar with MMT.

THE PRICE OF PROSPERITY: WHAT IS MMT?

This will be perhaps the most challenging section of this book because there are concepts here that are exceedingly difficult to wrap one's head around. To successfully do that, you're going to have to set aside virtually all of your preconceived notions of what money, credit, and debt are and how they function within the new economy.

When you understand what I'm about to lay out, you'll be miles ahead of 99.9 percent of the population, including all the financial "experts" you see on TV or whose blogs you read.

> From the outset: As I proceed, please bear in mind that **I am not proselytizing for Modern Monetary Theory**. I do not consider it the pinnacle of economic thought, nor that it will bring us a thousand years of stability and prosperity with nary a bump or bruise along the way. I am only the messenger (and please, do not shoot the messenger). What I personally think of MMT is immaterial.

I've said it before and can't say it enough: All that I do, as an investor and fund manager, is to deal with the reality that has been handed to me.

And at present, **FMC is the framework upon us**. MMT is around the corner if FMC fails. With the current political powers in place, if either the president or Congress fails, all fiscal and monetary roads will be moving toward MMT.

Thus, what follows is what *is*, not what you or I might wish it to be. Whether or not MMT's argument persuades you and me does not matter. The fact is that everything that happens now and in the next few decades in the financial arena will be determined by fiscal and monetary policy. To act as if the world is a different place is nuts and will be very costly to those who deny reality. I do not do that. Neither should you.

THE RUNUP TO MMT

To begin, it helps to have some knowledge of monetary history. I am not going to go into detail here; I decided that MMT is so important that it's best to dive into it right away and save a detailed examination of how we got to where we are for later. Nevertheless, a quick summary:

What we think of as "money" was invented around the seventh century BC. People needed something that would foster trade better than barter, and they settled on gold and silver coins, which had a lot of advantages over alternative choices.

Precious-metal coins continued to be the only money until the introduction of paper certificates, first in China in the seventh century AD, but not in Europe until the seventeenth century. In general, these certificates, or banknotes, were backed by a hoard of precious metals, at least in part, until the twentieth century. The gold standard theory was that the paper currency had a guaranteed value by the issuing authority and was backed by gold. Great Britain, Japan, Russia, Canada, Germany, Austria, China, and many other nations abandoned the gold standard by 1930. The United States kept its form for another forty years and was the last of the great nations to totally dump the gold standard when it did so on August 15, 1971.

The key to maintaining a sound monetary system was to keep inflation in check because people want their money to be worth about the same tomorrow as it is today. (Think of inflation not as a rise in the cost of products and services, but rather as a decline in the purchasing power of the currency.) Once any national or regional currency begins a downward value spiral in the marketplace, the whole system can unravel pretty quickly.

A monetary standard based on a precious metal(s) provides a natural brake on the kind of overspending that politicians love— but that ignites inflation—because gold and silver are always limited in supply. Thus, in nineteenth-century America, which vacillated between a gold and a bimetallic standard, there was an economic boom with no real price inflation.

Politicians and their economist buddies are never satisfied, always looking for ways to build a better mousetrap. It's in their nature, and it's self-serving. If a perfect system were devised, they'd be out of a job.

Many theories have evolved that purport to create monetary standards that will be most beneficial to an economy. They proliferated the more complicated economies became.

The most important was Keynesianism. John Maynard Keynes believed that when an economy hit a downturn, it wasn't necessary for it to work itself out in free-market fashion. That was a tenet of the so-called Austrian School of economics. Keynes contrarily believed that the best course was for the government to step in and inflate the currency, i.e., it should print more dollars, use them to goose the money supply, and pretty soon people would start buying again, and the economy would more quickly recover than if left to its own devices. Conversely, if inflation became a problem, the government should withdraw currency from circulation, reducing the money supply until it reached equilibrium with demand once again.

Now—and this is important—even though the Treasury printed the paper bills, in the US, the ultimate source of money has been the Federal Reserve since its inception in 1913. (The Fed has a long and tangled history that would take up too much space to go into here. For those interested, I'll present a detailed look at the Fed's history in Appendix I.) For now, what you need to know is that the Fed is not a government agency; it's a consortium of private banks.

From its inception, opponents of the Fed cried out that the creation of money should not be in private hands because that invited the banks to use their power for their own benefit—an entirely reasonable objection. But one of the Fed's primary selling points (and for the national interest) was specifically that it *was* independent. Proponents maintained that the private issuance of money was beneficial for the country precisely because it served as a mechanism to prevent politicians from overspending and indulging in excess money creation.

The Fed's independence will become a key issue, as we shall see later in this chapter, so keep it in mind.

Now back to Keynes.

Keynesian economics emerged in the 1930s and really hit its stride when Nixon took the country off the gold standard in 1971, after which his ideas held full sway for over forty years.

That brings us to Keynesianism's final successor, MMT.

THE ROOTS OF A MONETARY REVOLUTION

Okay, the one thing that Modern Monetary Theory is *not* is "modern."

Though MMT is an advanced evolution of Keynesian Economics that is already taking hold worldwide, it ultimately derived from a newfangled twentieth-century idea, the macroeconomic theory of *chartalism* (sometimes called *state money*). It was outlined in the early 1900s by economist Mitchell Innes. He championed a *fiat currency* (not backed by anything), which was heresy to the precious-metal-backed money enthusiasts who were ascendant at the time.

Chartalists led by Innes proclaimed that, "Fiat currency has value in exchange because of [government's] sovereign power to levy taxes on economic activity payable in the currency they issue."

He further argued that: "Credit and credit alone is money... Credit is simply the correlative of debt. What A owes to B is A's debt to B and B's credit on A... The words 'credit' and 'debt' express a legal relationship between two parties, and they express the same legal relationship seen from two opposite sides."

This was a radical break from a past in which people believed that the money supply was determined by the backing of something tangible—such as precious metals—that had value in and of itself. Governments (or private mints) could issue money in the form of coins and benefit from *seigniorage*, i.e., the difference between the face value of coins and their production costs. That relationship gave structure to monetary systems.

When paper replaces coins, then the cost of production falls drastically. When electronic bits and bytes replace paper, then the cost of production is essentially zero. Governments are incentivized to "print" as much as they like, which means a new way of defining money was needed. How could it maintain value if it wasn't backed by something tangible?

To the new way of thinking, money was seen not as something

to be coined and placed into circulation but credit advanced by the government for which there must be a debtor on the other side of the transaction. This was why the Treasury came to issue bills at interest. The ability to collect taxes was supposed to be the factor that canceled the credit issued, at least in theory.

Keynesians relied on the government's control of the old-fashioned printing press. It could be used to increase the money supply if the economy faltered. If the economy overheated, the government could contract the money supply by taking more currency out of circulation than it printed. In this way, equilibrium could be reached in which booms never got out of hand and busts never happened. Deficit government spending as a policy was okay because credit issued would result in economic growth, which would result in greater tax collection, which would offset the credit issued. The economy would push ever forward in a never-ending loop.

This loop was designed to be self-correcting. The money supply would expand and contract according to market conditions, and the economy would be kept running on an even keel. Backing this theory is the *efficient market hypothesis*, which holds that the collective decision-making by millions of market participants will always cause an asset—in this case, money itself—to find its true, intrinsic value level.

Well, theory is one thing, and the real world is another—as the central banks around the world would quickly find out.

With the advent of Keynesianism and abandonment of the direct ties of money to gold in most countries, governments in deep trouble (famously, Weimar Germany) came to believe that they could paper over (pun intended) their difficulties simply by issuing currency in amounts vastly beyond what productivity growth and taxes could cover. As a result, many countries experienced hyperinflation in the twentieth century; many currencies became worthless. At various points in the 1900s, Argentina, Germany, Hungary, Zimbabwe, Yugoslavia, and Venezuela all became poster children for the pitfalls of unlimited fiat currency creation.

The US dollar has been spared a similar fate. One of the main reasons for this is that while all of the world went off the gold standard by 1931, the US maintained a *gold exchange standard* for forty years, until August 15, 1971. This meant that, while American citizens were prohibited from owning gold or using it in domestic transactions, foreign governments were allowed to exchange greenbacks—acquired through international trade—for bullion. Another major reason was the upgraded infrastructure and supply chains and the strength of the US economy because of the relatively new large and powerful middle class. This resulted in a very long buildup of global confidence in the strength of the dollar relative to other currencies—think of it as the generation of enormous goodwill—culminating in its formal establishment as the reserve currency of the entire planet after World War II.

Thus, citizens in countries with currency issues have inevitably run to the most widely acknowledged safe haven, the US dollar. In general, this means they try to turn whatever assets they have into dollars, propping up the buck in the process and bolstering its supremacy.

KEYNES RUNS AGROUND

But behind the scenes, something else was afoot. As the last quarter of the twentieth century unfolded, the unit of account for a dollar became no longer a piece of paper, much less a metal coin.

It had morphed into an electronic digit, a necessary precondition for the transformation of Keynesianism into MMT.

Unfortunately, even in an economy as strong as America's, Keynesianism didn't work. It failed to prevent the stagflation of the '70s, the recession of the early '80s, the crash of 2000, or the near disintegration of the whole financial structure in 2008. It helps to know the role energy prices played on inflationary pressures: the Achilles heel to Keynesian economics. In Chapter 6, I cover how MMT, if applied correctly, can avoid a similar fate, in theory at least.

The financial crisis of '08 really stressed the system. A liquidity crisis brought it about fueled by the big banks, which had made some really boneheaded financial decisions. In brief, when their bills came due, they couldn't pay them. Interbank lending, which greases the system's wheels, dried up because lenders lost faith in borrowers' collateral creditworthiness.

Officials from the Fed, government, and the big banks gathered in a room in Washington one weekend to decide how to save the system because there was the very real possibility that Americans would wake up on Monday morning to find that their money market accounts had *poof!* disappeared and that ATMs would no longer dispense anything but hot air.

The Fed's response was to let some banks—like Lehman Brothers—go bankrupt while it saved others through *quantitative easing*, more commonly known as *QE*.

Under QE, the Fed created and lent money from thin air to the banks to re-liquify. Through very low interest rate loans or, through TARP, it did this with the purchase of some of the banks' more toxic assets, taking them off the banks' hands at par value (which many of them didn't deserve) and putting them on its own balance sheet.

This worked. The financial system slowly recovered.

But the world had changed.

What was intended as a stopgap measure never went away. QE persisted, albeit under different names. Yet, the perception in Washington was that even this wasn't enough to ensure financial stability. Something different, radical, and more far-reaching was needed, especially if there was a repeat financial crisis, or worse.

MMT is that something.

It is a *major* philosophical break from the past because debts no longer matter. MMT will make full use of the transition of "money" from coins, or even paper notes, to digits on a spreadsheet whose existence can only be described as evanescent.

HOW MMT WORKS, IN THEORY

With MMT, money or dollars are always available because, in theory, governments who have control of the levers of both monetary and fiscal policy cannot run out of money for payments in their own currency. They are the currency issuers, not the consumers or users of it. In a sense, they are the drug creator, not the drug user, not the drug dealer. Therefore, they cannot default on their debts—**as long as the debt is denominated in *their* currency**. This is the core principle. They can **always** create more currency to pay any debt in their own currency. The only macroeconomic constraint to MMT is inflation. Control inflation—primarily through stimulus, tax rates, and interest rates—and you can print as much money as you like.

There is no risk of defaults by government pension funds, social security, Fannie Mae, Freddie Mac, and Medicare because the government will backstop the shortfall. Most would accept that the government can do this by creating digits (or, as people still think, "printing" money) but would also expect that to be an inflationary event. Wrong. The government stepping in and creating all of these safeguards for society's betterment is not inflationary. The money was already invested by the recipients many years ago, expecting a future payout. That event has already been factored into the economy and thus is not inflationary. Many on the right, such as Stephen Moore, are championing the privatization of Social Security. I publicly challenged him on his thesis years ago, telling him that this will not happen as there is no need to do so under MMT. If and when MMT fails, then Social Security will be privatized, but not before.

You with me so far?

Now, as everyone knows, getting stuff without having to work for it has been one of humanity's enduring dreams: from the ancient myths of all-powerful genies who could satisfy your every desire to Jesus's ability to turn water into wine to modern state lotteries' promise of instant riches, we all love the fantasy of getting something for nothing.

MMT is as close to that as we'll ever get and is why critics of the policy derisively say that MMT really stands for "**Magic Money Tree.**"

However, proponents defend MMT as the best way to realize the Fed's two primary aims: to promote full employment and to control inflation—with no risks from a political standpoint, meaning it will keep society relatively calm and peaceful and prevent a descent into mass chaos. Or, to put it in a slightly more cynical way, a population with access to easy money is a complacent population.

And getting there is not hard. As former Fed Chair Alan Greenspan put it: "The United States can pay any debt it has because we can always print money to do that." Or, as Vice

President Dick Cheney famously proclaimed: "Reagan proved deficits don't matter." But John Connally may have said it best in late 1971 after Nixon closed the gold window and ended the gold standard when he told the G-10 Summit in Rome, "The dollar is *our* currency, but it's *your* problem." These dicta are taken as gospel within MMT's inner circle.

So, where is the Fed at currently?

The Fed is testing fiscal-monetary coordination out in a big way, perhaps even flirting with Modern Monetary Theory. The US is engaged in money creation at a staggering level.

June 2020, for example, saw government deficit spending of nearly a trillion dollars in one month. No amount of taxation could possibly cover that (and you will see later that tax revenue's purpose is not to pay back spending). It will never be paid down. And the policy will continue. In a July interview, Fed Chair Jerome Powell said that the bank is "not out of ammunition by a long shot" and would enlarge its existing lending programs for "as long as we need to." To the detriment of my gold bug colleagues, he is right. To repeat, the key line in the speech was "...we print digits." With that line, Jerome Powell confirmed to the world that the US Federal Reserve is pushing the limits of FMC and hinted toward MMT.

Both major American political parties are entirely on board as well. So, in terms of monetary policy, the results of any given election could not matter less.

Whatever the consequences of pedal-to-the-metal MMT might be, it is what we're going to have for...well, for as long as the Federal Reserve (led now by Jerome Powell and whoever is after him) wants.

So, we're looking at trillions upon trillions of new electronic "digits," known as dollars. They are being created out of thin air, in unimaginable quantities, for as long as the Fed "needs to." It's expected that they will continue to hold their value in the marketplace, jacking up the money supply and lowering unemployment, all the while not causing massive price inflation of goods and services.

How on earth does this all hang together? Or does it?

Economists Stephanie Kelton and Warren Mosler are the most prominent proponents of MMT today. I like both of them. Moller is a successful, self-made fund manager who comes from the "real world" of investing. Dr. Kelton is an economics and public policy professor at the State University of New York at Stony Brook and a senior fellow at the Schwartz Center for Economic Policy Analysis at the New School for Social Research. Formerly, she was chief economist for the US Senate Budget Committee and is an economic advisor to Sen. Bernie Sanders, Rep. Alexandria Ocasio-Cortez, and other "progressive" Democrats.

Both Kelton and Mosler have turned the common notions about economics on their heads. Those in the Austrian school of economists—who argue that policy from the gold standard economic playbook should equally be applied to a non-gold standard economy and currency—continually rant against MMT. But Kelton and Mosler demand that we take our thinking on a leap into what I call *quantum economics* (explained in a moment). In essence, both maintain that all classically trained economists—including some of the top names in the field—are clueless when it comes to the present day. They completely misunderstand how our system works. I am spending time on MMT in this book because I believe in the coming decades, it will become more of the norm.

For example, Kelton argues that when the Fed buys Treasuries,

"We think that the government has borrowed, and we think that this is real debt. And neither of those things is correct. If I walk into a bank and borrow money, I'm borrowing money because I don't have it. Right? That's why I went to the bank to take out a loan. The federal government is not borrowing money because it needs money. It's not borrowing because it doesn't have the capacity to finance whatever it wants to spend money on. It has the fiscal capacity; it can just spend. And not only that, the government sells the bonds. And by the time the government sells the bonds, the spending has already taken place. So, the bonds cannot possibly be the tool with which the government raises money in order to spend. It's selling the bonds after the spending had already taken place."

In my opinion, Stephanie Kelton has it right. This is where we are now. We have the evolution of Keynesian economic policy, where the government controls the printing press, to today's version of FMC and eventually to MMT, where the Fed meets the demand of the "market" by shifting digits back and forth across a credit/debit ledger.

MMT will become the future framework of not just the US Federal Reserve's policy, but that of all global central banks that maintain independent control of their monetary and fiscal policy—i.e., that can print and circulate their own money if the governments fail to upgrade their middle class.

Out of the total 193 countries globally, there are sixty-five that control their own monetary and fiscal destiny. All have pushed FMC to the limits, and many central banks have already embraced MMT.

The key difference between Keynesian economics and MMT is that the risk and responsibility of the debt taken out by borrowers—which are the pensions, funds, corporations, and individuals—**have now been transferred from those borrowers to the government** (if the debt is big enough, it becomes the central bank's problem). We have seen the central banks buying toxic debt, like mortgage-backed securities, at par value—even though they normally would not have been valued at par by the "free market." It happened a lot during the financial crisis of '08. The argument for the bailout was that the government guaranteed the mortgages backing those securities, never mind that it was the abuse by the banks—which bundled and rebundled the original mortgages until no one knew what they were worth—that caused the assets' toxicity in the first place.

And because the Fed prints "digits," the traditional mechanics of bonds have changed as well. In Keynesian economics, bonds were used to "borrow money" that the Treasury Department could then spend. In MMT, bonds should no longer be viewed as a financing mechanism but rather as an interest-rate-setting mechanism. In our present circumstances, bonds can be issued at will because they essentially promise to pay no interest at a time of historic low (or zero) interest rates.

An investment that essentially promises you no return? You may well wonder: who would buy such pieces of crap? Actually, lots of people because of *convexity*, which I explained in Chapter 2.

Investors, especially retirees, used to buy bonds to enjoy generous interest payments over long periods, after which they would get their principal back. "Living off the interest" from one's investments was a phrase commonly heard. Not anymore. No one buys bonds believing that they are loaning money to the government and getting interest payments in return. Not with today's microscopic interest rates (negative in some countries). But with convexity, investors are profiting from the increase in a bond's value brought on by falling interest rates (I'll cover how low they might go in a moment).

MMT will impact our concept of investments and national debt. But the fact is that MMT is the only economic framework we currently know of that can effectively battle the deflation that we face if fiscal-monetary coordination fails. Even so, interest rates are falling and will continue to do so, which will require even more stimulus. This goes even further against everyone's traditional perception of the economic rule book. That perception is a leftover from the days of a gold standard policy and is now out the window. But it is what we have.

DEBT AS A FUNCTION OF ENTERPRISE VALUE

Debt, under traditional economics (such as the Austrian School), is borrowing from the future. Under MMT, debt is not a burden on future generations because the next generation will consume what they produce. For example, have the debts of the Vietnam War or WWII been a burden on you? No. The standard of living of the present generation has been higher than either of the generations who took on debt to fight those wars. Higher deficits also do not automatically mean higher taxes for future generations nor that they must accept a lower standard of living. Instead, this is where one needs to think of debt and the deficit as "tapping into" the Enterprise Value of the Nation.

What does that mean?

Think of the US dollar as representative of the American goodwill that's been built up over the past century. Citizens have enjoyed an economy that's generally been strong, the nation has avoided the devastation of wars on its soil, and it has offered monetary assistance to help other nations rebuild after the destruction of WWII.

Winning WWII and the Cold War; staying on the gold standard forty years longer than any other nation; having the largest stock and bond markets; having the largest economy in the world, with the biggest and most innovative companies; creating the internet that has changed the world, from commerce to social media; enjoying the best universities in the world (that the world's foremost scholars and scientists come to); and maintaining the world's most powerful military—all of these have created significant goodwill for the US dollar. Not to mention that over 60 percent of all central bank foreign reserves are in US dollars, and most debt globally is priced in US dollars.

Moreover, the country's position in the world is furthered by other factors: the infrastructure it's built, alliances (think Saudi Petrodollar, etc.), the industries it's created and fostered, its intellectual accomplishments. Add it all together, and that's America's Enterprise Value. And you can see why there is such global affection for the US dollar.

Compare it to a company. Companies have a book value that's the total of their assets, minus liabilities.

The US is not a company, and it does not have a book value. But the closest thing is the country's total Enterprise Value. And what would that be? Would it merely be the sum of all corporate market caps, companies' stocks and bonds, land values, the physical stuff of industries, plus the savings of the people? Or would it include the goodwill, the education, the American Dream, the lifestyle, the resources built on, and in the ground, the dams, airlines, highways, and the electrical grid? In my opinion, it should.

Thus the US, by far, has the highest Enterprise Value of any nation in the world, which is well over $100 trillion and by far the largest in the world today.

This way, under MMT, digital money creation is not about loans expected to be paid back. It's about investments in the nation, the return on which cannot be limited simply to digits but has to include the element of prosperity itself. It is a *tool* used to enhance the national Enterprise Value, the nation's citizens' overall value.

THE QUANTUM UNIVERSE

Under MMT, spending is no longer spending, government debt is not real debt, and money is not money in the way we conventionally think of it. Hold on if your head is spinning. This is where you, the reader, will have to make the leap into the *quantum economics* that I referred to earlier. This is a term I coined to differentiate the radical new world of MMT from the linear economic world of Keynesian economics to which we are all accustomed.

It's a revolution comparable to the one in which quantum mechanics advanced from Newtonian physics at the quantum (subatomic) level because all the normal rules of logic get lost down there. For instance, matter can wink in and out of existence for no reason that we can know. That's a nice analogy for the monetary digits that jump from one side of a non-material ledger to the other (think government savings account to checking account), almost as if they have a life of their own.

In MMT, Treasuries are the interest-bearing component of the overall money supply of "digits" (think money) that the government spends (think invests) into the economy. And national debt, in Kelton's view, is merely a "stockpile of US Treasuries as a historical record."

Thus, in MMT, the whole national debt concept is viewed very differently from how it has been in the past. In MMT, the government creates "digits" (think printing of money) that eventually get "placed" into its member banks' reserves, which means the Federal Reserve is actually giving "credits" to those bank accounts as it debits its own account.

When the banks move that money into the economy, those bank accounts are debited. And when taxation returns money to the government, the debits it incurred from money creation move back to the ledger's credit side.

A deficit, in MMT, is nothing more than the difference between these two numbers. It means the Fed is marking up one account more than marking down another account. The government is responsible to the Fed, which creates the digits. But a government deficit is no longer viewed as "borrowing." Instead, it just means a net investment of dollars into some part of the economy that needs them.

But what about inflation? Yes, uncontrollable inflation would result if the Fed attempted to execute the amount of monetary inflation that MMT is permitting in a strong economic environment without increasing taxes to cool down the economy. The Fed will have no choice but to commit to MMT if FMC fails and the real economy continues to stay depressed. And MMT holds that a central bank can keep a lid on inflation—and this is key: **through the correct balance of stimulus, tax rates, and interest rates, the unemployment rate and thus inflation, will be controlled.**

In downtimes, such as now, a ZIRP (zero interest rate policy)— which in some countries has actually become a NIRP or negative interest rate policy—is sufficient to keep deflation at bay. At the same time, inflation remains tame no matter how many digits are created. (More on ZIRP and NIRP in a moment.)

The consequences of overspending and an incorrect balance of stimulus and taxes in MMT would result in inflation, or worse, hyperinflation, falling currency value, and interest rate risk. I've said for years and will demonstrate momentarily, that negative interest rates are deflationary. Interest rates globally have gone a lot lower for longer because of the decline in capital velocity. MMT will be the only economic framework that is a real option for central bankers to combat deflation.

Once deflation is defeated and the "proper" levels of inflation and unemployment are reached (according to the Fed), interest rates can rise once again. The money supply will contract, and taxes will increase, putting a cap on inflation.

In theory, MMT will continue until the US economy is fully recovered and beyond. Also, other nations will continue with their own version of MMT (think Japan and sixty-three other nations) until their economies are fully recovered. Or so the politicians will say. Unfortunately, for basic reasons like demographics and current debt obligations, not to mention the pandemic's ongoing long-term economic consequences, it will be a long time before the economy has fully recovered. Expect MMT, and as I've said, not just from the US, but from every central bank with the benefit of having an independent monetary and fiscal policy.

That means MMT is not a quick fix. If MMT does take hold, it will stay for a LONG TIME—just like Keynesian economics was initially meant to be a short-term boost to the economy yet became the foundation of all central bank policies in the twentieth century. MMT could play the same part during the twenty-first. We do not yet know how it will function once it beats deflation even if it does get us through the powerful deflationary forces at play.

However, in theory, MMT believes that as the economy

recovers and more people become employed, tax receipts will automatically increase as the economy grows. The deficit will automatically shrink as "digits" go from bank accounts to "government" accounts.

But tax receipts do not truly fund anything in an MMT framework. In MMT, taxes are used to create a demand for the currency and to help control inflation. Digits released into the economy are an investment. The return on that investment (ROI) is partly comprised of tax receipts but primarily comprised of the increase in Enterprise Value that the investment provokes, plus the decrease of social and economic inequality and an overall increase in the living standard. The difference between a personal investor and the government is that, as individuals, we only hope for an ROI that represents a profit; we could, of course, also take a loss. The government does not need hope because it never has to take a loss. It is *the* currency issuer, not *a* currency user.

You see how this changes the game, right? And do you also see how unlimited money creation via MMT could be very beneficial upon the foundation upon which the Rise of America can be built?

I am asking a lot, I know. But the world of finance will continue to be opaque to those who cannot or will not get a grasp on MMT. Again, refrain from judging it. It is what we *will have* going forward. Understand it and a lot of things that seem shrouded in mystery will become clear.

THE FAITH FACTOR

In Keynesian economic policy, the national debt size was a focal point and still is with most economists and politicians. Debt does matter with fiscal-monetary coordination, which is the current framework at hand. However, we have gotten used to politicians proclaiming that the government just does not have the money to fund some specific program or other. When, in fact, it does not need to "have" the money, it just needs to digitize the creation of the "money." That is essentially what has happened. And that is going to be magnified in an MMT world. In MMT, the national debt is not the limiting factor; the productive capacity of the economy is. This is the fundamental reason national debt is no longer an issue with MMT.

Under MMT, inflation only becomes an issue when the economy is being monetarily pushed beyond its productive capacity.

In fairness to MMT, Japan has essentially been using a form of it for the last two decades—with zero uncontrollable inflationary pressures. And it could be argued that both Ben Bernanke and Janet Yellen (former US Fed chairs) and now Jerome Powell have laid the groundwork for the same thing in America.

So, as I cannot stress enough, monetary policy has become nothing more than moving electronic digits from one column to another in the big American ledger book.

Again, MMT could take hold and become the go-to framework for central bankers because of deflation fears. Governments around the world are desperately trying to stave off deflation. So, before defining the limits of MMT and potential *in*flationary pressures, we first need to understand the current *de*flationary world in which we live. I want to hammer this point home. Deflation on the scale of the 1930s is what every government on the planet fears more than anything. In Chapter 2, I detailed the deflationary factors that are presently at work. There are a lot of them. And right now, the Fed is applying the fiscal-monetary coordination framework. However, if the FMC policy doesn't succeed like in the 1940s, a whole new batch of politicians will view MMT as the most viable framework to deal with the deflationary pressures. Before hyperinflation ever becomes a ghost of an issue, the Fed will have to deal with deflation and (quite possibly) negative interest rates.

Many believe that, even if the US does not have an imminent collapse of the dollar, its strength will be tested because of this deficit spending spree. As noted, MMT proponents dispute that on principle. But I believe there are some other countervailing tendencies of great importance. I think MMT will rule the roost for many years, most likely decades, and the USD will remain strong for longer than anyone else suspects.

I would also add that it is important to acknowledge that, nevertheless, there *is* a limit, and to me, that limit is not a matter of too much too fast; it is a matter of something entirely intangible: faith. A currency is only as strong as the people's faith in it. When faith is lost, the kind of hyperinflation that beset the US during the American Revolution, Weimar Germany, and Zimbabwe take hold. I will get to what I believe is the Achilles heel of MMT later in this chapter, but it will be a controversial perspective.

A crisis of faith can happen quickly, faith being a tenuous thing. It will happen to the US dollar at some point, as it historically has with all fiat currencies. We do not know when, but whenever it does, it will be ugly.

MMT has its fair share of detractors. And it wouldn't be fair to leave this subject without giving them some space.

Prominent among them is German economist Joseph Huber. Huber challenges the notion that money creation need not be limited:

"Just because modern money can freely be created, there must be some arrangement for making sure that there is neither too much nor too little money and that additions to the money supply keep within certain limits set by economic productivity and potential growth. Money and capital markets, contrary to what they are supposed to do according to efficient market hypotheses, perpetually fail to achieve the task because there are no effective limits to banks' deliberate creation of money on account, or intermittently, their deliberate extinction of credit and bank money."

MMT proponents would maintain that the policy does have a safeguard against excess money creation, the restraints imposed by supply and demand.

But Huber maintains that the primary central component of any currency system must be the separation of money and banking, an argument advanced by the Fed's original opponents over a century ago. "Banks can and should be free enterprises," he says, "but they should not be allowed to create themselves the money on which they operate." And, he laughs, modern "banking teachings, of course, they don't agree," by which he means MMT.

Thus, we have the hybridized American system, wherein the Fed with one hand maintains a tie to the federal government by monetizing its debt through Treasury purchases, but with the other hand, issues new currency units directly to its private member banks, allowing them to profit by being first at the spigot. By law, the Fed must turn any profits it generates for itself back to the Treasury, but that structure does not apply to member banks' profits. And that is a key component of the acceptance of MMT by the government. It works within the current laws.

Monetary reformists (anti-MMT economists) insist that this setup leads to all sorts of mischief and market distortions and that, ultimately, it will result in an unstable monetary system. Only time will tell.

Having duly considered both sides, where do I come down in this fight?

I don't.

It's my preference not to take a position on US monetary policy. It seems silly to be for or against it. Fiscal-monetary coordination is what we have, and MMT is where we are going; I can't change that. Accordingly, I much prefer to understand the actual workings of the flow of "money" and accept and work with it. My job is to figure out how best to exploit what the reality is and profit from it. I do not live in a theoretical world of "how the world should be in my eyes," but rather work with the "what it is in reality" world. That reality—and how it relates to the Rise of America—is what I am delineating in this book.

Where this policy will take us in the end, no one knows. But we do know this: the massive money-printing machine relentlessly drives bond prices higher and yields lower—not just in Treasuries but in private sector bonds, as well—all the way to the unheard-of extent of negative interest rates, the dangers of which I will consider shortly.

It also fuels a steep rise in the value of assets like stocks, real estate, fine art, fancy cars, rare wines, and, yes, precious metals and certain cryptocurrencies. The 1 percent (for lack of a better term) profits greatly—which is exactly the result we should expect when a handful of private banks create currency.

Among the main aims of MMT are to get unemployment near zero and to eliminate social and economic inequality gaps. But sadly, due to the Cantillon effect, we have seen the exact opposite happen. Although massive stimulus programs have kept the economy and society from melting down during the COVID-19 pandemic economic crisis, the inequality gap between the über rich and the rest of society has increased.

The Cantillon effect is not a new idea; it's been known for over 270 years. It merely states the obvious: If a central bank pumps more money into the economy, the resulting increase in prices does not happen evenly. In today's world, the banks and their über-wealthy clients are the closest to the flow of the digits newly created by the central bank and are the first recipients of the new currency that has entered the economy. They can put the new currency to work during suppressed prices of assets and services. This allows those with early access to the flow of newly created currency to have a much higher standard of living than those who do not have such access and must wait for it to trickle down. By then, inflation will have increased the price of assets and services. A few prosper, and the rest suffer.

Banks are receiving a flood of digits from the Fed, with little effect on Main St. Most of the money that is loaned out is being lent to low-risk, wealthy clients. Best customers first. Why? Because the big banks learned this lesson from the financial crisis of 2008: ordinary people are foolish and do foolish things (banks' perception, not mine). Thus, they present too high a risk, given the meager return (interest rate) the banks can now get. The margin is too thin. It is just not worth it.

So, the loan department is open to high-net-worth individuals, but Average Joe can take a hike. This despite the fact that nearly half of the Fed digits the banks have been credited with are ready and waiting to be used but aren't. This contributes to the velocity of money being near all-time lows, which is highly deflationary, as I noted in Chapter 2.

The big banks maintain accounts at the Fed; you and I don't have accounts at the Fed. So instead of moving through the economy, about half of those digits just sit there on deposit, rather than working their way through the economy and helping people who need them. The big banks can access those digits any time they want to, but right now, they don't want to.

What we have is kind of the inverse of our former fractional reserve banking system (which I explain in Appendix I). In brief, banks were formerly allowed to lend out 90 percent of the deposits they received, retaining only 10 percent on reserve in case a bunch of depositors all wanted their money back at once. To exaggerate to make a point, you can think of the nine-to-one lending game being cut by 94 percent to lending out of only 5 percent while keeping 95 percent in reserves. The point I am making is there has been a big change in all banks' lending velocity.

This pinpoints the big banks as choke points, preventing the release of new money into circulation. The Fed wants more money out there, to push inflation higher, to boost the economy, but the banks aren't cooperating. They are serving instead as yet another element of deflation. Ultimately, government spending on the economy is required to push inflation higher.

Okay, as I write this in late 2020, the global economy is in a major recession. No one disputes that. Across the planet, central banks are frantically trying to prevent that downturn from turning into a Second Great Depression.

Politicians abusing the fiscal and monetary framework is the biggest risk to the whole system.

Even now, we see massive street demonstrations in the US and worldwide, which are about wealth inequality as much as they are about race. The demonstrators may compel a change in some areas. Washington may move a little more to the left or a little more to the right politically, depending on who's in charge. But there will be no shift in monetary policy because of an election, meaning more stimulus and government spending ultimately leading to MMT. Democrats and Republicans alike are wedded to the status quo, which means more stimulus. That has become critical to preventing complete chaos and the spectacle of impoverished citizens fighting over bread.

Both major political parties are in lockstep. The only difference is that Republicans are a little more willing to let the market decide how to spend all these new currency units, while the Democrats want us to let them direct the spending. Both parties will take advantage of MMT to fund really expensive things like infrastructure repair and an overhaul of the energy sector. This will lead to the economic condition I call *crossflation* (see Chapter 2), and it will require even heavier deficit spending. If MMT is the correct framework for the economic environment, then that won't matter; we will be able to push the digital money supply to dizzying heights without having to worry about hyperinflation. And if MMT is wrong, well, we shall see…

TAXES

All of which leads me to a few further thoughts about MMT.

One key question is: What role do taxes play under MMT? Why do we need them if we can print digits until the end of time?

Good question. As we have seen, taxes play a role in moving digits from the debit to the ledger's credit side. They also act as natural inflationary control and a signifier of an increasing national Enterprise Value. But they have another, even more critical function: paying taxes gives our money itself value.

What do I mean by that? Remember that money has value only insofar as people have faith that other people will accept it and that it will be worth something when they spend it. The currency killer is hyperinflation—when nobody takes it because it is worth nothing.

Just imagine if the government printed all the money it needed to fund its own purchases of goods and services and gave you all the money you needed to buy the things *you* wanted. All of a sudden, more dollars—yours and the government's—would be chasing the same amount of goods and services.

That is inflationary and would soon turn to hyperinflation. Dollars you earn would rapidly decline in value, in comparison to what goods cost. Whoever spent the money first would get the lowest price of goods. Once the new dollars were spent, prices would rush higher. And they'd stay up because those new dollars wouldn't just disappear.

But you do not have unlimited money to spend. You do not even have what you have earned since a significant percentage of it is taxed away. That money flows back onto the government balance sheet as digits that offset debts that have been run up. If digits were only flowing out and nothing was coming in, then the dollar would collapse in short order. Taxes are the deterrent. As I said, they create a demand for the dollar and thus give the dollar value. Hence if the economy is heating up, taxes will rise to prevent inflation (taxes take dollars out of the economy and give them back to the government). Since inflation is not a key concern right now, those who have assets and cash should prepare themselves for wealth taxes in lieu of inflation. Wealth taxes will be sold as getting the rich to "pay their fair share." But as we have seen, under MMT, there is no such thing as a fair share. It's meaningless.

Next, many people confuse MMT and quantitative easing, but they are different.

Under QE, the Fed bailed out the banks under the belief that the banks would then inject money into the economy and things would get moving again. Under MMT, the Fed has not only provided digits to the banks; it has also made them available to the Treasury for **direct injection** into the system via payments to individuals and businesses that don't have to be paid back. This is the true "Magic Money Tree," where those citizens and companies are "enriched" without earning the money. Under MMT, it's justifiable because the alternative is out-of-control deflation—to be avoided whatever the cost.

You will recall that one of the justifications for having an independent Federal Reserve was that it provided a check on uncontrolled government (fiscal) spending. But MMT signals a beginning of a trend in which the Federal Reserve and government are increasingly merged. Once that merger is completed, well, you can see where this goes. It represents the ultimate blurring of the line between fiscal policy (government budget) and monetary policy (central bank), as self-serving elected officials demand control of both and seek to politicize the Federal Reserve.

The biggest risks to MMT are the inevitable politicians who will begin to attack the big banks and the greedy speculators on Wall Street as never before. The banks should not be able to profit from money creation, they will say. Ordinary Americans should pocket those profits instead. There will be a big push for universal job creation and 0 percent unemployment.

Under MMT, the US government could eventually, in theory, become the employer of last resort. This will happen through legislation for the unemployeds' rehabilitation, lifting them to a higher standard of living, which will be touted as a basic "human right." There will be a guaranteed income for those who wish to show up, participate, and want to work. A "job" for every single soul, paid for by MMT digits. This was a core promise of communism, lest we forget; thus, we should proceed with extreme caution. It's worth a try if properly thought out, planned, and executed, and it's a better option than welfare and food stamps. Or maybe if that fails, they'll just go for a guaranteed basic annual income for everyone. Who knows? Also notable is that, under MMT, low unemployment does not necessarily cause inflation, as we saw with the pre-COVID-19 historic low unemployment rates.

In their attempt to control the monetary policy, the politicians will offer to open up the system to public scrutiny. They'll promise to deal a death blow to the evil banks and their corrupt accomplices on Wall Street that have been robbing people forever and pledge to squeeze them out of the system completely. It's a platform that will have a very wide appeal, considering that the non-wealthy make up the citizenry's bulk.

Politicians will claim that this will be a net gain for society. Instead of a private Fed's semi-opaque machinations, they will be publicly accountable for where all that MMT money goes. *To the public good!* Of course.

Such proactive fiscal policy over monetary policy would be the dagger that starts the death spiral of MMT and, with it, the US dollar. Imagine the asinine and irrational decisions during an election year by officials in positions of power who have no understanding of economics. They would be the kiss of death for the currency. President's Trump insistence on increasing the proposed $600 stimulus to $2,000 without any policy or reasoning other than his opinion is a glimpse of what is to come. There may still be some who argue that citizens will elect the most capable individual, but recent elections around the world have stomped on that naïve notion.

If the politicians are in control of money creation, rather than the Fed, there are no longer restraints. Buoyed by the proven magic of MMT, they can spend to their collective hearts' content on whatever might be their favorite passion or popularity projects. Which they will, inflation be damned. They will spend those digits until digits cease to have value anymore, and faith in the US dollar will collapse. At that point, massive inflation, and perhaps hyperinflation, will become unstoppable. And with that, MMT will come crashing down.

It puts me in mind of the so-called Cobra Effect. During Britain's rule of India, there developed a perceived, dangerous cobra infestation. So, the Brits put a bounty on the snakes, paying people to kill them and bring in the carcasses. But a lot of resourceful Indians began breeding cobras and then killing them to claim the bounties. Once the scheme was discovered, the Brits responded by rescinding the bounties. And the Indians responded to that by releasing all their newly bred cobras from captivity—net result: more cobras than ever.

Politicians will let loose the equivalent of massive cobra inflation once they get ahold of the power of digit creation.

Fortunately, I think that moment is still decades away. We have time to figure out how to prevent it. MMT in the US will prevail as long as the country maintains independent control of its monetary and fiscal policies and averts uncontrollable inflation. If you think the US dollar's days are numbered, consider that the US is nowhere near the debt-to-GDP ratio of other countries, and remember that the US stayed on the gold standard for forty years longer than any other nation. To me, that suggests the US will have the ability to navigate MMT subject to Fed independence being maintained.

Since I originally wrote this chapter, we have had an election in which Joe Biden defeated Donald Trump for president. One of Biden's first cabinet appointments was Janet Yellen, former chair of the Federal Reserve, as secretary of the Treasury. This is significant. It sends the obvious signal that the Biden administration will be fully on board with fiscal-monetary coordination, and the foundation will be laid down for MMT policy. Yellen is in a position to influence the relationship between Treasury and Fed. It's possible that she would like that relationship to become cozier, but it's equally possible that she understands the value of carefully preserving the Fed's independence. We just don't know. But over the next four years, we're going to find out.

SOME MISCONCEPTIONS

Before I leave this crucial section of Chapter 3, I'd like to point out that there are serious misconceptions by some media commentators who don't understand economics. These fearmongers hold that countries such as Japan and China, who hold trillions of dollars in US debt (US Treasuries), somehow control the destiny of the US dollar. The fear is that the Chinese, especially, will "dump" their holdings and crash the value of the buck.

Trust me; this is complete nonsense.

First off, neither China nor Japan (or any nation, for that matter) has access to $1 trillion in $100 bills with which they can flood the world. All that China or anyone who owns a Treasury (US debt) has is an account with the US Central Bank. And in that account, they have a credit that eventually matures with interest. At that point, China, or any owner of Treasuries, can either switch them to "savings" accounts with the Fed or roll them over into new Treasuries.

China can't convert the "money" in its account with the Fed into gold or any other precious metal. It also cannot use those funds to buy any oil, asset, or service from any country on the US sanctions list, such as Iran.

China can purchase American goods or services from the US or another nation or corporation with an account at the Fed. With the digits transfer accounts, the US government maintains the demand for their currency and clips some fees in transaction taxes. The debt is in no way a threat to crush the dollar.

In addition, China somewhat pegs its currency to the US dollar. Even if they were to devalue the USD by "flooding the system with their US holdings" (which they can't), China would only be hurting themselves by devaluing their own foreign reserves.

The US dollar makes up a little over 60 percent of all foreign central bank reserves. None of those central banks has any interest in devaluing its holdings, contrary to what some alarmists may try to tell you.

At this point, you may also have connected the dots and seen that there is a benefit to running a budget deficit. As confusing and counterintuitive (or quantum) as that may seem, it is, in fact, the case for the US—and is also true for any country that can pull it off, such as Japan and many nations in Europe. Deficits elevate people's standard of living (they don't diminish it).

It comes down to a simple formula not much different from Adam Smith's. Smith (who opposed the gold standard) published his book, *The Wealth of Nations*, back in 1776 (coincidentally, of course, the same year as the US Declaration of Independence was issued). He maintained that overall wealth is the sum of all production kept in the nation and its imports minus its exports. If that figure is greater than zero, the theory states the nation's standard of living is increasing.

Following Smith's principle, there are real benefits to a trade deficit such as the one the US has with China. The US creates and issues the digital credit to the Chinese account at the Federal Reserve, allowing for the purchase of Chinese goods and services. China needs trade because it has a production economy. It thus becomes dependent on the US credit to increase its own savings of US dollars and keep its own flow of funds and economy going. It's only when China has a surplus of demand for its goods from other nations that it can work around the US credit of digits (currency).

That day is not coming anytime soon. The US is still the largest economy in the world, and in a depressed global economy, the current relationship with China will stand for years to come. China will use this period to ramp up and upgrade its infrastructure, supply chains, and military. America must do the same. During this period, there is little to no risk of China dethroning the US dollar as the reserve currency of the world for the reasons I have covered in this chapter. However, if the US does not upgrade itself, from infrastructure in all forms to supply chains, China could become a real threat to the dethroning the US dollar as the world's reserve currency.

A PARTING SHOT

MMT's success depends on Congress's and government officials' (whether appointed or elected) further involvement. And those individuals need to nail the correct mix of long-term stimulus injections and tax rates. To do so, the Federal Reserve (setting monetary policy) must forego some of its independence to create a unified framework and policy with Congress (politicians who decide upon fiscal policy). But not too much.

It's a tall order, but then, I never said MMT was a simple solution. It's the grand experiment that is not just underway in America, but across all the independent central banks in the world, in real time, which means *now*.

The sobering fact is that over 500 different fiat currencies went bust and were deemed worthless throughout history. In the long term, the odds are against the US dollar. But over the next few years and decades, it will remain unchallenged as the world's reserve currency.

The situation, you might say, is desperate but not hopeless.

FTDS: FINANCIALLY TRANSMITTED DISEASES

Let me add one further consequence of MMT: the global bond market has come to accept that we can move from zero interest rates (ZIRP) to the cloud cuckoo land of negative interest rates (NIRP).

NIRPs are something that was never even conceived of in any school of classical economic thinking—whether Keynesian, Austrian, or some other—much less as something that policymakers would actually put into practice.

Misguided bankers across the planet are touting NIRPs as the cool, new stimulus. The theory is that people will be discouraged from saving and encouraged to spend. Like magic, the economy starts charging forward again.

Stimulus? I call it a *financially transmitted disease*—an **FTD**.

I don't think average investors, or the financial talking heads in the media, or even the central bankers themselves truly understand the ripple effects that this FTD will have for everything from pension funds to retirees; from sovereign wealth funds to smaller, professional portfolio managers; from Wall Street to Main Street.

People have been misled. The notion is being promoted that NIRP is great. That mortgage costs will be declining, and people will be able to get access to cheaper money. That's not how it's going to work. Access to this cheaper NIRP money will be granted to just a select few at the top of the food chain. In China, you have the government rate and then the shadow market rate. I see that happening in the rest of the world now, and it' will have serious repercussions. A big risk is that the velocity of capital will slow down much more than it already has, and that's a big roadblock to prosperity.

NIRP GIVES US DEFLATION

Federal Reserve policy, which includes ZIRP and potentially NIRP, is geared toward promoting an "acceptable" price inflation level. The Fed does not want inflation to get out of hand, as it did in the 1970s when it hit double digits and interest rates rose to 20 percent. That was called *stagflation*, and it was partly due to fallout from Nixon's closure of the gold window.

But a revisit to the '70s is not really their worry. The Fed contends that those bad old days are permanently behind us. The policy is now designed to maintain inflation right at 2 percent. Somehow, these geniuses have determined that they can hold it right there if they wave their magic wand. Recall, earlier in the book, I mentioned how the central bankers around the world accepted a 2 percent inflation target as the goal based on New Zealand's success. The central bankers forget that the "natural inflation rate" during the gold standard era was 2 percent because that was the average annual increase of gold production. Of course, in a truly free market, where interest rates are allowed to float according to the demand for money, a stable inflation rate can't happen. Borrowers and lenders make that decision, not the central bank as prescribed in MMT. And besides, there is no magic wand. Powerful as the Fed is, it cannot possibly fine-tune inflation to within fractions of a percent.

For public consumption, Minneapolis Fed President Neel Kashkari put this out:

> "We say that we have a symmetric view of inflation. We don't mind if it's 2.1 percent or 1.9 percent, but in our practice, in what we actually do, we are much more worried about high inflation than we are low inflation. And I think that that is the scar from the 1970s."

I don't believe it.

Paul Volcker was the last Fed chair to take on out-of-control inflation, which he did by raising interest rates to nosebleed levels. It was painful, causing the recession of the early '80s, but it worked.

Alan Greenspan—Volcker's polar opposite—succeeded him. Greenspan—who, ironically, was an ardent gold standard enthusiast until he got his hands on the Fed's money spigot—pushed interest rates ever lower and turned on the spigot full blast. And he was followed by Ben Bernanke, a scholar of the Great Depression, who believed that the breadth and depth of that horrific downturn could have been prevented if only the government had kept ramping up the money supply. Many economists dispute this, but proponents of MMT would agree.

Thus, despite Mr. Kashkari's statement to the contrary, the Fed's obsession with controlled inflation stems from an absolute horror of deflation. The last four Fed chairs, and members of the Open Market Committee that sets policy, have made it clear that they will fend off a 1930s-style Great Depression, no matter what it takes. Given a choice between an inflationary recession and a deflationary one, they will opt for the former every single time.

Both are highly destructive to an economy in different ways. Which is worse is debatable. But the Fed has cast its vote.

So, considering the Fed's bias, it is odd that they would choose the path they've taken, which is heading directly toward NIRP. Because, in my opinion, NIRP is clearly deflationary (continue reading to see what happened to Switzerland). With NIRP, capital that is chasing ever-higher premiums (the *convexity* I talked about earlier) is capital that is not chasing goods and services; hence it's deflationary. Consider that NIRP also further depresses the velocity of capital, and you've got a double whammy.

A lot of people argue that a NIRP would simply be temporary, a short-term fix to goose the economy. Like quantitative easing (QE) was. Remember QE? They said it was just an interim measure to increase liquidity in the money supply. Well, it's hung around for an awfully long time. They just keep changing its name. (Do they think we won't notice?)

Remember that the lower interest rates go, the cheaper it gets for the government to finance deficit spending. Not that it matters under MMT, but the interest on the federal "debt" is declining. Soon, the government will only have to pay a token yearly amount (and eventually nothing) to roll it all over. It's like a credit card holder who only pays the minimum each month and carries the rest forward, only without credit card companies' exorbitant interest rates.

Yes, Washington's political class definitely has a big stake in this game.

All things taken into account, I believe we will get NIRP in America. I also believe it will last a lot longer and that negative interest rates will go much lower than anyone thinks.

Bond traders don't care. Once we get negative interest rates, they're not going to ask themselves who the hell wants an asset that's guaranteed to lose money. All they'll care about is that premiums are going up, and they're still getting their cut.

I will wager that negative interest rates can go *A LOT* lower for *A LOT* longer than anyone expects.

And that's a crazy train. Ten years ago, no one would have ever thought that this would happen, partly because of the Swiss experience of the '70s, but here we are, with people itching to get on board.

What happened in Switzerland is instructive. When the US went off the gold standard in '71, the world's currencies were suddenly deprived of something tangible to which they could tether their value. For the first time, all of them were left to float freely against one another.

This unsettled global markets. But amid the chaos, Switzerland loomed as a refuge. Historically, the country's fiscal conservatism and monetary stability had already given its currency a safe-haven reputation. The crisis made it even more desirable, and investors clamored to exchange their own currency—especially US dollars—for Swiss francs, driving up their value and setting the stage for a serious recession.

As a currency strengthens, exports necessarily become costlier. This was a disaster for the Swiss manufacturers of watches, chocolate, and precision tools. At first, the government tried capital controls, imposing reserve requirements on nonresident deposits. When that failed to stem the inflowing capital tide, they banned interest payments to nonresidents. And when *that* didn't work, they went to negative interest rates on foreign depositors, eventually imposing a 12 percent penalty on anyone bent on owning francs.

But the new fiat American currency continued to weaken and the franc to appreciate, up 70 percent in nominal terms between

1971 and 1975. Whatever you lost to negative interest rates, you more than made up for in currency appreciation.

Even after the government slapped a humongous 41 percent penalty on foreign deposits in January of 1975, money still poured in, and the recession continued. Industrial production fell 15 percent in 1975; plants worked well below capacity, and exports declined by over 8 percent in real terms. And get this: Before '71, official government figures acknowledged only *eighty-one* unemployed people—not a misprint—in a country of 6.4 million. The economy was so good that thousands of foreigners had to be brought in to fill jobs. With the recession, that unemployment figure rose to 32,000, but it would have been far higher had the Swiss not sent 150,000 foreign guest workers home.

Say this for the Swiss experiment: it did tame inflation. The country's rate for the second half of the '70s was minus 2.5 percent, the lowest in the world. Oh, and guess who benefited? Did you say Zurich's financial gnomes? Correct. All that money trading pushed bank profits up 15 percent between 1974 and 1975 alone.

Artificially low interest rates, massive unemployment, steep production declines, ballooning business bankruptcies, yet a booming financial sector. Sounding familiar yet?

Perhaps fittingly, the Swiss were among the first to go to NIRP in present times. At this writing, the Swiss National Bank has a benchmark three-month rate of minus 0.75 percent. And the answer to my original question, could it go a hell of a lot lower, is: sure, why not? If we're at negative three-quarters, why can't we get to negative one and a quarter, negative one and a half, negative two? Once the whole loopy concept is embraced, there's really no lower limit.

I can't stress this enough: NIRP is an FTD, and it will spread virally.

However: Negative interest rates will have negative impacts on real people.

This is where it gets really ugly.

It's going to be awful. People are injecting themselves with this FTD, thinking that it's going to help them. They think it's a steroid for themselves when it's the opposite, a virus for their portfolio.

For example, say you're a fifty-five-year-old dad, you're thinking to yourself, "Okay. I got a big mortgage; I can refinance it with low interest rates. My kid's a struggling artist, her boyfriend has moved into the basement and works odd jobs while finishing his degree part time, but they aren't paying any rent to help with my mortgage. And that's okay because I'll just refinance my house. I'm all for negative interest rates."

But you are not going to get a negative-interest-rate mortgage. Period. You're not going to get any of the relief.

Worse, pension funds are going to be significantly impacted. When they started their careers thirty, forty years ago, these pension fund managers expected the pension fund to average a gain of between 5 percent and 7 percent year over year. You could get that just investing in T-Bonds at that time, maybe mixing in a few higher-risk equities to get returns between 8 percent and 10 percent.

As bond yields drop, it's turning everything upside down. Most pension funds are not meeting their goals and expected payout ratios. In addition, their investment returns are going to shrink significantly. As a result of MMT, by the time the average person gets access to these newly printed digits, the average cost of living will have risen. Even if inflation is held at the magic 2 percent level, that's a problem if your income source can't keep up.

Pension funds are going to have to make riskier bets, overweighting in more volatile stocks. That can work if the stock market continues to move higher but could lead to bankruptcy in a market downturn.

The only other alternative is to tell pensioners that they're going to get considerably less than they thought they would, perhaps less than they can comfortably live on, with the payout perhaps even falling to nothing. Can you imagine trying to tell that to people who totally rely on you for income? NIRP means the wholesale destruction of nest eggs that were decades in the making. Now, that fifty-five-year-old dad who has been dutifully paying into his pension for thirty years has not only taken on more debt, but he is also carrying the costs of his adult kids living in the basement, and his pension may become worthless.

See why I call NIRP an FTD?

No one wants to face what is truly going on here. This is why the central bankers are kicking the can down the road, and the politicians are totally okay with pressuring the central bankers to absolve themselves of any responsibility. Politicians live on a little four-year cycle, and the bankers go along. Neither is factoring in the long-term implications or how to tackle them.

This conundrum is another reason MMT will be the go-to economic framework for the next few decades. It is the ultimate can-kicker. When in doubt, *print more digits!*

SOME FURTHER OBSERVATIONS

A WEALTH TAX

Like I said, no, there will not be negative-interest-rate mortgages. Banks can only lower mortgage rates so far. After that, if people still can't afford them, then I think you'll see an incredible expansion of subsidy programs, perhaps including a guaranteed annual income for everyone. Then we're really into the MMT version of a socialist state, and you're going to get taxed on your cash and all sorts of other things to "finance it." (Although, as we've seen, under MMT, that isn't really necessary. They'll do it anyway.)

In the years ahead, politicians across all spectrums and across the globe will push a "wealth tax." The masses will support it, and the politicians will do whatever it takes to stay in power. A wealth tax is nothing new.

A lot of people do not know that Great Britain (and its colonies that made up the Commonwealth of Nations like Canada and Australia), pre-World War II, used to ding their rich with a yearly "wealth" tax of up to 3 percent (known as a super tax) on anything deemed an asset in your portfolio. Back then, they would take your cash and your stocks, whatever you were holding, and charge you 3 percent to keep them. You would have to pay that in cold, hard cash every year.

In time, I do see an asset tax coming back everywhere because the pendulum sure is swinging that way. More government subsidies will result in ever more creative ways to tax. Such policies will be popular because they'll be sold as making the rich pay their "fair share." But you can be sure that *everyone* will wind up paying more.

Savers are the real victims in a NIRP world.

In a negative-interest-rate-policy world, people will have to face a new reality. It's only natural that, as people approach retirement, they start planning and becoming more conservative. But NIRP will add a new element of belt-tightening. People will suddenly realize that "Oh, crap, I'm going to retire, and I'm not getting the returns I expected to have. Maybe I haven't been fiscally conservative before, but I will be now because I need to figure out simply how to make ends meet."

That's going to have a ripple effect across the economy. You're not going to make those spontaneous purchases that you used to. You're not going to take the fancy vacations or spring for the big restaurant dinners. You'll buy cheaper wine.

NIRP will force people to save more than they did, instead of merrily running up the balances on their credit cards. As noted earlier, savings are already up under the austerities induced by the pandemic and widespread unemployment. The free ride is over, and that's a good thing. Living more within our means is healthy.

It's also deflationary.

Like I've been stressing, those in charge of monetary policy hate deflation. They *want* inflation. And they think that lowering interest rates to zero and then into NIRP territory will compel people to spend into the economy and pull us out of the doldrums. It won't, as I've explained. A lengthy, sluggish economy is going to drive them nuts.

When they don't get what they want, Washington's political class—which is economically ignorant to a tragic degree—will cast about for further ways to discourage savers, like raising taxes. And not just on assets, but also on financial transactions, inheritances, carbon emissions, and whatever they can manage. Hate to say it, but the government's going to screw you every which way, and that's just how it is.

WHAT ABOUT BONDS?

I see that the current uptrend will continue. As interest rates go further into negative territory, and they'll continue to do so, there's going to be a new junk bond era where the old methods of valuation that we're used to are being thrown out the window. For example, an Austrian bond was up over 55 percent at a negative 0.6 percent, and the bond managers were all over it. Then the next savvy banker will say, "Hey, we'll do a -0.7 percent bond, and we're happy with realizing 35 percent or 40 percent on the trading value of the bond."

As I said earlier, I see that trend continuing longer than most folks expect. People will have to put their money somewhere, and they're going to be sold on this new, lucrative bond market as well as an ever-rising S&P.

WHAT IS MY OUTLOOK ON COMMODITIES?

I think I've made it clear why I believe that MMT and SWAP Lines will keep the dollar strong for many years to come. I'll have much more to say about commodities in the later chapters. For now, here's a teaser: It's generally been the case, historically, that the dollar and precious metals have an inverse relationship with each other. I expect that to change. As the dollar gets even stronger in the coming years, I predict that precious metals will rise right along with the dollar.

DEMOGRAPHICS

Not to make matters worse, but the reality of the current demographic situation is that it's not overpopulation that is the problem for the global economy but rather population collapse. Worldwide, we see an increasing rate of slowing growth that will eventually yield to an absolute declining human population. Again, this is deflationary.

Why? Less demand for all the goods and services being created. The remedy: inflation. Via MMT, of course!

MMT FOREVER?

This will be hard for many to accept. Still, we are at a real inflection point in society, and MMT will become the most effective tool at hand for central bankers globally to deal with all of the deflationary forces I have outlined in this book.

As I've stressed, MMT isn't a short-term Band-Aid solution; but rather will be around for decades.

The psychology of the central bankers has changed by their full acceptance and implementation of MMT. The psychology of the bond market and equity investors has also changed as has the average person. For example, the saving rate of the average American household post-COVID has increased nearly 300 percent, to about 20 percent from 7 percent pre-COVID. The average person's psychology is changing, becoming more conservative, which is very deflationary for the economy.

With MMT, the funding will be available for corporations to reset their supply chains, meaning the start of de-globalization. As a result, the emerging markets' economies will feel more pain from changing behaviors than the US economy. This is mainly because the US is by far the largest economy in the world, with by far the most influential consumers. Now the supply chains for things that Americans need to buy will be from manufacturing hubs repatriated back home.

Again, this is deflationary for the rest of the world.

We may seem to be in a similar state to the 1930s, on the precipice of a new Great Depression. So many people are proclaiming it. However, in walking you through the Federal Reserve's monetary policy, I think I've shown how and why the central bank has adopted FMC and then eventually MMT as an antidote. And why it just might work, at least until it doesn't. But I don't expect that day of reckoning to arrive for years to come. There is a very strong possibility that the next two decades could be comparable to the incredible growth America experienced from the last time the Fed deployed FMC, which resulted in incredible growth from 1942–1962, which is known as the "golden era" of America.

The simple truth is that as bad as things are, America is still the place with the best schools and entrepreneurial spirit. It's where hard work and ambition are rewarded. As a result, America will fare better than other nations. The best minds on the planet will continue to come to America.

I know it's hard to think this way amid such gloom, but corny as it sounds, the American Dream is alive and well. America still leads in innovation. It's only in America where the son of a single teen mother can eventually create one of the world's largest conglomerates, the way Jeff Bezos has done with Amazon. Jeff Bezos's grandfather, Lawrence Preston Gise, was one of the first employees of DARPA (Defense Advanced Research Projects Agency), where many advancements to stealth technology, computing, communications, microelectronics, and surveillance were created. My point being, what you do today can influence your grandchildren in ways you cannot even imagine and perhaps even help make them the richest person on earth!

At present, the economy is sputtering, and there is still much instability in the markets. But progress will not dry up for want of money. If implemented, the changes in monetary policy that I've outlined here will fuel the Rise of America. It will be **THE** phenomenon of the next few decades, at a minimum.

MONETARY VERSUS FISCAL POLICY

One final question: Who is the most powerful person in America?

I think most people would say the president, and rightfully

so. Presidents can do things no one else can do, such as deploy the military to fight wars. They decide on the direction of federal spending through each year's federal budget (subject to congressional approval). They appoint judges to lifetime positions. They can veto any legislation coming out of Congress and, if they covet legislative powers of their own, can issue far-reaching executive orders, and so on.

But who is the *second* most powerful person? Some might say the Senate majority leader, and that's a reasonable choice. Personally, though, I would pick the chair of the Federal Reserve's Open Market Committee (FOMC).

The president and Congress determine the country's *fiscal policy*, i.e., what government funds—in the form of tax receipts plus borrowed money—will be spent. As such, they are beholden to the American people. If the people don't like what the president and their congressional representatives are doing, they can vote them out of office come the next election.

The Fed chair—and other FOMC members, who invariably go along with the chair's decisions—are presidential appointees. They cannot be voted in or out. In essence, they are accountable to no one. Yet, the chair controls the country's most important economic component: the determination of *monetary policy*.

There is a famous one-liner that's been attributed to any number of financial figures from the past. While we don't know for sure who first uttered it, no one denies its essential truth: *Give me control of a nation's money, and I care not who makes its laws.*

The power to create money and to determine its value is immeasurable. One could fairly argue that it is exceeded only by the power to wage war, which is why I place the Fed chair second only to the president among American authority figures.

It's also why I've spent so much space explaining policy tools like SWAP Lines, Eurodollars, and MMT. The Fed, and only the Fed, implements these in its collective wisdom. They were not devised by the president nor Congress and are not subject to the approval of either the executive or legislative branches of government.

The Fed stands alone when it comes to monetary policy. The chair sits atop the Fed. And his or her decisions reach into every corner of our lives.

As I've said before, it isn't up to me to pass judgment on these decisions. Their consequences may be relatively benign, or they may be catastrophic. I don't know—nor does anyone else. Only time will tell. But I can't change them. Neither can you, and for what it's worth, neither can the president. Yes, theoretically, the president can affect change by appointing a new chair—after Chairman Powell's term is up in 2022—with a different philosophy.

But he won't. The president and most members of Congress accept whatever the Fed dictates, partly because it's the easiest thing to do; partly because they believe in that collective wisdom of the FOMC members; and partly, perhaps mostly, because they lack enough understanding of economics to be able to devise effective counterarguments.

As I've said before, we have what *is*, and that's what we have to deal with, not *what we might wish for.*

SUMMING UP

This is a long chapter, I know. It's also dense with complicated material. Though I've simplified the subject as best I can, it is still not what anyone would call easy beach reading.

But I have done such a deep dive into MMT because—even though most people don't yet get it—it is the most consequential thing that can happen in the world of money moving forward. It's such a radical break from the past, and there's no reason to think we will experience particularly smooth sailing as the results unfold.

However, **the thing that distinguishes MMT from EVERY system that preceded it is its universality.** Write that on the wall. Take it to heart. Really do. MMT reigns alone, unique, as the biggest money experiment ever, mainly because in MMT, debts don't matter. Not just because of what it is, which is important enough, but also because there is a very high likelihood that **it is and will be implemented by nations around the world.**

There is no precedent...

CHAPTER FOUR

A SHORT HISTORY OF MONEY

IN THE PREVIOUS CHAPTER, I DEMONSTRATED HOW THE whole concept of money has changed with the onset of MMT. It's a lot to take in, I know. It shakes up the way we look at the present and, especially, the future. It's going to take time for us to integrate this new reality into our traditional worldview.

So, this is a good place for a brief detour into the past, specifically the history of money. It's a step backward in time to allow us to examine where we originated.

It will give us a chance to catch our collective breath and place the MMT revolution in context. The past, as they say, is prologue. By looking at our history, we can see where we are today and how we got here.

And we can project our thinking into a future dominated by the Rise of America.

IN THE BEGINNING...

We think of money in terms of paper certificates and coins, or entries in a checking account, or balances on a credit card, or the value of any one of a number of personal assets like your house or car. Even if we've heard about MMT, we still believe that we know the meaning of the word *money* when we use it. We feel secure when we have a lot of it and stressed when we're short.

Seldom, if ever, do we consider why, where, or when money first came about.

It feels like something that's always been around, not worth even a moment's casual thought. Of course, it hasn't always been there. It's really quite new.

Anthropologists' current consensus is that our species, *homo sapiens*, first appeared on the earth about 200,000 years ago. Those early humans had no money. Neither did any of their descendants, for most of the rest of our habitation of the planet.

For all those millennia, we made do with what we had. Occasionally, we would bump into another human group and, if we didn't immediately start killing each other, we might notice that they had food or a tool or some kind of fur that we didn't. And vice versa. Thus, barter was born. I propose to trade something to you for something I consider of equal value. You agree, the deal is struck, there's an exchange of *goods*, and we both go on our way with a satisfied mind. No killing required.

Most believe trade started with barter. But in his book *Debt, the First 5,000 Years*, David Graeber presents a stunning reversal of this conventional wisdom. Graeber argues that humans have used elaborate credit systems to buy and sell goods since the beginning of the agrarian empires. They are essentially dividing humans into debtors and creditors. Eventually, virtual credit money was replaced by gold, and the system as a whole went into decline.

The other argument we've been taught in school was that as

we became more sophisticated, barter could come to include nonphysical things as well, such as information. You know where the nearest water is; I know how to make a medicine to treat wounds. We exchange these intangibles, which would become known as *services*.

Barter served us well for a very long time. Even today, it has a place.

As a primary system of trade, it's suited to commerce among groups who are nomadic, engaged in hunting and gathering to survive. Everything is connected to the here and now. There is no futures market in the barter economy.

But there are some obvious drawbacks: the parties have to agree on the relative value of their respective offerings, and you have to be on your guard as negotiations proceed. The other guys might just be planning to attack, pillage everything you have, steal your women and children, and kill or enslave your men.

About 12,000 years ago, everything changed. Humans in the Middle East developed plant and animal domestication, and they began settling down into permanent communities. For the first time, there were surpluses of food in animals raised for slaughter and grains that could be stored.

Suddenly, the future existed. To a certain extent, barter was malleable, and it adapted. I could swap some of next year's grain for this year's goats. That was still cumbersome, and a less than bountiful harvest could ruin both parties. It also required the invention of record-keeping, an accounting system to keep track of who owed what to whom.

People realized that with transactions involving future goods or services, some sort of stand-in—a medium of exchange—had to be invented. In other words, *money*. Money was created as a "tool" to facilitate a convenient trading system.

Over the centuries, people tried to use all sorts of things like money. A non-exhaustive list includes seashells, beads, obsidian (think lava rocks), salt, tobacco, cigarettes, liquor, tea, cocoa beans, spears, swords, arrows and arrowheads, axes and ax heads, knives, animal skins, cloth, blankets, gemstones, jewelry, feathers, whale teeth, shark teeth, ivory, bone, cattle, camels, and, most shamefully, enslaved human beings.

Cattle, in particular, were as important as money. Historian Glyn Davies calls them humankind's "first working capital asset." Davies quotes linguistic evidence to show how ancient and widespread the association between cattle and money was. The English words *capital, chattel,* and *cattle* all derive from a common root. Similarly, *pecuniary* (think monetary payments) comes from the Latin word for cattle, *pecus.*

Davies cautions that "one should not confuse the abstract concept of an ox as a unit of account or standard of value, which is its essential but not only monetary function, with its admittedly cumbersome physical form. Once that is realized (a position quickly reached by primitive man if not yet by all economists or anthropologists), the inclusion of cattle as money is easily accepted, in practice and logic."

It was up to the Mesopotamians, circa 3000 BC, to develop some more modern systems. They were the first great merchant culture of the ancient world, and they kindly left us a written record of their monetary doings. They invented the first *commodity, money,* i.e., a physical thing that can be used as a medium of exchange for other physical things. Their money was called the *shekel,* a name still employed 5,000 years later in modern Israel. Originally, the value of one shekel was expressed as equivalent to a fixed weight of barley.

Mesopotamians were more than extraordinarily creative; they

were fussy and very detail oriented. They kept careful records of their transactions, incised into clay tablets. They created clay tokens that represented the three primary things traded: grain, livestock, and human labor. These are the first known instances in which a given amount of sweat equity was exchanged for tokens, which could then be exchanged for goods desired by the laborer. It's why you work nine to five for a paycheck. Not much has changed in 5,000 years, eh? But this is where it all began.

Eventually, sixteen tokens represented commonly traded goods like beds, bread, furniture, clothing, honey, and other products. And these people were the original bookkeepers. To keep track of their commerce, they were forced to develop the basic accounting principles we still use today.

With the shekel, the Mesopotamians established a monetary standard that could be applied over time. This was an utter sea change in the human psyche. Think about it. We went from a species that could only deal with things directly in front of them to a species capable of abstraction (agreeing today to future transactions' value and delivery). Our ancestors to be able to envision—and to express in language—what it is that money does:

> It enables you to hold an object in your hand that is essentially worthless at the moment but with a firm belief that it will be convertible into something that you want later on.

Truly revolutionary.

And as if all these accomplishments weren't enough, the Mesopotamians also bequeathed to us another familiar institution that would survive the passage of thousands of years: *banking*. As royal families came into being, their palaces provided secure places for the safe keeping of grain and other commodities.

Depositors would get receipts, which came to be used not only for withdrawals by the original depositors but could also be transferred to third parties in the settlement of debts. Or, in the birth of another modern tradition, confiscated by tax collectors.

Eventually, wealthy, nonroyal houses in Mesopotamia also got involved in similar operations and became the first private banks. Laws regulating them were included in the famous Code of Hammurabi that dates back to about 1754 BC.

At about the same time as money was being defined in barley units, precious metals entered the picture.

GOLD

No one knows when a human first plucked a gold nugget from a stream and carried it home to show the family. But it was probably a really long time ago. Archaeologists tell us that natural gold bits were found in Spanish caves inhabited by Paleolithic man about 40,000 years ago. But to be fair, it is doubtful that prehistoric *homo sapiens* used it for anything, and its presence in their living quarters could be purely coincidental.

Fast-forward thirty-three millennia or so, and suddenly we find definitive evidence that people had become engaged in transforming inert lumps of this strange substance into recognizable shapes. At that point, seemingly from nowhere, there appeared goldsmiths. Really good ones!

Now, gold was not the first metal to be worked on and shaped by our hands. The reason is simple. Gold in its natural state is relatively soft. It doesn't lend itself to toolmaking, and humans have always been developing new and better tools.

As we transitioned to fixed settlements based on agriculture, the stone implements of the long Paleolithic period were slowly replaced by metal ones. Copper was the initial metal of choice; thus, the new era is now termed the Chalcolithic (or Copper) Age. Isolated copper axes and adzes (a cutting tool like the ax) appeared in Anatolia and Mesopotamia as early as 5500 BC.

By 3000 BC, we were well into the Chalcolithic Age, and that's when smiths decided to see what they could do with gold. Obviously, that implies a concurrent demand. At some point, people had assigned value to the metal that was not based on real utility. And they did it far and wide. A near-universal perception of gold as extraordinarily beautiful and powerful, with perhaps magical qualities, developed.

It was not yet employed as money. But it was rare. It never changed and would not tarnish, corrode, or rust. Though you couldn't chop wood with it, things could easily be fashioned from it. It was amazingly malleable and ductile. One ounce of gold could be drawn out into a wire fifty miles long without breaking. It could be beaten until it is thin enough to see through without fracturing. For a special exhibit on gold, the walls of one room in the American Museum of Natural History were covered with approximately 300 square feet of 23-karat gold leaf created from just three ounces of gold—a volume equivalent to that of three US half-dollar coins. Gold could be embossed, hammered, cast, stretched, or twisted. In the hands of a talented craftsperson, it could be teased into a limitless variety of shapes.

While adornment may have been the prevailing usage for gold, it was not the only one. In early societies, gold jewelry was worn as amulets (like the Egyptian *ankh*) to ward off evil and protect against bad luck and illness. It was fashioned into symbols thought to give the wearer control over fertility, wealth, and love. It cemented political alliances. It served as an outward expression of nobility and, as more sophisticated religions developed, it identified the priestly class.

Gold was eternal and, indeed, akin to a god.

Perhaps most important was the early connection of gold with wealth. With the rise of the early agricultural civilizations came many aspects of what we now call society, such as classes, hierarchies, political rulers, defense forces, religious cults, and so on. Those at the top of the social structure became something never seen when we were all hunter/gatherers: *rich*.

Now, we can't go back and inhabit the minds of ancestors who lived more than six millennia ago. But given what we know of human nature, we can surmise that the *nouveau riche* probably wanted a physical way to express how much more they had—not to mention how much more attractive they were and how much more power they wielded—than everyone else. They also almost certainly wanted to own objects that would endure over time and be continually revered, giving their owners a surefire way to pass their riches down to their children, eventually creating royal lineages.

Gold filled the bill pretty early in the development of civilization. We can't know exactly how it gained such widespread acceptance as precious, but it did. Once that happened, people had a convenient, highly visible, nonverbal way of expressing who they were; showcasing their wealth, rank, political and religious affiliation; marking rites of passage; or even demonstrating affections toward someone else. And, at the outset, they didn't cast their gold into coins or bars and hide them away in a vault. They wore it.

So, smiths went to work fashioning gold ornaments.

Did they ever. And they were really skilled.

Even the very earliest works remain striking today. There

is a famous collection of jewelry recovered from a Chalcolithic necropolis excavated near the modern-day city of Varna, Bulgaria, on the Black Sea coast. Look it up. It is the oldest gold treasure hoard yet discovered in the world, found at a site carbon-dated to between 4560 and 4450 BC (~6,000 years ago). Many of the pieces—necklaces, bracelets, rings, stylized animals—could just as easily pass as items fashioned yesterday afternoon.

Egyptians were also early adopters of gold's symbolic value. It was used in jewelry there from the third millennium BC. They had access to a lot of the metal at sites in Nubia, which helped make them very wealthy by 1500 BC, and their goldsmiths were second to none. The craftsmanship that went into Tutankhamen's famed funeral mask, created in 1323 BC, remains a thing to be marveled at.

Nor was the veneration of gold confined to the Middle East. Far away, in China, squares of gold about the size of postage stamps became a form of money as early as 1091 BC. That this was the product of cultural diffusion seems unlikely, as the first contact between East and West that we know of today didn't happen for another seven centuries. It was probably an independent invention, which would be a powerful testimony to gold's universal allure.

Back in Mesopotamia, silver also came into usage for jewelry. Like gold, it was easily worked and came to represent a store of value. Though it never attained the same exalted status as gold, it was still quite popular.

The point is the connection between precious metals and money was established early. People could use their gold jewelry as a form of money to trade for other things they wanted. Silver even attained formal monetary status in Mesopotamia around 2500 BC. A shekel of silver replaced barley as the standard currency in the region. One shekel was defined as what would today be equivalent to one-third of an ounce of silver, and a month's worth of basic manual labor was rewarded with a single shekel.

Early economic traffic in precious metals was more convenient than using piles of grain, but it still had its downsides. Unless you wanted a particular product of the goldsmith's art, the metal had value only in terms of its weight. Gold and silver had to be weighed every time they changed hands. A lot depended on the integrity of the assayer. And there were issues of cheating by "blending" precious metals with base metals.

Clearly, there had to be a better system, one in which the precious metals came in a form that could, like cattle, be counted instead of weighed and that conformed to a widely accepted standard of authenticity and purity.

So, of course, humans being as ingenious as they are, they created:

Coins.

Especially gold and silver.

JINGLE, JANGLE

That gold and silver coins *became* money seems inevitable. They admirably served the three main functions of the whole concept of money as it was originally envisioned, namely that it should serve as:

- a **means of transaction**, making disparate things commensurable, thereby enabling people to conduct trade in goods that weren't physically present or didn't even yet exist
- a **unit of account**, so that records could be kept, and values determined

- and a **store of value**, so that money today will have the same worth tomorrow

Moreover, they fulfilled Aristotle's careful formulation, in the fourth century BC, of the characteristics ideal money should possess to commensurate goods and services, promote the flow of trade, and act as the ultimate equalizer:

- **Durable**—it must not weather, rot, fall apart, or become unusable. It must be able to withstand the test of time, which is one reason barley fell out of favor.
- **Portable**—it must be easily moveable and hold a large amount of universal value relative to its size, eliminating herds of cattle.
- **Divisible**—it should be relatively easy to separate and put back together without ruining its basic characteristics, which is why the *Mona Lisa* would not work.
- **Intrinsically Valuable**—it should be valuable in and of itself, and its value should be totally independent of any other object. Essentially, the item must be rare. Thus, for example, packets of dirt just will not do.

Aristotle maintained that everything could be expressed in the universal equivalent of money, giving the concept its first philosophical underpinning and establishing the basic commerce principle for thousands of years to come.

But back to coins.

The first precious metal coins were produced as early as 700 BC in the kingdom of Lydia, a powerhouse nation in its day. The kingdom was in what is now western Turkey, including the strategic passage from the Black Sea to the Mediterranean, and endured until being absorbed by the Persian Empire in 546 BC.

Lydia's coins—the *stater*—were made of electrum, a naturally occurring alloy of gold and silver. They established the foundations of most subsequent monetary systems. Precious metals would continue to serve as money for millennia, from ancient Lydia to mid-twentieth-century America.

The stater was made possible by advances in refining that allowed the kingdom to guarantee their authenticity and give merchants something convenient and standardized to use in their trade.

Now, I do use the term *standardized* loosely. Because soon after inventing coinage of a specific weight, the Lydians had one of the all-time great financial *Aha!* moments, with enormous and far-reaching consequences. They realized that they could easily debase their coinage by adding cheap copper to the alloy, with no one the wiser. So, they did it. More coins with less gold. *Et voilà*, an instant increase in the money supply—at least theoretically, as we shall see—and thereby in the kingdom's wealth.

Unknowingly, this long-vanished state gifted the world with one of history's ongoing monetary bugaboos: *inflation*. The notion that you could create more money from nothing—which I explored in Chapter 3—was as irresistible then as it is now. It was a temptation that would persist for the rest of human history, right up to the present day.

Gold and silver coins remained the definition of money in the West for about 1,700 years after the Lydians first stamped them out. Not so in China.

China had been using various bronze items as money since early in the first millennium BC. By the fourth century BC, coins cast in bronze or copper, with round or square holes in the center, were the realm's official money. Later, bronze and copper were replaced by iron, which was much more abundant. That resulted in more coins of lesser value. It was called *cash*, so the origin of our modern term comes from what is today China.

During the Tang dynasty (618–907 AD), the government was facing a shortage of copper. Somewhere around 800 AD, it decided to issue "certificates of deposit" against cash deposited in its vaults. Paper, invented in China, was already in use for hundreds of years by this time. Thus, it's only natural that the world's first paper currency was created there.

Merchants, who already dealt with the readily available but cumbersome iron coins, quickly adopted the use of the paper currency, as it was easier and safer to transport and transact. China was way ahead of the curve here. It'd be 250 years after the fall of the Tang Dynasty before the ability to make paper would finally spread to Europe—and Europeans wouldn't catch on to the idea of paper money until the seventeenth century.

These "receipts" were an instant hit in China. Everyone loved the new "flying money," as it was called because it conveyed credit across vast distances. It was convenient and easy to use, not to mention so much lighter than a bagful of metal coins. After all, while coins may be technically portable, they are pretty bulky and heavy if you have a lot of them. They jingle and jangle in your money pouch so that any sharp-eared thief in the neighborhood knows what you're carrying. Paper weighs little more than nothing. You can carry around a fortune in your pocket, and no one will know.

But from the government's point of view, the key attraction of paper money was that it was a breeze to inflate.

SINGING THE INFLATION SONG

Around 1000 AD, the rulers of the Song dynasty had an *Aha!* moment every bit as powerful and far-reaching as the Lydians had had 1,600 years earlier. And it was fully comparable since it involved the same concept: debasing the currency.

But unlike the Lydians, the Chinese weren't burdened with the tedious task of physically diluting the gold or silver content of their coins. They realized that there was no deterrent to producing more paper money than was backed by metal in the government vaults. All they had to do was print, and no one would ever know—unless all the depositors demanded their cash back at the same time, and what were the chances of that happening? All in all, it seemed like an expedient and risk-free way to solve any immediate cash flow problems. So, print they did.

To the extent that their paper's putative value exceeded the amount of cash in the vaults, it secretly became history's first fiat currency—defined as "money" backed by nothing but government promises. Today, all the planet's currencies are fiat, and so the term no longer carries quite the negative connotation it once did. But make no mistake. Dependence on a fiat currency that rests only on thin air is not risk-free, as countries throughout the ages have discovered to their chagrin.

> **Note**: It's important to keep in mind the meaning of the term *inflation*. Today, people tend to think of it exclusively in terms of the rising prices of goods and services in the marketplace. But it originally meant the expansion of the money supply beyond the simple need to meet demand. When that happens, you have an excess of currency chasing the same amount of goods and services, which drives the market price of them up. Thus, price inflation is a *consequence* of monetary inflation; it isn't so much a matter of prices going *up* as it is the value of the currency going *down*. (*Deflation* is the opposite; it is triggered by a withdrawal of currency from the economy.) And that's on purpose. As economist Ludwig von Mises put it: "The most important thing to remember is that inflation is not an act of God; inflation is not a catastrophe of the elements or a disease that comes like the plague. Inflation is a *policy*." As I explained in Chapter 3, MMT is that policy writ large.

In any event, those long-ago Chinese rulers not only gave us fiat currency by their overprinting, but they also committed the first instance of paper *currency inflation*.

And that's not all.

Concurrently, something else equally momentous happened. The Song dynasts found that they could also borrow cash from the vaults to buy off potential foreign invaders who would not take their paper money—and replace that cash with paper IOUs. Again, this would work so long as there was never a run on the vaults' physical metal.

Thus, was born the world's introduction to *fractional reserve banking*—a practice that has spread far and wide over the past millennium.

Obviously, it was still a novelty in eleventh-century AD China. But it really caught on. At that time, many private banks existed, and one of them in Szechuan warmly embraced the government's fiscal policy and started issuing deposit receipts above the actual cash it had on hand. Fifteen similar banks immediately copied the idea. Notes in circulation naturally grew much faster than the reserves of the banks. If they thought the public wouldn't notice, they were wrong. The people grew weary of the paper inflation and began turning in their receipts for cash. In 1032 there was a full-fledged run on the banks. All sixteen failed.

That crash spawned a widespread distrust of paper money, and the economy for a time reverted to using cash (iron and copper coins) for transactions.

And this is a scenario that has unfolded over and over throughout the history of money.

In 1189, the Song dynasty (which was still around) issued a "new" paper currency to push inflation down. But they failed to slow the printing presses. As the number of unbacked notes in circulation climbed, their value plummeted. By 1200, the people reverted to using cash (metal coins). Again.

By the mid-thirteenth century AD, the Mongols had taken over China, with Kublai Khan establishing the Yuan dynasty. And nothing changed. The new ruler issued the paper *mongol* in 1260 and outlawed competing money such as gold, silver, and copper. Kublai ran the printing presses nonstop, and the mongol's value suffered such a speedy collapse that in 1264 it was replaced by the *second mongol* at a 5:1 ratio (one new mongol could be exchanged for five old ones). But the presses never slowed their output, so in 1310, the dynasty issued a *third mongol*, exchangeable once again at a 5:1 ratio. This means that over fifty years, the mongol had lost 96 percent of its value.

And the people again returned to, wait for it, cash (metal coins).

FIAT MONEY HEADS WEST

In one of those odd coincidences that make history so interesting, it turns out that the adventurer Marco Polo was wandering through Kublai's kingdom at the time. As we know, Marco was a pretty keen observer. He'd never seen paper money before, but the canny Italian caught on immediately, writing in his *Travels*:

"You might say that (Kublai) has the secret of alchemy in perfection...the Khan causes every year to be made such a vast quantity of this money, which costs him nothing, that it must equal in amount all the treasure of the world."

Marco Polo was understandably skeptical of the Khan's grand scheme and wrote of the consequences of this early experiment in currency inflation:

"The best families in the empire were ruined, a new set of men came into the control of public affairs, and the country became the scene of internecine warfare and confusion."

(Polo, of course, took his keen observations back to the West. How much influence his writings may have had concerning this subject is unknown. Perhaps his warnings did, in fact, put people off. Anyway, all we know is that paper banknotes would not appear in Europe for nearly 400 years after he returned home.)

Fiat currency failure is the rule, not the exception. According to a study of 775 historical fiat currencies published on *DollarDaze.org*, there is no precedent for a fiat currency steadily holding its value. Ever. The study found that 20 percent failed through hyperinflation, 21 percent collapsed because of war, and 12 percent were destroyed by independence. Of the rest, 24 percent were monetarily reformed, and 23 percent are still in circulation, albeit subject to a steadily declining value. On average, the life expectancy of those 775 currencies has been a mere twenty-seven years.

Sweden was first to take the plunge, in 1661, with the Bank of Stockholm—under the direction of founder Johan Palmstruch—issuing *kreditivsedlar* (credit notes). With each note worth a fixed sum of *specie* (the generic term for physical money), these were modern-style banknotes, payable to the bearer on demand. Palmstruch believed that these would be a welcome alternative to Sweden's clumsy large copper coins.

Initially, there was a lot of resistance among officials and merchants who believed that this innovation would eventually destroy the country's monetary system. So, the government had to back the bank, guaranteeing the notes' redeemability, the banknotes carried sixteen certifying endorsements from prominent and trustworthy individuals, all signed individually by hand, to overcome the people's concerns!

Within months, other European governments and merchants—who could see the convenience of this new "money" as well as the boost it gave to the Swedish economy—followed along, issuing their own paper money. Moreover, everyone quickly realized that the entirety of the circulating banknotes would not be cashed in at the same time. All that needed to be done was to create the convenient fiction that there was enough gold and silver in a given depository to cover any demand. In a flash, fractional reserve banking had come to the West.

Complicating the situation was that the concept of paper money was so novel, most countries had no laws governing who could print money. Yes, anti-counterfeiting laws made it illegal to copy existing coins, and those were soon updated to cover paper money. But few countries had prohibitions against anyone issuing their own currency. Soon states, principalities, cities, banks, guilds, institutions, and even private individuals started churning out banknotes. The only questions were: did you have a printing press, and could you get the public to accept your offering as money? Answer *yes* to both, and you were in the fiat currency game.

With so much competition, the face value of many banknotes was an iffy proposition. Some notes might be issued and not accepted at all. Others were accepted only at a discount from face value. Still others quickly reached their innate value—zero. And a rare few banknotes circulated at more than face value, especially if the issuers were trusted to back them with the specified amounts of gold or silver (which, of course, themselves often fluctuated in value).

And what of poor Johan Palmstruch, the Swede who'd inadvertently set all these wheels to spinning? Yep, he succumbed to temptation and issued far too many Bank of Stockholm notes.

The bank lost the ability to redeem any significant amount of them on demand, and it collapsed. He was arrested, tried, and sentenced to prison—where he died in 1671, just ten short years after he'd dropped his grand idea on an unsuspecting public.

Across the Atlantic in the eighteenth century, the European powers began to establish their spheres of influence in the New World. It would be another hundred years before Britain's colonies determined to break away from the home country and establish a nation of their own. Their insurrection led to what we might term the Rise of America, version 1.0.

Like the current Rise of America I'm writing about in this book, the success of version 1.0 is also deeply involved with the nation's tangled relationship to money. The subject of the monetary history of the US is a fascinating one. It deserves a chapter of its own.

So, for readers who crave an in-depth exploration of that history or those who are just curious, you will find a lengthy exploration of the topic in Appendix I—from the Colonial days to the establishment of the Republic, from the nineteenth-century currency wars through to the evolution of the Federal Reserve, right up to the point at which MMT takes over.

One way of looking at monetary history is to note that virtually all Western currencies—from the first *kreditivsedlars* on—were at least partially fiat, even though many purported to be fully gold- or silver-backed. But it would take until the mid-twentieth century before every currency on the planet was 100 percent backed by nothing.

Especially not by gold...

CHAPTER FIVE

WHY GOLD MATTERS

THE YELLOW METAL IS SPECIAL.

It has mattered in virtually every monetary system since the Lydians introduced precious metal coins to the world over 2,500 years ago. It still matters today. And it will matter during the Rise of America powered by MMT.

Gold has exerted an irresistible pull on the human psyche, virtually from the point at which one of our distant ancestors first plucked a nugget from a local stream.

The history of gold is like that of no other element in the natural world. It is about greed and thrift; about prosperity and ruin; about empires raised to dizzying heights and reduced to ashes.

Gold has been the foundation of tyranny and the bulwark of freedom. It is the first thing pocketed by those fleeing for their lives and the last thing the miser will allow to be pried from his cold, dead fingers.

It's not my job to detail man's eternal fascination with gold here. That's a book in itself, maybe more than one. For those interested, I go into America's long involvement with the gold standard as part of my consideration of US monetary policy in Appendix I.

Nor is this book an investment guide. However, again for those interested, see Appendix V for some considerations about investing in the gold "paper market."

But here, I want to confine myself to a discussion of gold as it applies to the subject at hand. The critical fact is that, for millennia, gold has been, and remains today, one important thing—**money**. And despite the revolution launched by MMT, it still has a monetary role to play in the Rise of America. So, I need to briefly talk about the gold market as it exists in contemporary society. And what it will look like going forward.

THE WILD RIDE

Gold has not historically had such drastic price swings as in 2020 (except for the late 1970s and early 1980s, when people went mad for the metal after the ban on private ownership was lifted): up 40 percent between March and August, then selling off about 13 percent as of December. But I think we are in for a new normal that will regularly include such extremes well into the future. These are nervous times. And when people are nervous, they tend to go to extremes, spinning from safety to risk at dizzying speeds, not really knowing what they are doing, nor why.

On the one hand, gold is seen as a safe haven, a secure place to park money when there is uncertainty in other markets. That's truer now than ever because of ZIRP (zero-interest rate policies) everywhere and NIRP (negative interest rates) in many places. Formerly, many investors would avoid gold because it has carrying costs and doesn't generate any income. But now, as interest rates shrivel and even go below zero, that drawback is less significant, and gold has become more attractive to a much larger group of investors.

Traditionalists see gold as protection against a devaluing currency; an inflation hedge; a store of value; and something that might best be called calamity insurance. In times when people will accept nothing else in trade, they have always accepted gold.

On the other hand, gold today appeals to some not as a safe haven but as a way to speculate on economic uncertainty. Gold will entice those looking for high-risk/high-reward investments, which can be played on both the long and short sides of the paper market, as the gold price trends either upward or downward (see Appendix V).

As this book makes clear, I'm bullish on the inevitable Rise of America. But uncertainty will be with us for a while, depending on what happens with COVID-19 and how quickly the economy does or doesn't recover from the havoc the virus has created.

Expect volatility in the gold mining equity market and even in the price of gold. In the long term, people's desire to hold gold is not going anywhere for the reasons outlined above. Thus, as with any commodity, the market will primarily be driven by supply and demand.

SUPPLY

In the past, the supply of gold has lined up pretty well with demand. Not anymore.

Consider a recent report from Barrick Gold, one of the world's top producers. Barrick confirms what those of us immersed in natural resources already know: gold production faces a precipice of historic proportions.

The company estimates world production of gold in 2020

will be around 120 million ounces. It has been slowly rising in an unbroken uptrend since 2009 when about 80 million ounces were pulled from the ground.

The year 2020 represents the midpoint in time between 2009 and 2029, and Barrick predicts that it will also be the high point. From here, the company foresees a steady and continual decline, year after year, until 2029, production comes in at a little more than 60 million ounces, or barely half of what we're getting in 2020.

Here are some more numbers:

From 1990–2019, there have been 278 gold discoveries globally with a 2 million ounce or greater resource. Over those 278 discoveries, $95 billion was spent on exploration to find 2.19 billion ounces of gold.

In the past ten years, only twenty-five deposits of 2 million ounces or greater have been discovered. These twenty-five deposits contain on the order of 154 million ounces.

Put simply: Only 7 percent of the total gold found in the last thirty years was found in the last decade.

Here's another data point. $55 billion was spent in gold exploration over the last decade (2010–2020). That means the gold sector spent 58 percent of its expenditures from the last thirty years within the last decade, yet found only 7 percent of the gold.

Let me repeat this again...

The exploration dollars required to discover the 154 million ounces found in the last decade is $55 billion. Over half the total spending since 1990 has discovered only 7 percent of the gold.

Now let's compare exploration budgets to new discoveries. As a benchmark, we'll take the last really banner year, 2005. In that year, the overall exploration budget was less than $3 billion. But that was good enough to discover about 125 million new ounces.

The relationship deteriorated dramatically from there, hitting its low point in 2012, when companies spent $10 billion on exploration to discover less than 20 million ounces. In 2020, the exploration budget was $4 billion with *zero* confirmed new gold discoveries. The years 2017 through 2019 were also dismal, with around $12 billion spent and, while there were no confirmed major discoveries during the period, there were at least projected discoveries of maybe 40 million ounces. (Projected means the geologists think the gold will be there, but confirmatory drilling has yet to prove it.)

WHERE IS GOLD FOUND?

To make matters more challenging, most of the ounces that *are* being discovered lie in negative SWAP Line Nations. SWAP Lines are hugely important. If you need to refresh yourself on why, see Chapter 2.

Yes, the overall lack of new discoveries is alarming. But even more alarming is how little gold has been found in +SWAP Line Nations in the last decade. From 1990–1999, one billion ounces of gold were discovered at nearly a 50:50 split between +SWAP and –SWAP Line Nations. But in the last decade, only 76 million ounces—or 33 percent of the gold discovered—was in +SWAP Line Nations.

Put another way, only 28 percent as much gold was discovered between 2010–2019 in +SWAP Line Nations as was discovered in the same nations between 2000–2009. The trends are very clear. Less gold is being found every decade, and even less is being found in +SWAP Line Nations.

Look at the top ten largest gold discoveries: In the 1990s, six were in +SWAP Line Nations. In the '00s, only four were in

+SWAP Line Nations. And over the past decade, only three came in +SWAP Line Nations.

Production from –SWAP Line Nations is by its very nature insecure. In these countries, corruption tends to be rife, nationalization (and subsequent mismanagement) is an ever-present possibility, mining interruptions for various reasons are common, and infrastructure is generally subpar. Natural disasters are more consequential than they are in the more developed world, and politics plays a greater role in whether or not a given mine continues to operate.

Reliance on production in –SWAP Line Nations is iffy, but production costs in +SWAP Line Nations are usually higher. Both imply a coming supply crunch.

THE AK-47 INDICATOR

While we're on the subject of SWAP Lines, let me digress just a little bit and give you another rule of thumb I like to employ when looking at –SWAP vs. +SWAP Line Nations: the AK-47 indicator.

Let me explain.

The Russian AK-47 is the most widely sold, most widely used machine gun in history...and a mainstay of conflicts in the developing world, where *"cheap, simple, and reliable"* are the preferred qualities of firearms. It's estimated that more than 75 million AK-47s are in circulation around the planet.

As a resource investor, it can be hard not to get seduced by the excitement and drama that comes with investing in far-off lands. After all, many countries in Africa, Asia, and South America are less picked over by exploration geologists. You get to visit new places and meet interesting people. And the prospect of finding the next giant gold deposit in some forgotten patch of the jungle is just plain exciting. All these things got me on way too many plane trips.

Inevitably, I've seen my share of AK-47s, and then some.

You know what? Now, after many successes and many mistakes as a major investor in the gold sector, I tend to avoid places where you see people in the streets brandishing their AK-47s. I've learned the hard way to trade the excitement of new, exotic places for the boredom of places that honor the old concept of a *rule of law* and harbor a simple respect for business done the old-fashioned way: peaceably.

And you know what else? The AK-47 countries tend to be the ones with very few of the roads, bridges, power lines, railroads, and ports needed to get vital raw materials from the ground to the end user. That kind of infrastructure is critical for turning resource deposits into free cash flow. Worse still, AK-47 nations also often lack contract laws and property rights, and worst of all, they usually have little regard for human life.

If you're reading this, there's a good chance you live in the US, Canada, Australia, or Europe. As much of an SOB as you think the politician in your state, country, or province is, trust me, he has nothing on the average lunatic running a third-world country. If the American president doesn't like you, maybe he sends out a nasty tweet. If your average third-world dictator doesn't like you, he sends out a hit squad.

Increasingly, investors will put their capital to work in countries with long histories of respecting contracts and property rights, and which have the roads, power lines, bridges, and ports that are critical to extracting and transporting natural resources.

Unsurprisingly, the Fed agrees with me. It is not extending SWAP Lines to the AK-47 nations.

So much for the gold supply. Let's now turn to the demand side.

DEMAND

One measure of demand are inflows into an increasingly popular form of investing: gold-based ETFs.

For reasons of convenience, large numbers of investors prefer owning a promise that their gold is out there, somewhere, rather than owning the physical metal. I can understand. Taking possession of actual gold requires that you have a place to store it, which can entail risk (home storage) or yearly fees (offsite storage).

Buying and selling ETFs, on the other hand, couldn't be easier. They are traded on the major stock exchanges. They require only that you go to your regular broker's website, click a couple of buttons on your computer screen, and *presto*, you're a gold "owner."

It's simple, convenient, and basically hassle-free. Small wonder that investors seeking safe haven from COVID'S economic damages—as well as those simply wanting to participate in gold's developing bull market—have been piling into these products. Considering all gold-backed ETFs, the funds added a whopping $25 billion in investments between April and August of '20. (Since the funds have to buy gold with incoming money, another way of looking at the demand is to note the flow of gold into their vaults. In the second quarter of 2020 alone, that inflow totaled *434 metric tons*.)

Action in the ETFs more than offset a decline in demand in the consumer sector, especially with jewelry, which fell 53 percent year over year from 2Q19 after stores were shuttered. Makes sense.

More puzzling is that global bar and coin investment was

down 17 percent for the first half of 2020, year over year. But that's misleading. Yes, some of it can be chalked up to COVID-related lockdowns that curtailed physical gold shopping worldwide, with ETFs the main beneficiary. However, much of it was due to the fact that, with mints and refineries also being widely locked down, there were simply no coins to be had—as you well know if you tried to buy a Maple Leaf coin in April. Dealers reported demand that was many multiples higher than normal but had no stock to sell, or else were forced to saddle customers with very long wait times.

Moreover, the World Gold Council (WGC) noted a large divergence between the market action in different parts of the world in 2020. In Asia and the Middle East, selling dominated, probably because of profit-taking in the more affluent countries and economically strapped citizens' need to raise cash in the poorer ones. In the West, however, safe-haven buying, and investment momentum dominated. That led to "substantial growth" in bar and coin demand in Europe and North America, the WGC reported. Hence the shortage of physical metal in those places.

I expect fabrication demand to pick up as COVID lockdowns ease and for coin and bar demand to remain at a healthy level as the supply chain normalizes.

But I'd also like to add a couple of other observations relevant to demand.

THE EFFECT OF MMT

As I've been saying, MMT means massive injections of newly created currency into the economy. What have the banks done with this infusion of liquidity? You'd assume they'd be lending, but—as I explained in Chapter 3—they aren't. The banks' excuse has been that fewer people qualify for loans because of new, more stringent rules and regs imposed on them. I don't know how true that is. But much of this capital has certainly been flooding into the stock market, either through the deployment of loan money the banks have made available to their "best" clients or possibly through direct buying by the banks themselves. That has buoyed up the Dow and S&P, even in the face of such negatives as cratering GDP, plummeting corporate incomes, and swiftly rising bankruptcies. It also seems logical that some part of this money is being used to acquire the gold piling up in some banks' vaults.

That notion is buttressed by action at the COMEX warehouse, the clearance center for gold bars. As of late July 2020, a record 5.5 million ounces of physical gold had been delivered to the COMEX this year. The gold delivered in New York has been flooding in from spot markets such as Singapore, Switzerland, and Australia. (US imports directly from London are rare because, in London, 400-ounce bars are the standard for trading and the main futures contract in New York requires smaller, 100-ounce bars for delivery.)

One explanation for this level of delivery of physical metal to the COMEX lies in the potential for arbitrage. (*Arbitrage* is taking advantage of price disparities for the same asset in different markets; you buy low in one place and sell high in the other, and the difference is your profit.) Since March 23 of 2020, New York futures have persistently been trading above London spot, though the spread has fluctuated. As a result, when the spread is wide enough, the arbitrage opportunity arises.

What happens is that when futures prices in NY exceed spot in London, arbitragers buy physical gold at spot, sell futures contracts, fly the metal to New York, and physically deliver the gold. Thus, if the spread between spot and futures is $40 per ounce, the arbitrager's profit is $40 per ounce, minus costs for transport, insurance, storage, etc.

It's complicated, but you don't have to understand all the ins and outs. Suffice it to say that this is a risky business that requires conditions to remain favorable through the trade. And so far, in post-COVID 2020, it's obviously been worth it.

For our purposes, though, the larger question is: Who is taking delivery of the gold that the arbitragers are dumping at the COMEX? Someone has to be. Speculation is that they may be second-level arbitragers, playing the spread between the "near month futures contract" on the COMEX and the "next near month futures contract."

No matter. The COMEX warehouse is not a place where gold is stored indefinitely. Those millions of ounces are eventually going someplace. Somewhere along the line, those buying physical metal on the paper market will take actual delivery—and the COMEX warehouse is where they will go to pick it up.

So, someone big—perhaps one major bank like JPMorgan or several someone's—is stockpiling gold, which makes my case. It means there is serious insider money being bet on a continued bull market in the metal.

Additionally, low interest rates mean that people can really play the various markets. They can borrow for next to nothing and buy assets to turn them over in the short term for a quick profit. This works as long as markets are on the rise, which stocks, of course, have been. And gold, too.

I believe that this kind of speculative buying will continue for as long as the cost of borrowing is negligible and as long as gold moves higher—which I expect to be a very long time, indeed.

COVID-19

The pandemic has had a devastating effect on the mining business, putting many major operations at risk—and hitting the supply line hard.

The effects were felt almost overnight. Between early March and early April of 2020, there were about 120 gold mining shutdowns. Mines are being closed across the globe, either by government mandate or by the company, due to the health threat to workers. The mining world has never seen shutdowns at such a rapid pace.

The knock-on effects of these shutdowns will be significant. Mining is an economic essential in many regions of the world. In Namibia, to take one example, mining contributes 25 percent of the country's entire income, and with the virus panic, the whole industry was put on hold.

You might think that as the danger passes, mines will quickly reopen. No. In the real world, bringing back a mine isn't like turning the lights back on. You can't just flick some excavation master switch.

This will have a significant impact on many companies that are not sufficiently capitalized to weather the storm.

In the best of times, it's very rare that mines, when they are built, come online without hiccups (production delays and cost overruns). Obviously, these are not the best of times. So, at a minimum, expect the same kinds of obstacles in bringing back the mines that have been taken offline.

The truth is that many of the shut down mines will face financing hardships and will be at the mercy of their bankers. Some will probably be bought out; others may simply fail to reopen, ever.

Either way, the gold business will have to endure both short- and long-term supply shortages.

In addition to mine closures, back in the early days of COVID-19, there were mass shutdowns of refineries and mints. This—as you well know, if you tried to buy gold back then—produced the turmoil in the coin market I mentioned earlier. There was extreme scarcity, premiums went through the roof, and delivery times of six weeks or more were common. Some coins couldn't be had at any price.

Things stabilized over the course of the 2020 summer. Coins have become generally available again. But, at least as of this writing in late 2020, premiums remain relatively high. In "normal" times, you might expect to pay something like 3–4 percent over spot to get a 1-ounce American Eagle. As of November 2020, that premium has fallen from its peak in the spring, but it's still high, at around 6 percent. Where it goes from here is anyone's guess; it's totally dependent on future supply and demand.

I expect that the coronavirus may be brought under control as effective vaccines are developed and widely distributed. Or it may not. We don't know. What we do know is that this one event disrupted the entire supply/demand chain for gold. It could again. Or some other virus might.

As we've already seen, mine outputs will be steadily dropping for at least the next ten years. There will also, inevitably, be other disruptions from wars, natural disasters, financial woes, future pandemics, and whatever other black swans might alight.

Take crimps in the supply line, add in steady demand in the face of the economic uncertainties of a long-term crossflationary environment, and you have a pretty perfect storm for the rise of the yellow metal right alongside the Rise of America.

And that's a central idea in this book. In opposition to the mainstream financial opinion, I believe that this is baked in the cake: **appreciation in the gold price will proceed in tandem**

with the strengthening of the US dollar and then continue even after the dollar's rise eventually stagnates. Gold is money, and as such, it will outlast the US dollar, just like it has every other fiat currency (over 500 of them) before it.

But let me add one caveat: For those who delude themselves that the US will somehow get back on the gold standard, **forget about it.**

In January 1929, John Maynard Keynes laid out the argument best for why the gold standard wouldn't work, and he was right. In his report, Keynes cited the historical growth of gold production, which increases about 2 percent, at best, over time. But he stated that a 3 percent increase in the money supply was required to match the 3 percent pace of economic growth.

Keynes correctly predicted that it wouldn't be gold from mine production that would be the source of support for the gold standard in the future (for as long as it lasted), but rather a redistribution of gold from government holdings. After WWII, that was exactly the case, as it was the US's gold holdings that made up the bulk of gold entering the global central banks. Keynes also warned that gold production from mines was too inconsistent and risky to fix the available currency (aka printing) to the metal. This was borne out when, even though the gold price in the 1970s rose significantly in both real and nominal terms, gold production actually decreased.

And if you were the Fed chair, why would you give up the tangible, refined gold in your vaults when you can just create digits using the MMT framework? Maybe one day the gold standard will come back, but that day will not arrive in my lifetime.

However, it's worth mentioning that some countries (notably China) have floated the idea of an alternative, gold-backed currency to compete in the marketplace with fiat currencies. It's still just a rumor, but the rumor is supported by the fact that all of China's yearly gold production—and it's the world's biggest producer—is being kept in the country. If this idea of a gold yuan catches on, it would definitely affect the demand side.

SILVER

Silver deserves mention in the same breath as gold. It is gold's often-unappreciated stepchild—or, as I call it, blue-collar gold—for a simple reason: gold has worth primarily as a precious metal, a store of value for wealth preservation; silver is both a precious metal and one with a wide range of industrial uses. Most of the gold ever mined is still around. Much silver that is mined each year is used up.

Because silver is only sparsely viewed as a store of value, it is seldom accumulated for that purpose. When recession strikes, people run to gold as the safe haven. Silver's performance tends to be weaker because recession means a decline in industrial production, and any safe-haven demand will be perceived as offset by reduced industrial demand.

Conversely, coming out of a recession, investors expect renewed industrial demand. They tend to push up silver prices even faster than gold's, as happened in the aftermath of the 2008 financial crisis. Thus, from the November 2008 price low of around $9.50 per ounce, silver soared to a high near $48 per ounce in March of 2011 for a gain of over 500 percent (over the same period, gold slightly more than doubled).

And because industrial use continually depletes aboveground stocks, sometimes the miners can't keep up and supply shortages can develop that impact the production of coins and bars.

So, silver is more volatile than gold and a bit less predictable. Its price appreciation can languish, lagging gold for long periods of time, but then it can take off, as it did in 2020. On the other hand, when silver does explode, it can overshoot investors' optimism more than gold. Thus, while gold in 2020 easily eclipsed its former nominal peak, silver barely exceeded 50 percent of its all-time high.

Despite silver's potential for rapid price appreciation, most people prefer owning gold. It takes up a lot less room and is easier to transport. Still, it appears that silver has entered a bull market phase, and I can see that continuing.

What will drive it?

Well, for one thing, the COVID virus has caused silver mine shutdowns, as with gold. During that chaotic period from early March to early April 2020, when 120 gold mines closed, so did about fifteen silver mines. That's actually huge since there are far fewer silver mines in the world than gold. In fact, dedicated silver mines are scarce; much of the world's silver is produced as a byproduct of base metal mining. By the end of 2020, most of the base metal mines started up again, and the silver supply is back up again. We also have to factor in what the recession will mean for base metals. I suspect there will be an initial decline in base metal demand, although I see it picking up again as MMT is invoked to spur renewed economic growth.

Again, as with gold, the closure of mines, refineries, and mints led to a shortage of silver coins beginning in April of 2020. That may have been a catalyst to silver's rise, but it certainly wasn't the only one. Concurrent with the reasons already covered, plenty of others lead me to project that the silver bull market, concurrent with gold, will run for many years.

One important additional factor is the prospect of our present deflation yielding to inflation or, as I think more likely, what I have termed *crossflation*, as explained earlier in the book. I can't predict what silver might do under crossflation, but in serious inflation, it does very well indeed. Consider the highly inflationary late 1970s, for example. Between its 1976 low and 1980 peak, the silver price rose over 1,000 percent. If the same thing happened at today's levels, we'd be looking at a price over $4,000 per ounce.

Honestly, I don't really expect a move that's anything remotely as spectacular because that was the one-time result of the unleashing of pent-up demand that had been building for many years. But I would hardly be surprised to see silver in triple digits as the new normal begins.

One further factor impacting silver is that its futures trade on the COMEX, like gold, but in daily volumes a third less than gold. This is a *very* small market. If an entity like a big bank or a large fund decides it needs to bulk up its silver vault, which is far from improbable, it could drive prices up quickly.

It's also good to remember that both silver and gold have been the definition of *money* for a very long time. Even today, they are the only forms of money recognized and accepted everywhere in the world. If and when public confidence in our modern digital currencies begins to wane, then the value of silver as money will rise along with gold.

It's probably not necessary to say, but I firmly believe everyone should make ownership of some physical gold and silver a priority. This is not an "investment" recommendation. I don't buy gold to make a profit by selling it at a higher price, as I would a stock. I hold it as an asset safeguard against a real economic calamity. Having actual bullion accessible in emergencies is the ultimate insurance policy you can take out for yourself and your family.

Just don't show it off.

I have included this close examination of the precious metals because as the Rise of America continues, gold and silver will attract capital from those looking to diversify from fiat currencies into the oldest form of money: gold and silver. Contrary to what many others think, I believe that the rise of the dollar will be followed, in tandem, by the rise of gold.

In summary, as the US dollar strengthens relative to other currencies—which it will during the Rise of America—investors in those weakening currencies will desire gold to insulate their assets from the devaluation, and the gold price will benefit. At the same time, if the dollar experiences periods of weakness, then gold will benefit from those who want to hedge their US dollar devaluation.

Gold is one of the few assets that benefit from either outcome for the US dollar. And because it is and always has been money, it will maintain its status regardless of what happens in the world's currency markets.

CHAPTER SIX

ENERGY TO FUEL THE RISE OF AMERICA

OBVIOUSLY, THE RISE OF AMERICA THAT I'M ENVISIONING in this book is dependent on the country having access to abundant sources of energy. In that regard, the US is well-positioned to tap into existing energy stocks and benefit from advances in the sector that are happening at warp speed.

A LITTLE HISTORY

You already know that much of recorded history is a tale of the quest for energy.

For instance, on the morning of December 7, 1941, a destroyer operating off the coast of Hawaii, the *USS Ward*, was alerted to an object in its area that appeared to be a submarine.

The *Ward*'s skipper, Lt. William Outerbridge, and his crew had spotted a single periscope sticking out of the water. The *Ward* fired her four-inch deck gun at the object and dropped several depth charges. When it was all over, the sub was at the bottom of the ocean.

At that moment, no one in Hawaii, or the rest of America, had the slightest inkling that the sunken sub was merely a small part of a much larger attack headed its way. Just over an hour later, the sky over the nearby naval base at Pearl Harbor was swarming with attacking Japanese planes—and the day that will "live in infamy" began.

Only later did we learn that Japan didn't attack Pearl Harbor to send a political message. It didn't stage the attack because it was itching to engage the US in a massive global war. It was not the prelude to an assault on the American mainland.

The sneak attack on Pearl Harbor, one of the most audacious, infamous military operations in history, **was an attempt to secure natural resources—*specifically oil.***

In the years leading up to the attack, as Japan committed atrocities all over East Asia, the United States froze Japanese assets held within its borders and, along with its allies, instituted an oil embargo.

Japan is a relatively small island nation, with little in the way of domestic wells, so the embargo was a huge blow to its territorial ambitions. Since the dawn of the twentieth century, every nation's military has been dependent on oil. Without it, Japan's formidable war-making capabilities would be stopped dead in its tracks.

In a move born of desperation, Japan's military leaders decided to punch America in the nose, stagger the might of its Pacific Fleet (docked at Pearl), then make an unimpeded push to secure the huge natural resources of the Dutch East Indies (modern-day Indonesia).

You know the rest of the story. America mobilized in a short time and on an unimaginable scale. It devoted its enormous mining and industrial base to the production of aircraft carriers, submarines, battleships, guns, bombers, tanks, and fighter planes. America launched more naval vessels in 1941 than Japan did throughout the entire war. In 1944, America built more planes than Japan did from 1939 to 1945.

America's incredible mobilization is one for the history books, but it would never have happened without the country's huge domestic oil reserves.

On the other side of the world, energy was a major reason Hitler attacked Russia in one of World War II's pivotal events. Hitler wanted Russia's vast oil resources (and Ukrainian grain) to supply his war machine. The German army was crushed in its attempt to take them. Shortly after that defeat, Hitler could see the writing on the wall and committed suicide.

World War II is, of course, just one example. It, and hundreds of other conflicts, serve as bloody reminders: natural resources, and the energy required to exploit them, are the ultimate keys to economic and military power. He who has the resources makes the rules.

Even today's high-tech world of apps, tweets, and iTunes is built on a "low-tech" foundation of steel, concrete, copper, lumber, and aluminum. Every day, our cars, trucks, and airplanes consume millions of barrels of fuel. Our lights turn on because we burn coal and natural gas and split the atom in nuclear power plants. Feeding, clothing, and housing billions of people around the world consumes enormous amounts of agricultural products like corn, wheat, soybeans, rice, cotton, sugar, coffee, lumber, and livestock—and today's stunning production from the ag sector would have been impossible without energy, and lots of it.

Mining, pumping, planting, harvesting, processing, refining, and transporting vital resources is a *multitrillion-dollar business* that affects every area of your life. You are only reading these words because someone took a chainsaw to a tree or burned fossil fuels to produce the electricity that is powering your computer.

Humankind's constant demand for raw materials ensures that the natural resource and energy sectors will always be the world's biggest, most important industries.

It also ensures that *the ownership* of the world's resources will always be an indispensable source of wealth and power. Those who own the resources, or have the wealth to acquire them, will always enjoy incredible benefits and privilege. And those who aspire to be in that coveted position will have to develop ways to get what they need.

Part of what will power the Rise of America is, well, power: how we get it, how we distribute it, who benefits, what it will cost.

All of that is changing faster than most of us even imagine.

(There is, for example, a major development about to take place in the oil/gas patch. As I've continually stressed, FMC is running the show now, and I have another example of how it's going to be applied regardless of whether FMC or MMT is the framework being used. No one else is talking about this. But I will—a little later in this chapter.)

So, let me briefly review the major technological break-throughs that are taking place in the energy sector right now. Recession or no recession, tech is not going to take a breather. Newly printed digits are going to be pumped into the energy and natural resource sectors. And our lives are going to be the better for it.

HUMANS AND ENERGY

In the long saga of the human species, nothing was more import-ant than gaining the use of fire. It kept our caves warm at night, provided light so that we could see each other after the sun went down, gave us a means of cooking (and drying) food, and was a formidable new weapon against animal predators as well as other bands of humans that might not wish us well.

We discovered how to make and control fire at least 125,000 years ago (and maybe as much as a million, no one really knows). For most of that time, we mostly burned wood. It took a really long time, but eventually, we discovered other fuels: coal—about 5,500 years ago; natural gas—maybe 1000 BC; and oil—perhaps the fourth century BC. And that's still about it, with the sole addi-tion of uranium as fuel in the twentieth century.

After harnessing fire itself, the next giant leap forward was in 1752, when Benjamin Franklin decided to fly a kite. Franklin didn't discover electricity; that had happened a century earlier. But what he did was demonstrate that one day, we might be able to control this amazing force of nature.

Did we ever.

It may have taken a century and a half to figure out, but once we did, we were able to distribute energy anywhere with wires. In the relative blink of an eye, we had a network that sent electricity to every nook and cranny of the country.

Completing the grid was a massive achievement. When they were polled in 2000, scientists at the National Academy of Engi-neering voted the electrification grid the greatest engineering feat of the twentieth century, hands down. It should probably be considered the most important technological achievement of any kind in human history—no electric grid, no cities, for example.

Electricity wasn't shared equally across the planet, of course.

But where people did have it, standards of living rose immeasurably. All at once, half our days were no longer spent in darkness, lighted only by whale oil or kerosene. Or in the cold, heated only by physical flames. Our daily productive lives, and our leisure activities, were extended as far into the night as we wanted them to be. The very concept of *leisure* itself—something to be enjoyed by nearly everyone—had to be created.

The inventions of engines to do work—first with steam and then with internal combustion—were also milestones, to be sure. But the internal combustion engines that powered the twentieth century are on their way out. So are the fossil fuels they need to create energy.

Don't get me wrong. The employment of fossil fuels won't disappear overnight. They'll be around for a good long while, even as usage declines.

Overwhelmingly, though, the future is electric. Most people have no idea how far down that road we have already come, nor where we are headed. New technology is rising; old tech is being replaced or at least modified. And it's all happening at a speed that's almost incomprehensible if you weren't born into it.

The millennial generation has never known a world in which the internet did not exist, where you could not communicate, instantaneously and for free, with someone on the other side of the globe. It will be the same with electricity. It's going to become ubiquitous and cheap, and it's going to power every device we know today as well as many that haven't even been thought of yet.

Naturally enough, you ask: where is all that electricity going to come from?

Good question. Obviously, we can't just pull it out of the ground (although we *can* get it from water). So, we need sources, and we need methods and facilities for storage, and we need means of transmission.

We'll get them because the technological advances in the tech sector are coming fast and furious. But first, let me step back just a moment and say this:

The question of climate change is all over the news and on the minds of many people who care about "the planet." (How much so may be indicated by *Time* making its 2019 Person of the Year a teenage Swedish girl who is a political symbol of how younger generations have been harmed by the boomer generations' collective inaction.) Yes, the globe is warming.

My field *is* natural resources, and I know a couple of things for sure. First, billions of people on the planet do not have, but could certainly use, the same access to energy enjoyed by those of us in the developed nations. Second, we know that the continuing burning of fossil fuels is impractical. They are a finite resource, and they cause unhealthy levels of air pollution. Third, there is a huge impetus—among the public, but especially in government—to transition to so-called "green" energy, which is nonpolluting and comes from renewable sources.

For all of these, technology is coming to the rescue. As we go more and more electric, we can transition to cleaner energy. We can push atmospheric emissions of pollutants way down—which is good for public health—while at the same time bringing electricity to many people who now lack it. As we do this, the amount of CO_2 we pump into the air will drop, and whatever climate change is due to the greenhouse effect will be mitigated. It's a win for the planet.

And the thing is, green buildouts have happened so quietly that almost no one knows how far we have already gone in that direction.

But first, let's take a quick look at the current system (no pun intended).

THE GRID

While most people are unaware of this, demand on the electrical grid in the US peaked in 2008, after which it declined and has been flat ever since. The main reason is increased efficiency. New homes and office buildings are better insulated, while old ones have been retrofitted. Less power-hungry appliances have played a part. "Smart" electric household meters are becoming common. Even replacing incandescent light bulbs with LEDs has made a big difference. And of course, a rapidly proliferating number of buildings—businesses and homes—are generating their own electricity.

As noted earlier, the construction of the electrical grid was the greatest engineering accomplishment of all time. But it is old and creaky, and it's vulnerable—to natural decay, extreme weather events, even sabotage. Some of it dates back a hundred years. While it still works well, and many major improvements have been made over that time, it needs a major upgrade.

The first thing that's going to happen is the "smart grid," which is already in the process of being rolled out. This involves the use of sensors, communications networks, computational ability, and enhanced controls to improve the system's functionality. Utilities are moving away from being generators and becoming smart distributors. The result will be increased reliability; the optimization of resources (routing the energy where it's most needed at any given time); a lesser environmental impact; and the ability to manage assets most cost-effectively.

A smart grid will greatly improve what is already here. Not

only that, but it will also go a long way toward the prevention of the cascade effect, whereby an outage in one place has consequences across a much larger area. With a system of modern sensors, switches, and computer oversight, we won't again get a blackout that plunges the East Coast into the cold and dark.

All well and good, but the conventional grid, smart or not, doesn't address the transmission problems associated with wires. New, wireless-transmission technology will. In fact, in a very rudimentary way, it's here now. You're probably already familiar with wireless phone battery chargers.

Scale that up, and you get the future: microwave transmission. The proof of concept was demonstrated back in 2008. We're still just taking baby steps, sending electricity over distances measured in meters. There are kinks to work out. But those ultra-high-voltage power lines that crisscross the nation are going away—certainly by the year 2100—to be replaced by transmission and receiving towers.

HARNESSING THE SUN

Each day, the earth is drenched in solar radiation, enough to power the planet for an entire year. This is not news. We've long known that sunlight can be turned into electricity via the photovoltaic (PV) effect. The challenge has been to find a way to capture that energy and somehow convert it to usable electricity in a cost-effective manner.

That was the rub. PV cells were for decades hopelessly inefficient in terms of any honest cost/benefit analysis. Into the twenty-first century, they could still only operate in the range of 12–15 percent of captured energy put to use. Not good enough.

But due to a series of technological breakthroughs that I

needn't go into in any detail, experimental efficiency jumped as high as 40 percent in 2006. Researchers have their near-term sights set on 50 percent, and it's believed that 90 percent will eventually be attainable. Nothing like these numbers is available in the commercial market, which is still stuck in the 20–25 percent range. But converting experiments to practical applications is not far off.

Along with greater efficiency came other technologies that caused costs to fall off a cliff. Put together, those two factors ignited an interest in solar power that has exploded over the past fifteen years.

As recently as 2010, if I'd told you solar would emerge as a major factor in global energy production, you'd have laughed and said something like, "As if, dude." Everyone knew that solar panels were too expensive, too inefficient, and useless on cloudy days. You'd have claimed that they couldn't exist at all without government subsidies. But you'd have been wrong.

That's the thing about modern technology. One advancement tends to breed a dozen others, and soon you have an exponential growth curve. Today, solar panels are not only going up atop houses and on Wal-Mart roofs. They've jumped the grid. In many places, utility-scale solar is at or below the cost of conventional generation (coal, gas, or nuclear plants).

In the year 2000, total worldwide solar electricity generation was one gigawatt (GW). By the end of 2019, US generation alone was more than eighty-one GW, enough to power 15.7 million homes. That number is poised to soar past ninety GW by the end of '20. As of 2019, nearly 250,000 Americans worked in the solar industry, more than double the number in 2012. There were more than 10,000 companies spread across every US state. And for the year, the solar industry generated $18.7 billion of investment in the American economy.

Overall, 2020 investments in solar will likely experience a significant decline because of the coronavirus. No one can yet forecast the pandemic's impact. And the recovery time may be slow. Nevertheless, solar technology will keep progressing, and new forms of collection will continue to be developed. Here are a few things you can expect in the near future:

- New houses with rooftop solar panels standard, perhaps even government mandated.
- Electric cars with solar battery charging as you drive.
- Solar glass coatings that preserve transparency while they turn office buildings into giant collectors.
- Sprays that allow any surface to be turned into a solar collector.

The main problem associated with solar energy is obviously storage. Conventional power plants produce electricity 24/7. Solar must produce while the sun shines and somehow store that power to use at night or on cloudy days.

I'll address this issue in a moment, but there's one last thing to say about solar: it will be ported off-planet in time.

Space-based solar is the holy grail for collection of the sun's energy. Solar arrays placed in orbit could generate electricity continuously, with long lives, requiring little to no maintenance. They could beam the power back to earth via microwaves. But there are roadblocks. The transmission technology, as noted earlier, now works only across meters, not thousands of kilometers. And the high cost of blasting a large solar collector into space remains a major deterrent.

These problems will be solved, perhaps within a couple of decades. The Japanese Aerospace Exploration Agency (JAXA) is all over it. No surprise there. Remember that WWII in the Pacific began because the Japanese had no oil of their own. They still don't. And their nuclear industry was decimated by the Fukushima disaster.

So, Japan will lead the way with this new technology. They plan to launch a small-scale solar collection satellite by the end of 2021 and expect to have a 200-megawatt version in orbit by 2028. A one-gigawatt commercial pilot plant is projected to be operational by 2031. And a full-scale, commercial, space-based power industry will eventually be constructed, starting in 2037.

This is a mammoth undertaking. To get one GW of output at present efficiencies, Japan would have to deploy a solar collector weighing over 10,000 metric tons and measuring several kilometers across, sitting up there in geosynchronous orbit, some 36,000 kilometers from earth. Advances in collector technology will bring down weight and size, of course. And again, COVID-19 may alter this timeline. But it *will* happen.

Solar power is, of course, the big buzzword these days. But in terms of "green" energy, capturing the wind actually leads the sector.

A WIND IN OUR SAILS

The potential of wind power is enormous. As with solar power, energy generated in this way is vulnerable to off days (when it's calm). But contemporary wind turbines will turn in a pretty small breeze, and they're going to get even better. Plus, there are ideal places all over the planet where the wind essentially never stops blowing.

Like Scotland.

Few people even know this because the story hasn't gotten

much coverage in the mainstream media. But Scotland has become totally energy independent. In the first half of 2019, its wind turbines generated more than 9.8 megawatt-hour (MWh) of electricity. That's a great deal for a small country. It's enough to power nearly 4.5 million homes, which is almost twice as many as there actually are in Scotland. So, the whole thing is revenue-positive, as they can sell their excess electricity to neighboring England. This is "green energy" paying for itself.

In the US, the wind power revolution has also gotten little publicity compared with solar. The reason: The great majority of wind-generated electricity comes from utility-scale projects, which generally happen outside the public purview (unless they provoke environmental protests). There is nothing to prevent people from installing small wind generators on their roofs, instead of solar panels. The technology is ready—there are stand-alone and even hybrid wind/solar units you can attach to your roof. It's just not as much of a market as yet.

Thus, almost without anyone noticing, wind power emerged from 2019 as America's top choice for new power after 9.1 giga-watts (GW) of generation were added. That's big. It represents 39 percent of all new utility-scale power additions. At present, operating wind power capacity in the US stood at over 105 GW (vs. 81 GW of solar at the end of '19), and that's enough to power 32 million American homes.

That single, house-scale wind generators have lagged solar collectors will likely change. All that needs to happen is for an Elon Musk of wind to step up the way Musk has with home solar. Among the emerging technologies are small-scale units that ride on a maglev base and turn in the slightest of breezes. (Maglev means that the turbine is suspended in a magnetic field and turns without friction. You're probably already familiar with the high-speed maglev trains popular in France and Japan.) They're here now.

The same principle can be scaled up, too. China has plans to construct a maglev generator ten-stories tall. It will turn in a 3 mph wind and have a footprint of just one hundred acres, replacing 1,000 conventional windmills needing 64,000 acres. Since maglev turbines are cylinders and don't need the propeller blades of conventional wind machines, they are bird-friendly, too. (I don't know of any similar projects in the US, but if the Chinese experiment proves out, you can be sure that US entrepreneurs will follow.)

And their output is going to be way cheap. American designers project a cost of five cents per kWh as an achievable goal. That would be by far the lowest in the energy industry (the national average is now twelve cents), although some believe it's not a fantasy to see that reduced to just a penny. Nearly free.

None of this has yet been achieved at scale. But it will. Count on it.

Propeller-blade and maglev turbines are not the only options, either. Engineers are exploring a wide range of other alternatives. The details are more than I need to go into here, but just be aware that this is a field exploding with innovation. Readers with more than a passing interest in this stuff can do a Google search into the bewildering array of newfangled wind machines, such as vertical-axis generators, high-altitude turbines, bladeless vortex turbines, wind tunnel towers, and megaphone-style turbines.

Wind generation is a coming thing. Expect to see offshore farms emerging from the sea all over the place. In addition, vast numbers of people live in desolate places not reached by a power grid but where the wind seldom stops blowing; a few generators sited there will transform their lives. Even now, as America goes green, former oil patch workers in blustery North Dakota are being retrained for new jobs. As it turns out, it seems that the skills necessary for operating the derricks that frack for crude in the Bakken shale translate pretty directly into the skills required for operating the machines that convert the bitter winds of the high prairies into electricity.

The cost of wind, solar, geothermal, and hydropower has decreased enormously over the past twenty years. It is now cheaper than traditional fossil fuel power sources in many places. It's a trend that will accelerate even more with the coming advances in generation and distribution that will be funded by the government's adoption of printing digits for long-term funding of major upgrades to the infrastructure. The US now has the lowest cost of electricity in the industrialized world, and it will continue to decline. Falling energy costs will benefit individual users and increase the ability for American businesses to compete in the decentralized global economy, furthering the Rise of America.

Of course, with wind as with solar, the key issue is storage—meaning batteries. And here again, technology is on a roll.

BATTERIES

Materials science is not a term that's on everyone's lips. It's not as glamorous a field as, say, quantum mechanics or astrophysics. Yet, it's something that directly affects our lives every day.

These folks study various substances at the atomic and molecular levels to try to figure out what these things do, ways in which they might fit together, and how they can be made useful in the real world. Simply put, material scientists determine what stuff will be made from and how the component parts will interact.

One of the most impactful things they've done is to redesign the humble battery.

Now, this is not the place for an in-depth analysis of everything that's going on in the field of battery technology. But it's appropriate for me to hit a few of the high points.

It may be hard to remember a time before phones came with rechargeable batteries, and there were no EVs (electric vehicles) like Teslas. But it wasn't that long ago. (Yeah, I know, the electric car was invented in 1880. But it died out until its first modern descendant appeared in the 1990s.) The big deal was discovering the potential of lithium in the fabrication of a battery's cathodes. It wasn't until 1991 that Sony first married carbon anodes to lithium cathodes, creating the Li-ion (lithium-ion) battery. Almost overnight, a whole universe of new, battery-powered devices just sprang into existence.

Li-ion batteries still rule the roost. Tesla is pouring money into improvements for its Powerwall and Powerwall 2 home units. The company is also scaling up. In 2017, it finished building the world's largest Li-ion battery system in Australia. The installation has a storage capacity of 129 MWh and can deliver 100 MW of power.

Batteries are crucial to any renewable-based generation system, and Li-ion batteries still have plenty of limitations in terms of the amount and duration of storage. So, it's no surprise that materials scientists worldwide are working furiously to develop the next big thing in batteries. I don't have space (and, honestly, you probably don't have the interest) for me to go into all the theoretical constructs out there. Suffice it to say that future batteries will be bigger, better, higher functioning, and will feature higher capacities and storage times. Here's a small sampling of what's on the way:

- *Environmentally Friendly Lithium Batteries*—Current Li-ion cathodes contain toxic cobalt. More environmentally benign, high-energy density batteries are on the drawing board.
- *Carbon Nanotube Lithium Batteries*—Carbon nanotubes are the most exciting and versatile building material of the future. Nanotube-based batteries are projected to increase storage capacity tenfold over Li-ion. This research is proceeding in many different directions.
- *Liquid Metal Batteries*—Based on molten salt sandwiched between two layers of liquid metal, these are highly scalable and designed to be used for grid storage of power from renewables.
- *Lithium-Air Carbon Batteries*—Sort of like a battery that breathes. In tests, they've shown the highest energy density yet—about fifty times better than the best Li-ions.
- *Water Batteries*—Yes, you can store energy in water. These are projected to be ultra-low cost, long-lasting, and scalable to grid storage.
- *Graphene Batteries*—Graphene, like nanotubes, is another allotrope of carbon, the miracle element. It can be used to construct batteries that require a quick release of energy, as in electric vehicles, or to smooth out power availability from intermittent, renewable energy sources.
- *Nano-Built Batteries*—Researchers use viruses (yes, they're not all bad guys) as *bacteriophages*—tiny little assemblers—to construct entirely new materials from the atomic level up. Some are being used to make better-conducting electrodes.

This is not my field, and I'm sure other cutting-edge research projects are going on. The point is that, as alternative sources of electricity *ramp up*, storage has got to *catch up*.

And trust me, it will.

FUSION

I said earlier that space-based collectors are the holy grail of solar energy. But the holy grail of all energy holy grails is nuclear fusion.

Fusion reactions are how the sun produces its heat and light and radiates its energy to the earth, thereby making life possible. You get the reaction when hydrogen nuclei collide to produce helium. Simple. Your fuel is hydrogen, the most abundant element in the universe. But here's the catch: Hydrogen nuclei are positive, and they repel each other. The only way to force them to fuse is to accelerate them so that they smash into each other at very high speeds, which requires the extremely high pressures and temperatures formerly found only in stars. And under those conditions, it's extraordinarily difficult to get more energy out than you need to start the reaction.

So, there are some rather formidable obstacles to overcome. (I assume that so-called "cold fusion" is as impossible as it has so far proven to be, although you never know...) As a famous physicist once put it: "We say that we will put the sun into a box. The problem is, we don't know how to make the box."

Here is what the box must do: trap fusion reactions inside a plasma that has been heated to around 150 million degrees centigrade. Now, that's hot by anyone's standards. For comparison purposes, the surface temperature of the sun itself is "only" 5.6 million degrees C. You can see why getting more energy out than you put in is so difficult.

Still, scientists love nothing more than what seems to be an insuperable challenge. Several efforts are underway to create the first economical fusion reactor that produces more energy than it takes to superheat the plasma. The best results so far have been 30 percent short.

But as I said, this is the BIG *kahuna*. The promise is for nothing less than cheap, unlimited, nonpolluting energy. As such, the interest is universal. That potential has produced an unprecedented international effort based in France and backed by an alliance of governments from the EU, US, China, India, Japan, Korea, and Russia that are all too often at each other's throats. Imagine that. They are cooperating to build a huge experimental reactor that is currently half-finished. It's on track to reach a "first plasma" proof of concept in December 2025.

Meanwhile, there's a competitor. Researchers at the Massachusetts Institute of Technology (MIT) announced in late 2020 that they are collaborating on a new "compact" fusion reactor that could be ready to test in four years and online within just ten. There's plenty of skepticism about that, but we shall see.

If (or perhaps *when*) fusion works, and if it can be made economical, there is no end to the number of human problems it can solve.

THE NUCLEAR RENAISSANCE

In recent years, there has been renewed interest in nuclear power plants. Some call it a *renaissance*. As of May 2020, there were fifty-four facilities under construction, with China (eleven) and India (seven) leading the way. It's a boom everywhere but in the US, which has only two units under construction, with another six permitted (as opposed to thirty-seven facilities permanently shut down as of February 2020).

These plants cannot be phased out altogether in the US, as some nuclear opponents would wish because then lights would go out all over the place. Nukes currently provide about 18 percent of the nation's electricity. That contribution would not be easily replaced. But adding new nuclear capability in America is problematic for three reasons: skyrocketing construction costs: $7-plus billion for a new unit, which makes them less competitive with alternatives; a long and difficult permit process; and opposition from both environmentalists and the general public.

Thus, the most recent plant to come online was in 2016. *That* was the first new one since 1996. And *that* one was the first to break ground since 1977.

Public opposition in the US stems from the near disaster at Three Mile Island in 1979. Those negative feelings were strongly reinforced by the Chernobyl meltdown in 1986 and then taken over the top by the catastrophe at Fukushima in 2011.

In addition, there is the ongoing problem of the disposal of highly radioactive nuclear waste (where "not in my backyard" is the most common mentality) and the association of nuclear fission with weapons of mass destruction. There's little that can be done about these two things. Waste is a big problem, given the materials' long half-lives. And the second is only natural, given the historical record.

That history includes why we have uranium reactors in the first place. We could have opted for thorium reactors instead; they're safer and produce less waste. But when nuclear reactions were first proven out in the 1940s, the emphasis was on winning a world war. Uranium fission produces plutonium, the basis for bomb-making, as a byproduct. Thorium doesn't. The US committed to uranium and never looked back. So did every other nation.

(Incidentally, thorium reactors are getting a second look, primarily in China and India, though the US is unlikely to follow suit.)

As to that other issue, *risk*: nuclear plants have progressed along a pathway to ever-greater safety over time. The first ones constructed were Generation I. Since then, we have moved through Gen II to Gen III (and III+), with Gen IV now on the drawing board. All of the accidents that make people wary of nuclear power occurred with aging, Generation I or II reactors. They were built using technology from the '50s and '60s (Gen I) and the 1970s to late '90s (Gen II). The last Gen I reactor shut down in 2015, and Gen II reactors (the final one has been built) should probably all be scrapped, especially those near their original expected forty-year operational life.

Gen III reactors feature substantial improvements in life expectancy, maintenance requirements, and spent fuel reduction—and they're designed to withstand a direct hit from a bomb or missile. Most important, they are *way* safer. They feature *passive nuclear safety*, which means that they do not require any active intervention on the part of either the operator or any electrical/electronic feedback to shut down the reactor in the event of an emergency.

The difference in generational safety is very significant. As revealed by core damage frequencies, the best measurement of safety issues: sixty core damage events are the average for the standard model Gen III and just three core damage events for Gen III+, both per 100 million reactor-years. Compare those to the 1,000 core damage events per 100 million reactor-years experienced by Gen II.

Unfortunately, you can't just retrofit a Gen II reactor and turn it into a Gen III. You need to start from scratch. That's what is happening with the few new reactors being built in the US. With the old ones, the Nuclear Regulatory Commission has been approving rehab efforts or merely extending forty-year reactors' licenses to sixty years. This is a stopgap measure, at best, and it generates some serious safety concerns.

However, the future of nuclear power in the US may lie with *small modular reactors* (SMRs). These "micro-nukes"—which are designed to pump out around sixty MW of power vs. one GW for conventional plants—have many advantages. They're small. They can be fabricated at a central assembly plant, then trucked to the construction site. They're much safer. And they can be linked in arrays that are far cheaper to build than a Gen III nuke with comparable output. One SMR could run a small town, a large neighborhood, or even an individual business. Google, for instance, might purchase one to power a massive server farm.

The impact they may have could be profound. Proponents note that, in addition to cost savings and ease of construction, entities running one or an array of SMRs—especially if they are in remote locations—would not need to tie into the grid. Inefficient long-distance power lines could largely vanish from the landscape.

The trouble is, SMRs do not yet exist. So far in the US, a bit surprisingly, there's only one company seeking to license and build an SMR. As with much new technology, China is further along, while Russia, too, is in the game. SMRs are not a near-future thing, but they will happen.

URANIUM

Because the nuclear energy industry has been the most unloved sector of the American economy for twenty-five years, US domestic uranium production has fallen to almost nothing.

This is a serious problem.

As noted, the country cannot do without nuclear energy, for which, obviously, a uranium supply is needed, to the tune of some 50 million pounds annually for civilian use and another 5 million for military purposes. But little will be mined in America. The US produced a total of 170,000 pounds U_3O_8 (triuranium octoxide concentrate) from all domestic sources in 2019 (that is one-third of 1 percent of its domestic consumption for 2019)—some 89 percent less than in 2018 and far from its peak of 43.7 million pounds in 1980—according to the Energy Information Administration. (U_3O_8 is one of the most stable forms of uranium. In the enrichment process, it is converted to uranium hexafluoride—UF_6—the primary nuclear fuel feedstock.)

When you get into the supply/demand situation with uranium, you take a deep dive into international politics. It is the most important factor, and many games are being played within the nuclear arena. The demand side is relatively stable. But the supply side? Well, where to get uranium from is a sticky problem for US companies and officials.

In fact, it's such a complex issue that it takes quite a while to explain it, and I fear that putting that explanation in here would bog us down. I want to move forward to the revelatory things I still need to get to in this chapter. Nevertheless, this question is still important and probably of interest to more than a few readers. So, for an in-depth look at the international uranium supply chain, please see Appendix II.

THE OIL PATCH

I have consistently maintained that oil demand would not exceed supply and that I expected downward pressure on the price of oil, as the whole idea of peak oil proved to be false. But it's important to understand the causes of the unprecedented oil correction in the spring of 2020.

The production cut standoff between Russia and Saudi Arabia created a massive sell-off at the same time that COVID-19 caused the largest decrease in demand since the end of World War II. From March through April of '20, global oil demand fell continuously as economies slowed to a crawl. The demand for refined crude oil products like gasoline and jet fuel dropped by more than 50 percent.

The longer shelter-in-place guidelines apply, the longer the demand shock will stay in place. The massive supply build from March through late July led to an oversupply of some 60 million barrels.

AN EXPLANATION FOR OIL PRICE CHAOS

The major disconnect between crude oil production and crude oil consumption caused immense pressure on the front month oil price.

Crude oil for May 2020 delivery hit -$38 per barrel. Yes, you read that right: negative thirty-eight dollars per barrel. Oil was under significant pressure, and prices were in the dumps, but that was not the cause of the negative oil price. The price got pushed negative due to over 100,000 futures contracts being sold during contract expiry. It was more of a "financialized" value rather than a "physical" one. So no, a supplier was not going to pay you to take the oil off their hands.

Still, with on-land storage approaching maximum capacity, companies and traders needed to put the oil somewhere. The next best option to keeping it in the ground is to load crude oil onto tankers and store the oil at sea (known as "floating storage").

As of October 2020, about 200 million barrels of floating storage worldwide are being reported and tracked. That's a record, amounting to 5 percent of global carrying capacity, though that number will fall as the negative effects of the pandemic abate.

THE OPEC+ AGREEMENT FALLOUT

Clearly, the market is telling OPEC and its partners that the cut was insufficient.

The new agreement, announced on Easter Sunday (April 12) of 2020, called for reducing 9.7 million barrels of oil per day (bopd). It was a joint cut between OPEC and its "plus" counterparts (OPEC+), namely Russia.

In addition, countries like the United States and Canada suggested that their national production will decline naturally by several million barrels per day.

The thought process was that the virus would be controlled within a few months, and then the cuts would balance everything out.

Early on the morning of April 13, President Trump tweeted that the real number being negotiated was 20 million bopd—more than twice the 9.7 million being reported.

Trump was correct when he said a deal would be cut between Russia and Saudi Arabia. But could the actual production cut be 20 million bopd? Saudi Arabia has openly stated that everyone would have to share the cut equally. I doubt that's even possible, for some physical as well as political reasons.

Russia is the obvious OPEC+ member that could not comply with such a production cut. That's because of the type of production the Russians have: more than half of Russian production is from wells that, if shut down, would never come back online without major reworkings of the well. This would make production uneconomical at oil prices below $40 per barrel.

Thus, those wells will pump away. It doesn't make sense for the Russians to shut them down. They are old Soviet wells that will continue to produce regardless of whether the oil is $10 or $100/barrel.

Oil wells become exhausted over time, so drilling cadence is very important. All oil companies will expect natural production declines if they don't drill new wells to replace production from existing wells.

Even for a market that is commonly plus or minus 1 million barrels per day over- or undersupplied, the magnitude of the recent oversupply is something the sector has never seen before. This has been a deadly combination of events for the oil and gas sector, which sent prices crashing from the mid-$60s to that brief period of negative oil futures per barrel.

It's been an enormous shock. Without question, oil and gas companies are still feeling the pain—or worse, already preparing for bankruptcy.

Unfortunately, the pain in the oil patch endures, as the sector as a whole is in the "Echo" phase of my Boom, Bust & Echo framework (see Appendix IV). Do not try to catch a falling knife; you will get cut by this one. As much as President Trump strived to bring confidence into the market, the demand shock is far from over. It will stick around for much longer than most realize, which means rangebound prices over the near term, at best.

THE FEDS "DIGITS" ARE HERE, TOO

Throughout this book, I've emphasized how much the Fed's framework (whether fiscal-monetary coordination or Modern

Monetary Theory is going to influence the economy going forward. And at the beginning of this chapter, I promised to show you one thing it's going to bring that you won't read about elsewhere. Here it is:

I project that the federal government will ticket about $20 trillion in new digit stimulus money for infrastructure work over the next twenty-five years. Some of this will go toward obvious upgrades to the transportation sector.

But there will be another benefactor, and that's the oil patch—just not in the way you would expect.

You see, when oil and gas wells close down because they're exhausted or no longer economical, it's not like turning off a light switch. Over 3 million wells in the US are now shut in, and many of them are seeping pollutants into the environment. Casing and properly reclaiming these wells so that they no longer pollute is a huge undertaking.

It will be undertaken. The money will be made available as part of the commitment to the green revolution. This will be no mom-and-pop operation, either. It will require the services of large oilfield outfits—American companies employing American workers—that already specialize in servicing the fossil fuel industry, and those will be high-paying jobs that will support middle-class Americans. As the "oil and natural gas exploration and production" industry winds down, these companies will be able to remain working in the oil patch, with a big boost coming from remediation of past producing wells instead of drilling wells. They'll be happy because they'll be less tethered to the old boom/bust cycle. Think of it as a new "undrilled sector" within the oil patch.

It's an easy, nonpartisan governmental decision. Republicans and Democrats alike will get behind the project. The public will embrace it as environmentally friendly and a jolt to the economy by creating high-paying jobs, jobs, and jobs.

It's a classic win-win situation.

THE FUTURE OF GBOES

To close this chapter, I want to set forth something that, again, you will not be reading about anywhere else. No one else is even thinking about it at present. I believe it's going to be *huge*.

Many years ago, I wrote a paper on why the supermajor oil companies will have no option but to expand into the green energy sector. People scoffed. But we are now seeing this in real time.

I began with the concept of BOE—*barrels of oil equivalent*—which is a number that the oil companies carry on their books, to define a meaningful relationship between their diverse holdings of oil, measured in barrels, and natural gas, measured in mcf (thousand cubic feet). This is useful for investors trying to evaluate an energy company's assets. Since 6,000 cubic feet of natural gas contains the same amount of energy as one barrel of oil, then 6 mcf gas = 1 BOE. One million cubic feet of natural gas is abbreviated mmcf, one billion as bcf, and one trillion as tcf.

Once I realized that the oil majors were going to have to move into green energy, I also understood that these companies had to have a way to express the relationship between oil and green energy. So, I invented something called **GBOE** (green barrels of oil equivalent). It'd be out of place here, but for my nerd friends, the step-by-step math for creating green barrels of oil equivalent can be found in Appendix II.

The important part is my breakthrough. The math that allows natural gas to be included on an energy company's financial books as BOE (barrels of oil equivalent) **also allows for green**

energy produced from solar, wind, or geothermal fields to be similarly evaluated.

(The math formula that can also be applied to nuclear energy—currently the world's most undervalued sector as well to bring its valuation into line with other energy sources.)

I expect the GBOE concept to gain traction; it's too useful not to. Eventually, it will be packaged by Goldman Sachs and the like. They'll get bankers and management teams to accept the GBOEs on the balance sheet just like they do BOEs (which also took time to be accepted). That's fine; I hope they do. And it will be the savvy bankers who convince their counterparts at the central banks to fund the green revolution in taking over the oil patch using the GBOE metrics and funds from the long-term digit printing.

The big advantage of the past oil majors (low cost of capital) is completely gone. The world's largest oil companies are down over 50 percent or more over the last decade.

Conversely, green energy companies are flush with cash, have a much lower cost of capital than the oil majors, and will be supported by FMC and eventually MMT to **buy out and own the oil companies.** Yes, you read that right. They will. It's another thing no one else is saying, but I stand by it. Though you may not believe it now, a revolution is coming.

The loudest voices on the environmental side insist that we need to phase out and shut down the oil patch now. There is nothing more telling than the fifth-generation Rockefellers who have launched BankFWD, with other powerful and wealthy individuals and institutions, to prevent banks from lending to oil companies.

That isn't the solution.

Instead, the way to shut down the oil patch is first to own

the oil patch and extract the cash flow from production to fund economic, renewable GBOE production and *then* phase out the production.

The green energy companies can buy the oil companies now at historic lows. Everyone wins from this concept. The green energy producers will benefit from owning the oil companies, as the phase-out of the oil assets over the next fifty years will be controlled.

Let me give a real-world example. Brookfield Energy is the Exxon of green energy. With the help of low interest rates and the current FMC framework, it could easily gobble up some of North America's largest oil producers. Buying the oil companies at historic lows would have incredibly positive benefits to the free cash on Brookfield's balance sheet, which could fund green production growth at the same time as it funds the phase-out of oil production. All the while, the green energy company would still maintain its GBOE-positive (more green energy than carbon energy) status.

This means that, ironically, the future of clean green energy could rely on cash flow from the oil patch.

Every barrel of oil would be used toward creating a new GBOE. But it's not a 1:1 match. It's much better since each barrel of oil would be used to create multiple GBOEs because of their renewable nature (unlike fossil fuels, they aren't used up).

Rather than reinvesting into drilling oil wells to produce more oil, production in the green energy company's hands will channel the oil cash flow into green energy to maintain its GBOE-positive metrics. Everyone's happy because we will have:

- Controlled phase-out of oil assets
- Conversion of carbon to green energy for the future, funded by current oil production

Oil is needed for more than just energy. It's about lubricants, plastics, medicine, etc. So, it isn't going entirely away. But owned and managed by green energy producers, the whole oil patch would be working toward becoming GBOE-positive.

And what will fund the capital required for a green takeover of the oil patch? You guessed it—the US government and the Fed. This shift will strengthen the energy companies' cash flow and balance sheets, improve the environment, and provide high-paying jobs. It will also eliminate any price shocks to energy that cause inflationary pressure to the economy, such as the oil price shocks of the 1970s.

The evolution of the "energy patch" fully supports the Rise of America.

CHAPTER SEVEN

CRITICAL METALS FOR THE RISE OF AMERICA

BASE METALS

Copper, nickel, and cobalt are three of the metals that will be critical for the Rise of America.

Let's start with copper.

There is an expectation that the big copper mines in Chile and Peru will be shutting down due to the virus.

Combine that with the market's belief that China's government will stimulate their economy and thus buy all the copper they can get their hands on, and the conclusion is that the strong run-up in copper prices will continue.

I've received a lot of feedback on my long-term stance on commodities, base metals, and precious metals—especially true for my +SWAP vs. –SWAP Line Nation thesis (see Chapter 2 for my analysis of the importance of SWAP Lines).

And the biggest counterargument that I've received from management teams, analysts, and investors is that:

The market has already priced in the geopolitical risk.

Wrong.

I've examined hundreds of instances where analysts are using the same discount rates for projects in both high-risk, emerging-market nations and politically stable jurisdictions for comparable projects. And that's across all the different stages of the project life cycle (production, development, or exploration stage assets) for precious and base metal commodities. Too often, the market is valuing peer-comparable assets more highly in risky jurisdictions compared to similar projects in the US, Australia, or Canada.

My point is...

I've never seen the market, market pundits, and investors so complacent about geopolitical risks to their investments in my career.

The mantra of "go wherever the gold/copper/silver/oil is" has firmly taken hold of the resource sector. But I believe the most successful resource projects over the next twenty years will be ones whose top-tier assets are in a jurisdiction where the rule of law is still in place.

But the risks aren't being discounted correctly in their valuation models. To me, if you're investing in mining in, say, the Democratic Republic of Congo, you'd better be acknowledging a much higher degree of risk than with mining in, say, Nevada, USA. Yet many investors are ignoring reality and not pricing in that risk. And that's just crazy.

THE COPPER BAROMETER

Global (and especially Chinese) economic activity took a nosedive in Q1-2020. That was one of the main drivers behind plummeting copper prices. As expected, the drop in share prices of copper miners was magnified. While copper's price fell about 15 percent, the miners received a 45 percent haircut.

However, Chinese industrial demand has begun to tick up. The country's swift post-coronavirus economic recovery and its resumption of industrial activity have led to a strong price movement higher in copper and other industrial metals.

If copper continues to catch a tailwind...

You can bet that desperate countries with budget shortfalls will look to "return to the people what's rightfully theirs." This is the geopolitical risk I'm discussing.

You can see the tag line that'll make it happen:

We Will Redistribute Our Mineral Wealth *to the People*!

Now, do you see the enormous implications for +**SWAP Line Nations** vs. –**SWAP Line Nations**?

Governments will feel the deflationary pressures in their local economies and experience significant unrest among their people. There will be pressure to put their citizens first, and redistributions of wealth will happen all over the developing world. Not that this is something new. Corrupt governments have always been eager to seize resource assets after foreign investors with advanced technologies have developed them, often leading to disaster (as with the Venezuelan expropriation of its oil fields). But such actions will be greatly magnified during a global deflation as desperation spreads.

Copper is particularly vulnerable, as 72 percent of the world's production comes from regions without US SWAP Lines in place.

In raw numbers, the top fifty copper mines produce 28.6 billion pounds of copper annually, equivalent to 64 percent of annual global copper production. Non-SWAP Line countries produce 22 billion pounds of that copper, compared to +SWAP Line regions, which produce a paltry 6.6 billion pounds. Among the twenty-five largest producers, thirteen of them—including CODELCO, the largest—operate entirely in non-SWAP Line Nations.

I believe expropriations will become a global focus issue as the less-developed nations continue to electrify and modernize, forcing them to seek additional revenue sources.

MY COPPER OUTLOOK

Currently, Peru and Chile do not have US SWAP Lines but produce just below 40 percent (17.6 billion pounds) of the world's copper each year.

Both governments are right leaning currently, favoring mining development with international assistance. But I've seen video footage of union meetings at very large mines in Peru and Chile suggesting some serious issues at the mine sites there. I wouldn't be surprised to see the current government parties lose to more left-wing factions in the federal elections in Peru and Chile in 2021.

This is a dicey situation, to say the least. The prospect of everything from increased taxes to outright nationalization of large mines is real—and I believe it will happen.

Gazing ahead, I have no doubt that there's much potential for serious economic headwinds that could slow global growth and subsequently copper demand in the near term. Yet copper prices and copper-focused equity share prices remain strong. The long-term thesis for copper is very bullish and the outlook remains bullish.

To be clear, I'm bullish on copper, too.

I'm just also cautious about the potential risks still present in the current macro global economy and I am concerned about the high valuations many base metal companies are already getting, especially those in politically shaky jurisdictions.

The real issue that will cause copper prices to soar will be the obstacles to permitting large copper projects. It will only become more expensive and take more time for world-class, large copper projects to come online. The Pebble Project's copper/gold porphyry program in Alaska is a perfect example. I have been to the site. I know many engineers with decades-long experience who have been to the site and believe the mine should be put into production. But the reality is, the project will not be built for many decades because of politics, not science.

Many such projects have the size and economics to come online, but political issues have held them back. As companies and investors in America start losing their producing assets in emerging markets, the push and momentum for developing world-class assets within the US will build momentum.

I believe that this is inevitable and that the government will support domestic production. In addition, there are large deposits in +SWAP Line Nations like Canada, and there are also plenty of smelters in +SWAP Line Nations. The US must secure its copper supply needs without depending on –SWAP Line Nations. It will.

Concerning nickel and cobalt, we are well supplied, and where there might be potential shortages (particularly with cobalt), substitutions are possible (see next section).

That is not the case with the rare-earth elements. They are indispensable to the Rise of America, yet there are serious supply questions. We need to take a close look at the issues.

RARE EARTHS

The rare-earth elements (REEs) sector will become one of the most sought after, highly competitive marketplaces in the world.

Why are REEs so important?

It's simple. rare-earth elements provide the building blocks to produce the best magnets in the world.

Now when you think magnets, you likely envision the one on your fridge that holds up your kids' or grandkids' pictures and artwork. Those aren't the magnets I'm discussing.

The most important type of magnet is called a "permanent magnet." There are permanent magnets in your cell phone and MRI machines. There are 920 pounds of permanent magnets in an F-35 Lightning II stealth fighter jet.

But as important as their military applications are, REEs are crucial to wind turbines, military equipment, 5G, and electric vehicles (EVs).

Because of their incredible magnetic properties, permanent magnets are replacing the gearbox for direct-drive wind turbines. And in electric vehicles, permanent magnets act as the drive unit and provide the torque and precision required for the electric motor.

In other words, if nations want to go green, they *must* have REEs. And it's not just the United States that is trying to go green. So is Europe, so is China, and so are many other developing nations.

Both direct-drive wind turbines and electric vehicle motors require a permanent magnet called neodymium-iron-boron (NdFeB). The element that is the most crucial component is rare earth: neodymium (which in the magnet is in the form of a compound called neodymium-praseodymium oxide or NdPr).

The average electric vehicle's motor requires one kilogram (2.2

pounds) of neodymium-praseodymium oxide. Each direct-drive wind turbine requires 200+ kilograms (440+ pounds) of this same neodymium-praseodymium oxide material.

Direct-drive wind turbines are forecast to account for 30 percent of connected onshore wind turbines.

Is neodymium-praseodymium oxide production keeping up with demand? Well, yes. But only for the moment. In the year 2020, production of the compound was approximately equal to current consumption. However, a gap between supply and demand is opening up, and it's going to become a chasm over the next twenty years.

By 2040, global production of this key compound is projected to increase by about 50 percent. But demand is projected to more than double. In raw numbers, this adds up to a shortage of about 150 million pounds.

SUBSTITUTION: A WORD OF CAUTION...

To be sure, there are many examples of niche metals where dire predictions of shortages never come to pass—because of substitution.

Cobalt is an excellent example.

It's a metal that improves the conductivity and chargeability of the lithium-ion battery. But several years ago, supply became a serious issue because the primary source was the Democratic Republic of Congo (DRC). The next best source was Russia, also shaky. There was no real mine outside of these two that could provide tangible production of volume for the EV industry.

The industry could see that it would be too expensive and too risky to bet the global EV revolution on an AK-47 nation. And no one wants to be beholden to Russia.

But technological progress breeds innovation. Within two years, scientists discovered that by increasing the nickel in the battery, manufacturers could achieve the same positive outcomes on chargeability and conductivity that they got with cobalt.

In short, there was a substitute for cobalt.

It makes for a good cautionary tale, but I do not see the same type of scenario playing out with permanent magnets.

You see, neodymium magnets have the highest magnetic force among all magnets in the world. In addition, they offer excellent heat resistance and coercivity (resistance to demagnetization). There is no substitute, although not for lack of trying. For example, Toyota has done deep dives on removing some neodymium from permanent magnets and substituting lanthanum and cerium, two "cheaper" rare-earth metals. The swap resulted in lower performance and higher deterioration.

Tesla has actually moved away from an induction motor in its cars, replacing it with a permanent magnet motor. Elon Musk has continually been ahead of the curve; there is no reason to think otherwise with the motor change. And today, every single major car manufacturer is moving toward producing EVs using a permanent magnet setup with the neodymium-praseodymium oxide compound.

UNDERSTANDING THE SUPPLY SIDE OF REES

The supply of rare-earth ores and finished goods is perhaps the least transparent segment in the commodity space. Why? Because China controls the entire vertically integrated supply chain, and the country is notoriously secretive. We know China is far and away the largest producer of rare-earth metals, both at the mining and refined product levels. It accounts for 60 percent of mined output, 85 percent of refining, and 90 percent of manufacturing.

Among other rare earth miners are the United States (12 percent of global production), Myanmar (10 percent), Australia (9 percent), and Brazil (5 percent).

I know those familiar with the rare-earth market will say that the US doesn't produce any rare earths; we import them all. That statement is *sort of* correct.

US mines *do* produce a very basic rare-earth concentrate. The problem is that this concentrate is not useful for anything. It must be further refined into oxides or alloys, and there are no facilities on American soil capable of doing that.

It almost all gets sent to China, which refines the concentrate and sells the finished product back to the United States. Thus, China accounts for 80 percent of all US rare-earth imports.

That the US is 100 percent dependent on outside sources for its refined rare-earth products is ironic. The fact of the matter is that, for much of the twentieth century, the United States of America was the world's rare-earth powerhouse. This changed in 1995 when China began to expand into the market aggressively. Shortly after the Chinese expansion, America's largest mine, Mountain Pass, changed hands several times and eventually went into bankruptcy.

Unquestionably, rare earths are already a matter of national security for the United States. And the issue becomes an order of magnitude greater as politicians push for "Made in America" electric vehicles and wind turbines.

Think about it... The US already imports 100 percent of finished rare-earth alloys, most of them from China. And as the country wants to ramp up the production of electric vehicles and wind turbines domestically, **the surge in demand for rare earths will be enormous.**

Yet government officials seem oblivious to the shortage problem that's looming—especially when compared with their Chinese counterparts. On November 17, 2020, the United States Department of Defense (DoD) announced a $13 million subsidy for the US REE sector. That's pathetically low and shows how little the DoD understands the current situation. Consider that China subsidized their domestic rare-earth sector to the tune of US $20 Billion in 2019.

Think about that for a second.

Chinese government investment in REEs is more than 1,500 times greater than the American investment. Talk about the shortsighted view of those in the US administration. In addition, I'd bet that the Chinese get at least two times more bang for their money than in America.

This is huge, and the US government needs to *wake up*! Of all the threats to the Rise of America—not to mention the advancing electrification of the globe—this is arguably the most serious of them all. It is the real Achilles' heel to the Rise of America.

But it is a problem that money can solve. The question then becomes: Is the US even capable of mining REEs? The answer is *YES*, with time and capital. And if you include +SWAP Line Nations, it is an even more resounding *YES*. The light and heavy rare-earth resources in the US and their allied nations are sufficient to meet the growing demand, provided that there is adequate investment to build out the operations.

How so if China is so dominant?

FUTURE RARE-EARTH SUPPLY

One of the things to understand about rare earths is that they're a bit misnamed. They're actually not rare at all as a component of the earth's crust. The reason they're called rare is that they are very thinly distributed around the planet. There are very few places where they are concentrated enough for profitable commercial mining.

The rare-earth market is heating up, yes, but it hasn't nearly peaked yet. So, it's more important to figure out where the best untapped primary deposits are in the world. We want to find the deposits in the feasibility or later stage, keeping in mind the amount of time required to get a project into commercial production.

Going from grassroots discovery to production is a tedious multistep process, with loads of red tape and each step consuming big blocks of time. The total could be well over ten years. Even projects at the development stage will take five or more years to reach commercial operation.

Okay, so where are future rare earths going to come from? Let me do my analysis in the context of the SWAP Lines I've been stressing the importance of throughout this book.

Of the eight primary rare-earth mines that have completed a feasibility study but are not in commercial production, half are in –SWAP Line Nations (China, Vietnam, Tanzania, and Angola). This is not good for the United States or Europe, both of whom would greatly prefer the transparency associated with a project in a +SWAP line nation. However, you have to play the hand you're dealt, not the one you wish you had. (Well, unless you're bluffing. But there will be no bluffs in this market.)

The developed world will aim to source their REEs from the remaining four that are in a +SWAP Line Nation. They include one, Mountain Pass in California, which was once the world's leading producer. The other three—in Greenland, Australia, and Canada—are newly identified deposits, promising but without any infrastructure, meaning a lot of capital will be required to put them into production. They are most likely uneconomical using current rare-earth prices.

The good news is that we're not facing a serious shortage of neodymium-praseodymium oxide anytime soon. Long term, there is abundant supply at the right price. Given REEs' importance going forward, price is not going to be an obstacle.

US PRODUCTION

Still, the rare-earth market is nearly always on a knife's edge in the short term. With China having complete dominance over the supply chain, any hiccup in US/Chinese relations could send the market into a frenzy or a tailspin.

In the most extreme example, China flexed its muscles by shutting the doors on rare-earth supply in 2010. When it did, the price for neodymium-praseodymium skyrocketed from $10/pound to nearly $90/pound in a year. The price recovered when the door was opened again but never fell to 2009 levels. Similarly, when the US/China trade war broke out in 2018, prices climbed nearly 100 percent.

The antidote to a supply crisis is a supply chain alternative to China. And Mountain Pass, idle for two decades, is back in the game.

Currently, Mountain Pass produces a very basic rare-earth concentrate, which is sold cheaply to China. This was planned for the project's Phase 1. Management's goal is to now move further down the supply chain. Phase 2 involves a $170 million upgrade to the existing facility. This upgrade will provide the ability to extract neodymium, praseodymium, and other rare-earth oxides from the concentrate. Management expects Phase 2 to come online in 2022. The upgrade is really a retrofit and realignment of the current operations within the existing separation facility.

Mountain Pass is ramping up to become both a producer as well as the only domestic refiner. This is a giant step away from dependence on China, making Mountain Pass the odds-on favorite to become the next big thing in REEs. I cannot stress enough the advantage it enjoys by having most or all the necessary infrastructure already on site. It saves years of expensive development headaches.

And after Mountain Pass, we can look forward to Australia, Greenland, and Canada coming online—eventually. So, the future is not nearly as bleak as it may have seemed.

RARE EARTH'S FRACKING MOMENT

Plus, there's another wild card that's mostly hidden from view right now, but that may burst into the public consciousness in a big way. It involves a revolutionary new technology and one in which the US could compete with China.

There is a mineral called monazite. It is found throughout the world in mineral sand deposits, with big deposits in Australia, SE Asia, and South America (and even some in the US). It contains neodymium-praseodymium (NdPr)—but is also impregnated with radioactive uranium and thorium. The question has been how to recover the rare earths from the sand.

Tech to the rescue. A procedure has been created by which monazite will be able to be "cracked and leached," with the radioactive material separated, leaving a rich concentrate that can then be processed. It's a breakthrough similar to how fracking changed the oil industry, though few have noticed.

This is, unfortunately, not a simple matter. Because of the

radioactivity, exploitation will require licenses to transport, handle, and process the radioactive monazite and handle the material post-cracking and leaching. That takes time. Plus, all of this is expensive. It's going to take an investment of billions to get this new industry up and running. Private concerns will not foot the bill initially; the government must step in and subsidize the effort.

Which it should. This is a national security issue, and it's entirely appropriate that the Department of Defense become involved. Monazite processing gives us access to the neodymium-praseodymium (NdPr) that magnet manufacturers (and thus the defense industry) need. It helps overcome the dependence on China that impedes the Rise of America.

But I have to say, this development comes with a giant neon *Warning* sign: China knows exactly what's happening in the new monazite market and is moving to lock up the major monazite deposits before the new process fully comes online. Chinese state-owned enterprises are investing billions of dollars in all aspects of REE production to preserve their strategic advantage with REEs. It knows that its dominance in this area is a sword that it holds over the rest of the world. That sword can be fully weaponized at any time of China's choosing.

Given China's big head start with REEs, the US government cannot afford to sit idly by and let that country pad its lead. Domestic REE production must proceed on all fronts, whether from conventional mines or monazite processing. This is not something that is going to happen overnight. It will take time and a lot of capital investment, but it is *not* optional. It *must* get fast-tracked in America.

Consider this a challenge issued.

CHAPTER EIGHT

THE RISE OF AMERICA WILL RAISE THE REST OF THE WORLD

WITH THIS BOOK, I HAVE TRIED TO, AS SUCCINCTLY AS I can, alert you to a few of the many developments in the world today—and especially in the US—that will deeply affect your life going forward and will, not incidentally, contribute to a Rise of America that now sits right there on the horizon, ready to launch.

The next ten to twenty years are going to be interesting, tumultuous, often crazier than a lake full of loons. A lot is happening already that most people don't know about—especially if they haven't read this book. There is a lot that, as an extension of current trends, is baked in the cake. And there will also be a lot that takes us completely by surprise.

Dissatisfaction with the present is in the nature of our species. We are ingenious and innovative and given endlessly to tinker with our received reality. We're on the move, usually forward, occasionally back, but never still.

Human life on this beautiful blue ball of a planet is in the process of changing profoundly and forever. In fact, it is likely to change more in the coming two decades than it has in the previous two millennia. Granted that we are on an unpaved road, there will be plenty of potholes along the way. There will be great advances. There will be setbacks. There will be turmoil. But on balance, I couldn't be more optimistic.

Just a few things we know for sure:

· New technology will continue to evolve exponentially.
· There will be a major reshuffling in the geopolitical sphere.
· We will live longer, healthier lives as most serious diseases are brought under control.
· A demographic decrease in populations will be the rule across the globe.
· The importance of fossil fuels will fade, while new energy sources will make electricity cheap and plentiful on a global scale.
· The race for control of space is on.
· MMT will be the most daring experiment in money creation in all of human history and, if done properly, has the potential to fund the Rise of America.
· The obstacles to the Rise of America will be lack of faith in government due to its failures, media manipulation, and alienation of those who lose jobs to technologies like robotics, 3D printing, and artificial intelligence.

Let me first review the most critical points I've made. Then I'll discuss a few more things that I haven't yet covered either in the main text or in the Appendices, but related to my main themes.

MONEY AND ECONOMICS

If you take away nothing else from this book, take away this: As I explained in detail in Chapter 3, economies worldwide are on the brink of operating according to the principles of Modern Monetary Theory (MMT). This is the most radical change in the history of money since the invention of money itself. However, almost no one has fully grasped how or why MMT works, nor for how long it will, nor its implications.

Many mainstream economists refuse to concede that it's happening at all. No one at the Fed has endorsed MMT. Most have already consigned it to failure. Yet it's unfolding in real-time, right in front of their faces. After reading this book, you now know more than they do.

In essence, MMT theorists are making the case that the digitization of the money supply, on which the growth of prosperity depends, has changed the nature of the game. That is, they contend that the money supply can be increased indefinitely and in unlimited quantities without provoking the hyperinflation that has laid waste to most previous fiat currencies. It is the realization of one of humanity's enduring dreams: an endless flood of money with no negative consequences.

Whether in the long run MMT is a viable economic framework, I don't know. No one does because this is the first time it's been tried. What I do know is that MMT is here, worldwide, and it will be with us for the foreseeable future. I don't make the rules; I just figure out what they are and then work to see how to profit within the framework at hand.

I do believe that the current framework of fiscal-monetary coordination (FMC), if done right, will provide the framework for the Rise of America as it did for America from 1942–1951. I worry that Congress fails to work together and politicians do what politicians do (not much) and screw up the fiscal and monetary framework.

MMT would then be the last framework implemented. It behooves us to arrange our personal financial lives so as not to try to fight the Fed.

Call me an optimist, and even though I believe the politicians will do very little right, I believe FMC will do what it's intended to do, and the Rise of America will be even greater than I am projecting in this book.

THE US DOLLAR AND THE WORLD

The second most important takeaway from this book concerns the US dollar, its position in the world, and its effect on the political alignment of nations.

The USD is—and has been for seventy-five years—the reserve currency of the world. That has been extraordinarily beneficial for the country. With all international commerce, especially the oil trade, proceeding in dollars, there has been an insatiable demand for the currency. If you don't have dollars, you don't get to play. Among other things, this has allowed the US to run enormous trade deficits, bringing in boatloads of cheap, foreign-made goods and paying for them with money that it can print at will. Best deal ever.

Now, many "experts" are shouting in the media that the USD's long reign is coming to an end.

To which I say, *NO*!

Here's why: to paraphrase Winston Churchill, *the dollar is the worst currency in the world—except for all the others*. The dollar is king. And will stay that way for decades to come. It still makes up over 60 percent of all currencies held across the globe. What will challenge it? The next strongest currency, the euro, is being propped up by, you guessed it, the USD. The euro is on very shaky ground, its very survival depends on the fractured European Union not breaking apart (don't count on it). Do you see anyone clamoring to conduct trade in yuan or rubles? Didn't think so.

The USD is not only going to remain the go-to currency in international trade, but it's also going to strengthen its position. The world is awash in a mountain of debt, and the vast majority of it is in US dollars. That debt has to be paid back (or written off—which is significantly deflationary) and paying it back means acquiring the means to do so, i.e., to accumulate dollars. It's a self-fulfilling loop. Anyone who wants to benefit from international trade has to pay to play—and pay in USD. That is the ticket to prosperity. The rest of the world knows it, and it isn't going to change.

What are the implications? They're far-reaching. The continuation of the USD as the strongest global currency means that, as the saying goes, other countries are *either with us or against us.* Here's where the SWAP Lines I detailed in Chapter 2 come to the fore. Understanding what the Fed is doing with them is crucial if you want to see where we're headed. Nations that align with the US will be extended USD credit through SWAP Lines; those opposed to the US will be going it alone. This forms a potent monetary alliance that will then determine geopolitical alliances for years to come. If you don't have access to dollars, you'll struggle; if you do, you'll prosper. It's just that simple.

Do you see how Eurodollars—and we're talking trillions here and in the future—yet further reinforces other countries' dependence on a strong dollar? By now, you should.

Put these things together and, by themselves, they already make a strong case for the Rise of America. But there's more.

GEOPOLITICS

A lot is going on besides the alignment of the US with the +SWAP Line Nations.

For example, a radical realignment in the Middle East is underway. Israel, largely through support from the US and its own military, has become a technology powerhouse second to none. It will continue to thrive with USD support and send its innovations America's way, and the US will continue to support it. Technologies and applications crafted in Israel are so ubiquitous that the country features the second greatest number of companies on the tech-heavy NASDAQ stock exchange, trailing only the US. Overall, Israeli companies in all sectors are the third most-listed companies on American stock exchanges, after the US (first) and China (second).

But traditional alliances in the region are shifting.

In 2020, the UAE, Morocco, Bahrain, and Sudan moved to normalize relations with Israel, and Saudi Arabia will follow. America benefits the most from the Saudi/Israeli trade agreement that is coming. Saudi Arabia provides the capital, Israel provides the technological expertise, and America provides the marketplace and guarantee of military backing.

This is inevitable because, as oil becomes less important in the world, the Saudis will become even more US dollar dependent. Saudi Arabia will be forced to join the *rapprochement*—fostered by America—among Israel and the Sunni Arab nations, allying against Shi'ite Iran and the extremists it funds. Iran will become ever more dependent on Russia and China, but that won't last. I believe Iran's religious regime will eventually fall, and it will revert to the kind of secular state it was before 1979. Someday it might even be invited back into the US-dominated world once again.

These are all incredible positives, but there is also the other side to the geopolitical ledger—and over there, it's not all rainbows and daffodils.

Russia has become little more than a bit player on the global stage, but it still has a huge military, thousands of nukes, and a pretty sophisticated cyberattack force. It will try to bully its way to the international prominence it believes it's entitled to and it represents a destabilizing element that's always dangerous.

Vladimir Putin has brought Russia back from the abyss after the collapse of the Soviet Union by reigniting his people's sense of nationalism. But the fact is Russia's main sources of income—namely natural resources, and specifically oil and natural gas—will continue to be under pressure due to falling prices as fossil fuels are phased out globally and demand withers. This does not bode well for the country's economy.

Moreover, although Russia has a strong defense and aerospace sector, they have not expanded as much as they would have due to the brain drain that occurred when scientists and engineers fled to America and Israel as the Soviet Union imploded. This was not a situation that can be reversed quickly, but Russia is in much better shape today than twenty years ago. Putin is planning for the future by making sure that plenty of money flows to software engineers and designers of military hardware. And he has already started preparations for Russia after his leadership, which will continue the trajectory he put the nation on.

Then there's China, the world's second-place power. Many observers seem to think it will supplant the US for the top spot. But I have some very relevant things to say about that.

Yes, China wants to be No. 1. It hopes to get there with its Belt and Road Initiative (BRI)—the most ambitious infrastructure project ever undertaken—designed to facilitate trade, expand the international use of Chinese currency, the renminbi, and "break the bottleneck in Asian connectivity," according to President Xi. While there is no official count, it's estimated that about sixty countries are actual or potential participants in the BRI.

It won't happen as planned. Fact is, many of those sixty countries are close economic or military partners with the US. They are not about to switch their allegiance to an untrustworthy Communist country with a currency few nations will fully accept in trade. Others, like India, have ongoing hostile relations with China and are keen on opening their own US dollar SWAP Lines. China's influence will largely be confined within its own borders.

Remember also that the renminbi is pegged to, yes, the USD and that the country carries over $1 trillion of Treasury debt—denominated in dollars, of course. The heads of the Chinese Communist Party (CCP) know they cannot fool around with the peg without the global markets devaluing the renminbi. This has significant implications for their economy.

Furthermore, please pay no attention to those shrieking worrywarts who maintain that China could destroy the American economy by wholesale dumping of its Treasuries into the marketplace. It couldn't do that without destroying its own economy. I mean, if it sold Treasuries, what would it get in return? Right, *more US dollars*! Which would do the Chinese no good except to use those dollars in trade, which they already do, anyway. Besides, the Fed would stand ready to soak up any Treasuries China proposed to sell, maintaining the financial order. Although China is a threat long term, the risk China will crush the US dollar are impotent.

And for those who think China will go back to a gold standard by making the yuan convertible to physical delivery of gold, I say: *think again*. First, let's assume China did make its yuan convertible to gold. Do you think it will allow the gold to leave China without significant "taxes" and filing fees if it even allowed it to leave the nation at all?

Or take the case of rare earths. Foreigners can buy refined rare earths in China but getting delivery outside of China without an agreement with existing corporations and government approvals (and significant permit fees and taxes) is essentially impossible. Delivery is at your own risk. Similarly, that would be a best-case scenario if the yuan ever went to a gold standard.

But in my opinion, a yuan backed by gold just will not happen. China has been doing its own form of MMT by propping up state banks for decades. This, in turn, props up SOE (state-owned enterprises) and other companies that are of strategic importance to China. Trying to revert to a gold standard would blow up this whole structure. That is decidedly NOT what President-for-Life Xi wants.

China will experiment internally first with DCEP (China's National Digital Currency), as will other countries. But the how, when, and what convertibility of such national digital currencies are still in their early days.

Remember always how economics and politics are totally tied together in China. The government allows capitalists wide latitude in their entrepreneurial efforts (in some ways, there are fewer regulatory roadblocks to starting a business than in the US). However, it is still a communist state with the CCP in ultimate control. No one bucks them.

The case of Jack Ma serves as a telling example. Ma—one of the richest men in China and founder of Alibaba (China's version of Amazon)—in late 2020 intended on doing a large and fully subscribed $38 billion IPO of his company called Ant Group. The IPO, set for November 5, attracted $3 trillion of interest from retail investors and was projected to have an initial market cap north of $300 billion. It would have smashed the record for the most valuable IPO, seizing the title from Saudi Aramco—and demonstrating, among other things, the ongoing shift from oil to data as the world's most valuable resource.

Ant Group is a fintech company that has been somewhat in direct competition with the Chinese state banks, siphoning off millions of customers. Moreover, Jack Ma made a *big* mistake. The billionaire tossed off some negative comments attacking the state-owned banks. He publicly snubbed China's financial regulatory system at a Shanghai conference on October 24, 2000, declaring its rules to be ill-suited for fostering healthy innovation. He also demeaned the regulators who enforce China's international banking rules, calling them "an old man's club."

Uh-oh.

It doesn't matter if he was right or not. You just don't *do* that, not in China.

Officials suddenly introduced some new regulations and said that there were "major issues" with Ant's listing under the new rules. *Bye-bye*, Comrade Ma. The Shanghai exchange suspended Ant's IPO on November 3, and the company willingly pulled its listing in Hong Kong on the same day.

Ant Group may return *if* it can satisfy regulators. But most observers believe it will look significantly different and face a much-diminished IPO.

Here's my point: if you (an individual or corporation in China) challenge the CCP, you will lose, no matter how important, innovative, and profitable your company is. But these incidents have consequences. Foreign capital looks very negatively on heavy-handed government actions such as this. Due to its companies' lack of financial transparency, China already has little goodwill in the global markets. It has much work to do before it gives any comfort to foreign capital. In contrast, American markets are highly respected across the planet, and the result is the world's most liquid and largest market.

China has much work to do to replace America as the global finance capital.

As a final note, no discussion of China is complete without looking at what is happening in cyberspace.

China is a unique experiment. It has committed itself to rapid capitalist development while at the same time maintaining an unprecedented level of social control through the CCP. Surveillance is ubiquitous, and punishment for breaking the rules is swift and severe, intending to create a docile, obedient population. Modern technology allows for an Orwellian environment of frightening proportions beyond what even Orwell could imagine. One's social credit score—which is computed continuously based on one's "good" and "bad" actions—is of paramount importance in everyday China. If you stray too far, you will be publicly outed and branded as a malcontent, and your mobility within the society will be sharply curtailed.

A very real concern that Americans should have about China is that the US will follow in its footsteps and become a more authoritarian state to the detriment of its citizens.

Another concern is cyberwarfare. Like Russia, China is becoming very skilled at it. The great land wars of the twentieth century, which stretched across vast areas, are anachronisms. Today, you can wreak more havoc manipulating electronic digits than you can with an aircraft carrier.

The future of cyberwar is fodder for a whole book on its own but suffice it to say that cyberspace is the new global battlefield. Because of the very low barrier to entry vs. the outsized rewards, online threats are flooding into the US daily by the *millions*. They may come from major adversaries like Russia and China or minor players like Iran, N. Korea, and other nations not in the US circle.

The risk is more than just someone hacking into your Gmail or PayPal account to steal credit card info. It's more than using hacked facial and vocal recognition to create fake "live events" and influence elections. We are building out an electronically linked and controlled infrastructure that will always have vulnerabilities to a determined adversary. Thus, the Fed's and Congress's printer will be used, to whatever extent necessary, to pour money into cyber- and digital security. Count on it. It is not optional. On the plus side, blockchain technologies may unlock incredible protection from such threats. But they will take time to be created, tested, approved, and adopted.

CENTRAL BANKING

Central bankers have been determining monetary policy for the nations that have them since founding the first (and longest enduring) one, the Bank of England, in 1694. However, fiscal policy—determining how the money is to be spent—has been the province of politicians.

This is changing. Especially in the US, the line between its central bank—the Federal Reserve—and the government is blurring. If this blurring loses sight of the debt's size, it's both supportive initially of MMT and an eventual threat to its success.

The Fed (which "prints" America's money) is a consortium of private banks, much to the chagrin of its critics who claim that this is a blatant conflict of interest. True enough. This means that newly minted money goes first to the Fed's member banks and its affiliates (friends). But at the same time, the Fed has kept the power of money creation away from politicians who are dead certain to abuse it to promote their pet schemes.

MMT holds that massive government deficit spending, and the money that funds it, will not cause havoc in the markets so long as inflation is held in check—and that the Fed has the tools to accomplish just that. But that nettles politicians who believe that *they* would be better stewards of money creation. Increasingly, they will make populist arguments, calling for the squeezing out of the private banks, which work "against the people," as they will say. They will make a case for themselves to take over and become the direct beneficiaries of the "magic money tree" and the direct distributors of its largesse.

Even MMT's strongest proponents admit that it has limits in terms of money creation. Should the Fed and federal government merge, expect politicians ignorant of economics to push spending beyond those limits, risking ruinous inflation. Hopefully, that won't happen.

DE-GLOBALIZATION

As noted in Chapter 1, the pandemic has forced a heightened awareness of global supply lines' fragility. At the same time, the attractions of outsourced production have waned with rising wages overseas; the skyrocketing use of robotics and AI in manufacturing; just-in-time product delivery; more efficient warehousing and transportation systems; and the declining cost of energy.

Now add in FMC and eventually MMT, which will be used to provide government infusion of capital to "retool" the US manufacturing sector, and you get an undertaking that both political parties will agree on. Before long, products *designed in California, assembled in China* will give way to products *designed and assembled in the USA.* New facilities will be located where they are treated best, offering a potential new vitality to the nation's formerly depressed areas.

But with robotics and AI, millions of American workers' skill sets and labor will become obsolete. In an ideal world, the universal income will provide the financial comfort for those individuals to learn new skill sets and obtain the training required to make them value-added employees, rather than just another form of welfare. The administration and criteria for the universal income will be critical to ensure the most efficient use of the funds and prevent fraud. The spending of universal income, whether on training services or the purchase of goods, if done properly, will be a net positive for the economy.

But universal income will be a failure if it creates a population dependent on politicians as a way of life. Hopefully, instead, the funds from MMT will be used to empower individuals to better themselves. If this experiment fails, socialism takes root. It is already the professed end game for some shortsighted politicians ignorant of history.

GOING GREEN

We are going green and not looking back. I don't need to repeat the whole energy chapter here. Suffice it to say that while fossil fuels will still be with us for a good while, that era is ending. We're undergoing an extensive and permanent shift in the way energy is produced and distributed as well as in the nature of the companies that produce and distribute it.

Further, there is going to be not just an emphasis placed on ethically sourced materials, but mandatory proof demanded. This has never happened before. It is a must.

Technology will improve for the exploration and extraction of our traditional raw materials. At the same time, amazing new materials—many of them carbon-based—will be produced without disturbing the land at all. Clean air and water will be protected, and our overall environmental quality will increase manyfold. Utility-scale battery storage is coming and will enable green energy to meet both commercial and residential needs.

MMT will bankroll green innovations and growth in the sector. Because of the PPAs (power purchase agreements) and long-term financing of projects by the utilities and governments, the big energy price inflations of the past will be tamed. Inflationary pressures—caused by dependence on imported oil (such as in the '70s)—which formerly crippled the economy will be eliminated by ultra-low-cost sources of renewable energy that power everything. It isn't coming tomorrow. It will take many decades, but it will happen, and it will prevent the energy price shocks we've had in the past.

We will never run out of food. Logistics and distribution will be the issue. We're already producing more food on fewer acres than ever before, and that trend will accelerate with computerized crop-raising and the spread of efficient indoor production facilities.

The new green landscape of long-lived, cheap power will be a huge net positive for the Rise of America.

THE DIGITAL SOCIETY

As noted, the incredible rise of computing power over the past twenty years has had life-changing effects. For one thing, it has made the Chinese model for the surveillance state possible. Not in the future, but right now, a central government can track its citizens' behavior to an astonishing degree. The government can know where you are at any given moment, whom you're talking to, and what you're saying. It knows who your friends are, what entertainment and foods you like, where you shop and what for, what your religious, political, and social views are. Increasingly, *privacy* is becoming a quaint, old-fashioned word that no longer has meaning.

Moreover, it isn't just government. We have *volunteered* masses of information about ourselves through social media—information that it would have taken the government an enormous expenditure of time and money to collect. We give it away for free. No wonder we have seen the rise to power of companies whose sole purpose is to harvest this data and use it to manipulate people through the social media websites they frequent. It started with pushing products and quickly moved into politics. Their ability to guide your opinions—subtly, powerfully, and without your awareness or consent—is well documented.

This is not new news. But the Rise of America depends to some extent on a continued free flow of information and innovation. That should be enough of a warning. This is an incredibly complex issue. But just like Rockefeller's Standard Oil was broken up due to regulation, the same will happen with the largest social media and technology companies. Today's digital colossi have been able to amass incredible power as they operate within a framework ahead of the laws. Expect an array of new laws that will change the dominance of the tech giants.

Another result of supercomputing is that the Fed and government will track citizen consumption rates—or, better put, take the exact pulse of the economy—in real time in any market, big or small. Such economic tracking has not kept pace with the technological advancements at hand, but it will catch up. The government will not have to resort to the lagged responses it's always employed. This real-time data stream is analogous to catching cancer in its early days vs. late stage. The chance of full recovery is much higher.

Today's technology was not available during the financial crisis of 2008. With this tech will come more effective use of stimulus packages and improved timing in their implementation. This dovetails nicely with MMT-directed spending, meaning those who need the help the most will get it when and in the amount they need. The benefits will be positive not just to low-income earners but also to specifically defined regions of the economy and the small businesses who may not be getting funds like the bigger companies that are getting their bonds financed and redone. A real-time stimulus can be invaluable if something bad happens in a particular pocket of the economy, with funds targeted to support jobs and prevent the spread of the problem.

Meanwhile, across the Pond...

As leaders try to formalize the digitization of their currencies, you will see massive pushback against such moves. The European Union has openly stated they are exploring the possibility of launching a digital euro. For reasons mentioned in Chapter 3, they will eventually get their way, especially when universal income takes hold. Christine Lagarde, the president of the ECB (European Central Bank), will have to deal first with nations with heavy cash economies. Countries such as Italy, Spain, and Greece—which have anywhere from 20–30 percent cash economies—will stubbornly resist this change. It's no coincidence that those three nations are heavily indebted to the EU, but with MMT, as I've shown, the tax revenue doesn't need to cover the debts. Eventually, the ECB will win out because the payments will seize up if the holdout nations don't capitulate. Much more chaos and pain can come from the lack of digits (in this case, euros) than bullets, and the ECB knows that.

Despite the remaining resistance to full-on digital money, cash as we have always known it, is on the way out. Hardly anyone uses physical coins anymore, and bills will be next to go. Liberty lovers will oppose a system in which every commercial transaction is digitized and trackable. They will decry the loss of privacy that will come with the elimination of cash transactions. Sad to say, they will lose. Most will surrender to the inevitable and even embrace the convenience. A few will rebel by turning to cryptocurrencies (see below).

The intrusion of cyberspace into our lives will increase until it is ultimately accepted as being as "normal" and "real" as our physical reality. AR (augmented reality) and VR (virtual reality) are already here and becoming more sophisticated by the day. You can explore the world in 4D and surround sound and never leave home. Hollywood will set up shop in your living room (with a small device and a monthly streaming fee), providing you with an immersive experience without the threat of catching a virus from the coughing guy next to you in the theatre. Instantaneous electronic language translators allow you to read foreign newspapers and converse with anyone, anywhere in the world, any time you want. And so on. You can find whole books on this subject, as well as endless opinions as to whether ubiquitous cyberspace is actually good for us.

Finally, there is the communications revolution. America does have some catch-up to play in this sector, but it will catch up and lead the way. I see global high-speed connectivity—with 5G cellular and satellite networks that bring the internet to everyone on the planet—as a net positive. But as stated earlier, the US administration has failed miserably thus far, not just on securing the resources but also technology. This is an area of much concern moving forward.

AMERICAN POLITICS

Expect continued division and strife. There will be an inevitable conflict between politicians who embrace change and those who preach a return to some illusory past "golden age." The latter group will lose. Hopefully, a new party enters the picture down the middle and covers most Americans' needs, not the far right of either side. If there is one thing we know for sure about genies, it's that they cannot be put back in once out of the lamp. The real golden age is going to be the one produced by technology that benefits all.

In the near term, though, the growing wealth inequality gap—not just in the US but around the world—will cause political havoc. Governments will be implored to "do something," and they will try to find ways to close the gap. But the real solution won't be any specific policies the bureaucrats created. Rather it'll be the new technologies and the application and acceptance of these technologies that will close the gap. If anything, it's the politicians and bureaucrats who will stand in the way and may prevent the early adoption of beneficial technologies.

When it becomes crystal clear that new tech is raising everyone's standard of living, a lot of what now seems like permanent political friction will just melt away.

Companies such as Amazon that have successfully executed their business plans, and disrupted their whole sector across the world, will be branded as not paying "their fair share." They will be subject to new taxes and levies. This is no different than what happened to the gold companies after the 1849 California Gold

Rush. Like Amazon today, the gold companies paid essentially no tax to their state and federal governments. That changed. The gold companies were not just taxed on their earnings at the state and federal level but were also hit with a "per ounce of gold" levy to be paid to the government. The same still holds true today.

I use Amazon only as an example, but it's a good one because it pays essentially no tax while benefiting from the United States Postal Service infrastructure. This will change. Amazon and its peers in online commerce will be levied "per package" or delivery fees in some form, and new taxes will be applied to them.

Also, expect the tech giants to pay a tax/fee that will contribute to government-created funds used to train workers who have become obsolete from their technology. Think of this just like the resource companies that have to contribute to a bond (pool of capital) that covers the reclamation of the project after the project ends to return the environment to a better level than before the operation started. This will essentially be a digital bond established to help out workers displaced by technology.

THE RACE TO SPACE

Like the Fed is backstopping the markets with MMT, the Space Force (controlled by the Department of Defense) will guarantee NASA the funds it needs to finance internal space projects and joint ventures with private companies such as Space-X, Blue Origin, Lockheed Martin, etc. The race is on to innovate and control the space on and around the moon.

This effort will be staged and presented as a quest to bring valuable information and technology back to earth (which it will). Still, the true goal is to prevent the weaponization of the moon by China, Russia, or an alliance between the two.

The nations working with the US on the space race are also nations with +SWAP Lines. Coincidence? I think not.

On the other hand, China and Russia are focusing on strengthening the 1967 Outer Space Treaty, which was signed at the height of the Cold War and which the US does not support or recognize.

Regardless, they are in the space race. Unlike with the Cold War's arms race, the space race is not about who has the biggest or the largest number of nukes. Rather it's about which side can control the area around and on the moon. Trillions will go into the attempt to gain dominance.

Those trillions of dollars will be delivered by MMT—and they will trickle down to private companies like the ones above, along with many other private and public companies in the US and its allies.

A Sino-Russian alliance may try to keep pace, but America is by far in the lead in this race and will continue to outspend its rivals. The Treasury, using MMT money from the Fed, will make sure the DoD has no funding shortfalls.

While fulfilling the DoD's agenda, the space race will be sold as in the interest of all Americans because of the technological advancements it will spawn. They are probably unimaginable— in the same way that no one could have imagined what would happen with another former DoD project, the internet.

In the end, technological advancements from the space race will enhance the standard of living for all, not just the US. US first, of course, but other nations will benefit, too. The military will fund research and development in nanotechnology, medicine, materials science, advanced computing, wearable technologies, human augmentation, and much more. And as we know from past experience, exotic new products and processes that originate in the military eventually become available to every citizen.

To take just one example, technologies embedded in your clothing (or on your body) will continuously analyze your vital life signs and warn you to get to a hospital before a major incident like a heart attack. This is deflationary for the medical system. The real damage is done, and the bill is run up after the heart attack. Prevention is better and cheaper. Your personal data will transfer wirelessly to your primary physician and the medical professionals at the hospital. That will help save lives while decreasing healthcare costs.

I want to say it's simply the free market and capitalism that triumph here, but without the government, they won't. The key to the US advantage is that the government's balance sheet will back the private sector's innovations. China is applying a similar strategy, but the communist regime won't allow as much of a free development platform as in America.

POVERTY AND PEACE

The technological revolution that is being led by American innovation has the potential to usher in a new world of plenty. The long-elusive goal of the eradication of poverty is within reach. So is a new era of peace. Technology cannot erase conflicts that arise from the likes of ethnic and religious differences. But as the means of attaining a universal prosperity spread, they *can* eliminate one of the primary causes of war: the desire to take by conquest what your neighbor has and you don't.

DEMOGRAPHICS

Many think the world is overpopulated. The opposite is true. We have a demographic problem to the downside, not on the upside.

As people are lifted out of poverty, they have fewer children. Birth rates have fallen dramatically in all developed nations across the globe, to the point where many countries are not breeding at even replacement levels. (Ironically, this includes the US, which would have a declining population were it not for the immigrants who are the objects of so much misplaced scorn.) But the global economic system is based on ever-expanding consumption when technological advancements are increasing output and decreasing waste. This will be a serious issue unless innovation can be retooled to focus on better stuff rather than more of it. Luckily, we have a lot of time before that day arrives.

Most people are unaware that demographics also support the Rise of America. Let me explain. China will reach its peak population by 2024 at 1.432 billion people. China's fertility rate is 1.5. This means that, by the year 2100, China will have about 732 million people, a decrease of 48.9 percent of its population from its peak. The same can be said for Japan and most of Europe.

America will not reach its peak population until the year 2062, with about 362 million people. America's fertility rate is 1.8. By the year 2100, it is expected that the US will have about 336 million people, a decrease of 7.2 percent from its peak and a 1.5 percent increase from its population in 2020.

It will be America, not China, that benefits from shifts in global populations. America will attract the best and the brightest among immigrants. China is attracting the best immigrants, but the Chinese Dream has a long way to go before it replaces the American Dream in the world's imagination. This has been a trend true for the last hundred years and will continue to be true for the next hundred years.

The average purchasing power of individuals in China will increase with time, but demographics will shrink its domestic markets and soon. What is important to remember is that America's population is more stable. The US currently has the largest economy in the world, and it (not China) will remain dominant in the future.

BLOCKCHAIN, DISTRIBUTED LEDGERS, AND DIGITAL COINS

Blockchains and distributed ledgers are very disruptive technologies. They've already arrived. I won't bother exploring the subject in any detail here; you can find plenty of information online with a simple search. I'll just say that they will become increasingly employed as unhackable recordkeepers. And they can also be used to create a kind of money.

Bitcoin is an obvious example. It's been around since 2008 and doesn't look like it's going anywhere. In fact, mining for new Bitcoins, which requires enormous computing power, now consumes more electricity worldwide than the total yearly amount used in a nation like Switzerland. Much of that electrical generation is from the high-pollution-emitting power sources such as lignite coal in China.

The field is still in its infancy, and who knows how it will play out? But a lot of very bright minds are involved, and a lot of capital has been invested. Suppose cryptos do go mainstream and become legitimate currency alternatives. In that case, they will boost the velocity of US dollars outside of the Fed, and my hunch is that those dollars are greatly needed. They will also return the concept of privacy to commercial transactions. But there are obstacles.

First, of course, is government. The government does not like competing currencies, and none but the dollar is recognized as legal tender that must be accepted in trade. So far, Washington has not moved to ban or even regulate the likes of Bitcoin, and that's probably, at least in part, because it would be so difficult to do. Bitcoin resides on a blockchain distributed across thousands of nodes (computers). It was specifically designed so that no bad actors can gain access to and modify the chain. That doesn't mean the authorities won't come after Bitcoin someday if it becomes perceived as a genuine threat to the government's monetary hegemony—just that an effective clampdown will be difficult. There is a major concern about crypto being a source of US dollars for money laundering, financing terrorism, and supporting malign activities that threaten US national security interests and the integrity of the US financial system (mainly SWIFT). This is especially true of organizations and nations on the US sanctions list or are in a position of desperate need for US dollars. Another major negative with crypto is the incredible amount of pollution created by the crypto mining companies that consume low-cost electricity to power the computers to create the crypto coins like Bitcoin (usually the dirtiest and worst emitters of pollution such as lignite coal to produce electricity in China). I have been shocked how investors have not connected the crypto coins to their horrible environmental footprint, especially with the institutional investors and millennial investors who focus on ESG. It's relatively easy to follow on the blockchain where each coin was digitally minted, and all institutions should avoid "dirty coins." This should also eliminate bad actors who have set up crypto mining farms (in the crypto sector, farms are nothing more than a large number of computers—in the tens of thousands—in one large area, all connected, working toward creating coins) not following the highest environmental protocols. This would never be accepted in the gold, mining, or energy sector in North America by investors. Why is it being accepted in the crypto sector?

Acceptance is also an ongoing issue. As I wrote earlier in this book, the viability of all money is a matter of faith. When people have faith in a currency, it endures; if they lose that faith, it can collapse in a heartbeat. For Bitcoin to truly succeed, people have to endow it with value by having faith that it's "real" money. And for that to happen, it will have to show more stability than it has at present.

The fundamental issue with all cryptos including Bitcoin is that without its "network," including being connected to the internet and having a power source, it is worthless. Why? There is no way to verify how many Bitcoins (or any other crypto) without being online and having access to the network. Compare this to, say, gold or silver, which have many ways to be verified without dependence on any existing network or internet.

Making a deal in Bitcoin means assuming the risk that tomorrow it may be worth only half of what it's worth today—as has happened all too often with Bitcoin. Few people want to take that risk. Of course, the flip side is that it can also rise steeply in price and frequently has. So, I think it's probably safe to say that most Bitcoin owners are in it as a speculation. The volatility will have to decrease before it becomes a store of value or a currency for buying things. And it's important to remember that any appreciation in Bitcoin's value doesn't exist outside its relationship to a national currency like dollars (or euros, yen, or whatever). You profit from Bitcoin only when you convert it to something else. And that brings us back to the main concern: that a vast majority of the mining of the crypto coins occurs in China, Russia, and Iran, where individuals, corporations, groups, or nations may lack US dollars. How ironic that the coins being created in those nations are using investors' lack of faith in the US dollar to trade US dollars. They send coins, you send US dollars, and everyone ignores the environmental footprint. The irony is fitting.

Could Bitcoin or another crypto develop into a genuine currency that's accepted by merchants everywhere? Perhaps.

For that to happen, though, Bitcoin will have to overcome not only the hurdles I've laid out here but another one that looms even larger. For some time now, it has been rumored that the Federal Reserve has been toying with the idea of creating its own blockchain and using it to market its own cryptocurrency. Call it Fedcoin. (All of the central banks are contemplating a similar move.)

That is a highly logical government response to Bitcoin. You don't have to ban or regulate something if you can introduce a competitor that wipes it out. That's what Fedcoin would do to other cryptos. It would see immediate and widespread adoption because it would have an insuperable advantage over other coins: it'd be legal tender, especially important to those on universal basic income. Expect the government to make it mandatory for companies that received any support from the Fed bond-buying program to accept only Fedcoins.

Because Fedcoin would be under the government's control, you can bet your last physical dime that the Fed's blockchain will have a built-in trapdoor that allows for government access. It will host the ultimate perfect surveillance system.

Yes, there would still be some diehard privacy lovers who would shun Fedcoin in favor of some other crypto. But the great bulk of the population would opt for the convenience of the government offers.

STORES OF VALUE

In the brave new world of MMT, people are naturally going to want to hedge their bets by putting at least some of their ghostly digits into tangible things that promise to be stores of value. Gold and silver have served that purpose for millennia, and I don't see that changing. I'd suggest putting up to 5 percent of your net worth into physical gold as insurance against MMT being abused by politicians and inflation occurrences. In fact, I believe that we're in the early stages of a monster bull market in precious metals. Socking away some physical gold and silver is a very prudent thing to do right now.

Other stores of value will be unique, like fine art, or scarce, such as rare stamps or certain wine vintages. Real estate will remain valuable provided that it's the kind where limited supply is meeting rising demand. But city apartments and office buildings are likely to suffer as people move out of urban areas and work increasingly from home. While not yet widely used in everyday transactions, Bitcoin is emerging as a legitimate store of value; it will become more accessible to investors as it gets adopted by more mainstream institutional platforms.

MY FINAL WORDS

While you will find a wealth of useful supplementary information in the Appendices, I hope that in this book, I have already convinced you that the Rise of America is *the* unstoppable force of our time. Not everyone is going to welcome this, some not at first, and some not at all. But eventually, the benefits will become crystal clear.

And those benefits will spread inexorably. Technology invented in the US and Israel (and in conjunction with American

SWAP Line allies)—combined with the funding impetus from FMC and possibly MMT—will create an engine capable of powering the planet's future, pulling people everywhere out of poverty.

There is no precedent in all of human existence.

Make no mistake, the Rise of America will be good not only for American citizens, and not only for its allies, but also for the rest of the people of the world.

APPENDIX I

HOW WE GOT HERE: AMERICAN MONETARY HISTORY

TO FULLY UNDERSTAND WHERE WE ARE CONCERNING THE global financial structure and America's role, it helps to be aware of the country's past experiments with money that led us to our current situation.

COLONIAL DAYS

When Great Britain began to colonize the newly discovered continent of North America, its citizens back home used coins as money for over 700 years. The coins—primarily the *penny*, the *shilling,* and the *crown*—were struck at mints all over England and were made of silver. The *pound sterling* concept derived from this early coinage, as one pound of silver pennies by weight (240 of them) equaled the value of one pound sterling. (Actual pound notes would not arrive until 1694, concurrent with the Bank of England's founding, history's first central bank.)

In 1663, Charles II introduced a gold pound coin (also known as the *guinea*). This established an official bimetallic system of *specie* in the country. (The term, *specie*—also known as *hard money*—denotes metal coins used in commerce, as distinguished from paper currencies and our contemporary system of electronic digits.)

Over in the colonies, there was a chronic shortage of money. America was looked down upon by the haughty home country. At best, it was considered a primitive backwater that existed solely to be exploited, like any other colony in the emerging British Empire. Its inhabitants were second-class citizens—if they were lucky enough to be freeborn, that is; slaves were no-class citizens, merely property.

The official money was the pound sterling, but whatever pounds found their way across the water didn't stay there for long due to a balance of trade that intentionally favored Britain. American industry had barely begun, and the colonists were heavily dependent on importing finished goods from the homeland. They paid for these with raw materials like cotton and tobacco, but those exports' value was far less than the value of all the imported goods.

Thus, the colonies were insufficiently supplied with enough coinage to conduct internal trade and were legally prohibited from minting their own, a crime for which one could be prosecuted for treason. They were purposely impoverished by their masters and kept that way, with many existing in dire poverty.

Even if local money had been suddenly allowed, the colonists had not yet made any native gold or silver discoveries from which to fashion coins. So, any English coins that made it across the Atlantic were quickly recycled back.

Outside of whatever coins the colonists could lay their

hands on, they had to improvise. Barter was very common, of course. Furs became one unit of currency. Other settlers adopted wampum, the shells used by some Native Americans, but the British quickly put an end to that. Most useful were coins from countries outside of Britain. They were relatively plentiful and circulated freely especially silver Spanish dollars. The famed "pieces of eight" became the *de facto* coin of the realm.

In the South, tobacco was king. But because organic products left to the weather quickly rot, public warehouses sprang up. They soon began storing, grading, and issuing "certificates of deposit" for the leaves. These *tobacco notes* served as bearer bonds that could themselves be traded. They were popular and well-trusted and long served as the principal currency in Virginia. In fact, in 1727, the government of Virginia even authorized them as legal tender.

During the eighteenth century, local colonial governments turned to paper money. One variety, *commodity money*, was directly equivalent to and convertible into a specific amount of some physical asset. In some places, as noted, that might be tobacco. Elsewhere, it could be traditional gold or silver coins. But since the scarcity of gold and silver was the main problem to begin with, that didn't work so well.

A good alternative was the one asset the early settlers had the most of: land. So, several colonial governments created land offices that issued paper money backed by real estate. This allowed colonists to take out loans in paper notes, using their land as collateral—these notes circulated in the local economy as currency. The loans could then be paid back, plus interest, with either the same form of paper money or gold or silver (if they could find any). Failure to repay the debt incurred resulted in foreclosure on the land.

Land-backed currencies were most popular in the mid-Atlantic colonies of Pennsylvania, New York, New Jersey, Delaware, and Maryland. In fact, the interest that accrued from these loans provided their governments with the funds needed for government administration's ongoing costs, sometimes even eliminating taxation.

The other form of money tried was, yes, *fiat currency*.

By the mid-eighteenth century, most of the colonies were printing their own paper monies. These were all "bills of credit." The colony would authorize printing a specified quantity of notes, which it would then use to pay creditors. The creditors would, in turn, use the notes to make other purchases and so put them into circulation.

With each currency emission, the colony would also authorize an equivalent tax. i.e., for each note they issued, they would issue a tax for the value of the note. Quite a smart idea. It served two purposes. It strictly limited the quantity of notes in circulation, thereby keeping a lid on inflation. And two, it balanced the budget, which used to be thought of as important.

Such currencies circulated freely and helped ease money shortages. And they worked just fine as long as they were limited in quantity to the amount of anticipated future tax receipts.

The thing is, it's never long after the introduction of paper money, just about anywhere, before authorities get to monkeying with the system. And so, it was in eighteenth-century America. Some local politicians came up with the idea of offering a 50 percent discount on taxes paid in gold or silver. Others followed more conventional tracks: issuing fiat money in excess of anticipated future receipts; printing new notes before earlier ones had been collected and destroyed; or failing to include a specific date or method for retiring the money.

All of which contributed to a steep increase in the number of notes in circulation, aka inflation—with predictable effects.

Prices rose as the value of the notes depreciated, marking these fiat currencies as failures as either a dependable store of value or a reliable unit of exchange.

So, the people did what the people always do. They reverted to conducting their business with whatever precious metal they could lay their hands on. Enduringly popular were those Spanish pieces of eight, also known as *pesos*, which were minted in Mexico and made their way north in trade. They became the most trusted form of money in the colonies, even though the British refused to recognize them as legal tender.

As an aside, the words *Spanish* and *peso* came to be abbreviated into an S and a P with one written over the other, which is the origin or our dollar ($) sign. Additionally, merchants would make changes in the marketplace by cutting the Spanish dollar into eight pieces or *bits*. This is why we came to call a quarter of a dollar "two bits."

And then there was war.

REVOLUTION

Most people associate the start of the Revolutionary War with the signing of the Declaration of Independence. But it actually began more than a year before that. Shortly after the fighting began, on June 23, 1775, the Second Continental Congress approved $2 million in a paper fiat currency called the *Continental*.

That $2 million was supposed to pay for fighting the entire war. After the war was quickly won—they were nothing if not optimistic, our revolutionaries—the Continentals would slowly be fully backed by *specie* (gold or silver coin) acquired through the collection of taxes over the four years following the war. Continentals were initially pegged at a 1:1 ratio with the Spanish silver dollar, and the promise was that they could be exchanged at that rate.

By November, just three months after they were introduced, the 2 million in Continental dollars had been spent. So, Congress issued another $3 million, and extended the tax collection needed to back them a further eight years into the future. In February 1776, just three months later, the government was insolvent again. So, they issued $4 million more—but this time without any pledge to secure them with future taxation.

To that point, the new paper money had pretty much retained its value, and it still traded at a 1:1 ratio with the Spanish silver peso. So, when the government went broke again, in August of '76, Congress had no problem printing up another $5 million to cover the mounting cost overruns. But the essence of confidence in a fiat paper currency is trust, and that began to wane.

The fledgling nation had embarked on the rockiest of journeys, its first experiment with a true national fiat currency. If the public should have learned the hazards from the earlier trials of local fiat currencies, well, it didn't.

By September of 1778, an average of $10 million in new Continentals was being created every month, and that pace kept up until the exhausted printing presses were finally shut down at the end of 1779.

Wars are expensive. This is a lesson that has been retaught throughout American history. And yet, we've failed to learn that seldom do you have enough money to fight them with tax dollars alone. Usually, you either borrow or create fiat currency from thin air. If not both.

Paying for the Revolutionary War was more of a burden than the colonists could bear simply through taxes. In total, a staggering 242 million in Continental paper dollars were eventually put into circulation. When the British surrendered after the Battle of Yorktown in 1781, the Continental's value had fallen so much that it now took 1,000 of them to buy just one Spanish silver dollar. And by the official end of the war, the currency had plummeted to its ultimate inherent value, zero—and the term "not worth a Continental" became the common, uniquely American way of disparaging the value of something.

ESTABLISHING A PRECIOUS-METAL STANDARD

In 1785, presumably for lack of a better idea, the Continental Congress accepted the Spanish silver dollar as the United States' new official money. Further refinement came in 1786 when the Board of Treasury—with memories of the Continental fiasco fresh in their minds—adopted as the law of the land:

- That the official money of the United States would be precious metals—silver and gold,
- That the basic unit of value would be called a "dollar" and consist of 375.64 grains of fine silver. and
- That all other coins, both foreign and domestic, would be evaluated in terms of this official silver dollar.

George Washington was not only the hero of the Revolution; he was also no stranger to the perils of fiat currency. In January of 1787, two years before becoming the first president, he issued this warning:

If in the pursuit of the means we should unfortunately stumble again on unfunded paper money or any similar species of fraud, we shall assuredly give a fatal stab to our national credit in its infancy. Paper money will invariably operate in the body of politics as spirit liquors on the human body. They prey on the vitals and ultimately destroy them. Paper money has had the effect in your state that it will ever have to ruin commerce, oppress the honest, and open the door to every species of fraud and injustice.

Four months later, representatives from the sovereign states gathered in Philadelphia to replace the Articles of Confederation with the Constitution. Given the experience of the Continental, Washington's opinion was generally shared among the delegates, which is why they wrote their preferred definition of money into our founding document. Right there in Article I, you'll find these words:

The Congress shall have the power to...coin money, regulate the value thereof, and to fix the standard of weights and measures [Section 8, Clause 5]. And, No State shall...coin Money, emit Bills of Credit, or make anything but Gold and Silver Coin a tender in payment of debt [Section 10, Clause 1].

Congress established March 9, 1789, as the date for the nascent nation to begin operating under the Constitution that the about-to-be-president, anti-inflationist Washington would be the first to swear to "preserve, protect, and defend."

Of course, it did occur to the founders that it would never do for Americans to try to run their own economy using some foreign country's money, such as Spain's. So, one of the first issues to be taken up by the new Congress was establishing official money for the United States. The resultant legislation was the first Coinage Act, passed in 1792, which established the United States dollar as its standard unit of money. Dollars were expressed only in precious metals, not paper. It reflected the Continental-stoked fears of the era that the Act actually invoked the death penalty for anyone debasing the money.

The Act also created a United States Mint, where gold and silver dollars were to be coined, commencing in 1794. The mint was sited in Philadelphia, then the nation's capital. Among the Act's other provisions:

- Gold eagles were to contain 247.5 grains (16.04 g) of pure gold and be worth ten silver dollars. Half eagles (worth $5) and quarter eagles (worth $2.50) would be minted, with a proportionate amount of gold.
- Silver dollars would contain 371.25 grains (24.1 g) of fine silver. The 371.25 grains resulted from Alexander Hamilton's taking the average weight of a large sample of Spanish dollars already in use.
- Half dollars, quarters, dimes, and half dimes (*disme*, from the French, later shortened to *dime*) were authorized, containing a proportionate silver amount.
- Pennies and halfpennies were to be made of copper.
- The ratio between gold and silver was not allowed to seek its independent market value but was fixed by statute at 15:1.
- Free minting privileges were granted to all citizens. Anyone could take either gold or silver bullion to the mint and have it minted into coins, a permitted practice for nearly eighty years until 1873.

So, America, at the outset, opted for a bimetallic standard. However, the decision to fix the silver/gold ratio instead of letting it float caused problems. At 15:1, it was soon out of sync in favor of gold, and much of the American gold stocks sailed east, purchased with European silver.

That situation was reversed by the Coinage Act of 1834, which reset the silver/gold ratio to 16:1, moving the mint price for silver to a level below its international market price. Europe began buying silver, returning the gold it had previously accumulated. This brought gold stocks back to the United States, and from then until the Civil War, the nation was, for all practical purposes, on a gold standard.

During the government's first seventy years, sentiment remained strongly opposed to any national paper currency. But events of the period from 1810 to 1860 tested that resolve. The War of 1812, the Mexican War of 1846, the Panic of 1857—all of these strained the US Treasury. That meant deficits, and to finance them, the federal government issued so-called Treasury Notes from time to time. They were simply promissory notes that earned interest and did not circulate as official currency, except for a brief time in 1815.

As America was expanding, pushing its boundaries ever westward, it was hard for coinage to keep up. The discovery at Sutter's Mill hadn't happened yet, and available gold was simply inadequate for financing the kind of growth the new nation experienced. Some substitute had to be devised as a medium of exchange. Thus, for the first sixty years of the nineteenth century, numerous banks and other businesses issued their own paper currency. Although the states themselves were theoretically forbidden from creating their own money, there was no explicit prohibition on private banks. So, they exploited that loophole. Hundreds of private firms and thinly veiled "state" banks got into the money business, producing what became generally known as *broken bank notes*.

Should the country have a central bank, like the Bank of England? This was a question that came up early and often. It led to experimentation with the nation's initial two national banks. The First Bank of the United States (FBUS) was chartered in 1791 and was jointly owned by the federal government and private stockholders. FBUS was a nationwide commercial bank that served as the bank for the federal government and operated as a regular commercial bank acting in competition with state banks. When depositors brought state bank notes to First Bank of the United States, it would present these notes to the state banks, demanding gold. This constrained the state banks' ability to issues notes and maintain adequate reserves.

Thus, it was no surprise that, when the FBUS's charter came up for renewal in 1811, the state banks mustered a great deal of opposition. The renewal legislation failed, and the FBUS ceased all operations.

The Second Bank of the United States (SBUS) opened in January 1817. The War of 1812 had drained the Treasury to the point that it had difficulty financing military operations. The credit and borrowing status of the Treasury was low and had to be shored up.

SBUS's charter was for twenty years, and, once again, the state banks opposed it. Since it served as the depository of the federal government's revenues, that made it a political target of state banks that both objected to and envied the SBUS's relationship with the central government. They got their champion in Andrew Jackson, who hated the SBUS as much as they did.

Jackson made abolition of the SBUS one of the centerpieces of his political platform. He believed that *specie* (gold and silver) were the only true monies. Vesting power and fiscal responsibility in a single bank would inevitably lead to inflation and other financial ills.

In 1833, President Jackson issued an executive order that ended the deposit of government funds into the Second Bank of the United States. After that, deposits were placed in the state-chartered banks. It was a mere formality that the SBUS's charter was not renewed in 1836, and it joined the FBUS in history's dustbin.

From 1837 to 1860 is sometimes referred to as the *free banking era*, with its genesis in Michigan. Previously, a bank charter could be obtained only by a specific legislative act. Still, the Michigan Act of 1837 allowed chartering of banks without the state legislature's consent. The following year, New York enacted similar legislation, and other states soon followed. These banks could issue notes backed by gold and silver coins, and the states regulated the reserve requirements, interest rates for loans and deposits, the necessary capital ratio, etc. Free banking spread like wildfire, and from 1840 to 1861, all banking business was done by state-chartered institutions.

It was a golden age of the gold standard and represented the states' point of maximum financial freedom from regulation by the federal government.

GREENBACKS

Those freewheeling days came to an abrupt end with the onset of the Civil War. As continually noted, wars are expensive. Governments never have enough gold in their Treasuries to finance them without creating some new currency out of thin air. And so, it was in the US as it went to war against itself.

The American Civil War started in 1861. Soon after it began, both the Union (the North) and the Confederacy (the South) levied taxes, raised tariffs, and borrowed heavily by issuing all sorts of bonds.

Within two months, the Confederacy started printing its own currency. Shortly after that, the Union's treasury was running dry, and President Abraham Lincoln needed a way to pay the troops. At first, his administration sought loans from major banks, mostly in New York City. But the banks demanded very high interest rates, on the order of 24 to 36 percent. Lincoln refused to borrow on such terms and called for other solutions, and Treasury Secretary Salmon P. Chase obliged by designing a new currency.

In July 1861, Congress authorized $50 million in Demand Notes. They bore no interest but could be redeemed for *specie* "on demand." They were not legal tender (before March 1862) but, like Treasury Notes, they could be used to pay customs duties.

Unlike private and state banknotes, Demand Notes were printed on both sides. The reverse side was printed in green ink, and so the Demand Notes were dubbed *greenbacks*, an appellation that has survived to the present day.

Initially, greenbacks were discounted relative to gold, but being fully redeemable in gold was soon par. In December 1861, the government suspended *specie* redemption, and they declined in value. Chase then authorized paying interest on Demand Notes, which served to prop up their value.

Demand Notes could be used to pay customs duties or interest on the public debt, along with gold. Importers continued to use Demand Notes in place of gold. In March 1862, Demand Notes were made legal tender. As Demand Notes were used to pay duties, they were taken out of circulation. By mid-1863, about 95 percent of them were gone.

Concurrently, Lincoln realized that the number of Demand Notes issued was completely insufficient to meet the government's war expenses.

What to do?

Enter Colonel Edmund Dick Taylor—an Illinois businessman serving as a volunteer officer—who met with Lincoln in January 1862. Taylor suggested issuing unbacked paper money. He told the president: "Just get Congress to pass a bill authorizing the printing of full legal tender Treasury notes...and pay your soldiers with them and go ahead and win your war with them also. If you make them full legal tender they will have the full sanction of the government and be just as good as any money, as Congress is given the express right by the Constitution."

Lincoln had come to office as an advocate of sound, metal-backed money. Now here was a guy peddling the notion of an unbacked paper currency. This did not sit at all well with him. But war was raging, and there was mounting pressure from Congress to do *something*. If the government didn't print its own money, it was destined to go into deep and never-ending debt to foreign creditors. That seemed the only other option, and it sat even less well with the president. So, in the end, he capitulated and called on Congress to get it done.

It wasn't easy. Opponents argued that Article I, Section 10 of the Constitution implied that the federal government did not have the power to issue a paper currency. It had always been interpreted that way. There were still Americans around who remembered the Continental and believed in gold as the only true money.

But proponents argued that "extraordinary measures must be resorted to in order to save our government and preserve our nationality."

Resistance faded away and, on February 25, 1862, Congress passed the first Legal Tender Act, which authorized the issuance of $150 million in United States Notes.

US Notes became the new greenbacks and the first American fiat currency since the Continental. Though originally called a Demand Note, the printed promise of payment *on Demand* was removed, and the statement *This note is legal tender* was substituted. The legal tender status was important because it guaranteed that creditors would have to accept the new notes even though they were not backed by gold, bank deposits, or government reserves and bore no interest. They were the precursors of today's Federal Reserve Notes.

However, their validity was not universal. They could not be used by merchants to pay customs duties on imports and could not be used by the government to pay interest on its bonds.

The Civil War also gave us the 1863 National Banking Act. It encouraged private banks to apply for federal charters, thereby making them "national banks" and making their printing efforts legal tender.

These newly chartered national banks used their funds to buy Union bonds (thus raising money for the war effort). They deposited the bonds with the Treasury in Washington, DC, and then were allowed to issue National Bank Notes for up to 90 percent of the bonds' value on deposit.

It worked. During the Act's first year, 179 private banks went national. By war's end in 1865, that number was nearly 2,000. And it continued to grow. When the issuance of these national bank notes finally ceased in 1935, over 14,000 banks had become members. All of them issued paper money under their own name, and, at least in theory, it is all still legal tender today.

A CROSS OF GOLD

As originally proposed, greenbacks were only supposed to be a temporary wartime currency. Many politicians believed that the Legal Tender Acts were unconstitutional in peacetime and should be voided. The House of Representatives agreed and, with a return to the gold standard as a goal, passed the Funding Act of April 12, 1866. The bill authorized the retirement of $10 million in greenbacks within six months and up to $4 million per month after that.

This proceeded until $356 million remained outstanding in February 1868. But then the recall stalled. Economic recovery from the war was sluggish, there was a poor crop harvest, and an economic panic in Great Britain jumped the ocean and caused a sharp drop in prices in the United States. The money supply contracted, and deflation's ugly head arose for the first time. American debtors—forced to repay debts in more expensive dollars—were hurting, and they successfully petitioned for a halt to the notes' retirement.

By 1869, due to the high price of silver, little of that metal was circulating. But the authorities foresaw that the development of the Comstock Lode and other rich silver-mining areas would lower the price, causing large quantities of silver dollars to be struck and the gold standard to be endangered.

But making changes was highly controversial because what was proposed was, in effect, the death knell for bimetallism in the US. The debate raged in Congress for three years until the Coinage Act of 1873 was finally signed into law in February of that year. In addition to ending the silver dollar production, it forbade citizens from exercising their former right to present bullion at the US Mint and walk away with coin—as those who tried it discovered to their chagrin.

The Act set the nation firmly on the gold standard and ushered in the second golden age of gold.

Other countries quickly joined the party. By 1876, most of

Europe was on gold, and by 1886, there was only a small handful of holdouts.

And why not? With most currencies on the planet redeemable for a fixed amount of gold, they were now pegged at fixed rates to one another. With stable exchange rates, something magical happened. International trade and foreign investment exploded! Countries found it more advantageous for their economies to end the protectionism that was considered normal and engage their neighbors in trade. Barriers fell, tariffs were eliminated, and a new era of international business and prosperity was ushered in.

It was the age of classical economic liberalism. For the first time, there was a global consensus that open markets and free commerce ought to be the default state of affairs, with political systems interfering only in the case of direst public need or correcting minor problems.

What is more, for four decades, there was no overall inflation... *none, zero, zip, nada.* Imagine that. Sure, there were still booms and busts, but it averaged out as a zero-sum game from the beginning of the international gold standard to its end because gold is the great equalizer.

The utility of the gold standard should have been obvious to everyone. But it wasn't. Its adoption also led to a bitter clash between two large and opposing forces in the US. On the one hand, were those who favored the deflation that the gold standard promoted; on the other were those who believed free coinage of silver to be the necessary engine to drive the inflationary economic prosperity that was busting out all over in the wake of the Industrial Revolution. It was a pitched battle that would be continually fought for the rest of the nineteenth century.

In January 1875, Congress authorized a contraction in the circulation of greenbacks to a limit of $300 million, and required the government to redeem them for gold.

As a result, the currency strengthened, and by April 1876, the notes were on par with silver coins, which then began to re-emerge into circulation—even though they were no longer produced and bimetallism was defunct, they were still honored. On May 31, 1878, the contraction in the circulation was halted, and the amount of paper currency stabilized at $346,681,016—a level which, amazingly, would be maintained for almost a hundred years.

As of 1879, the Treasury held sufficient *specie* to redeem notes upon request. This brought the value of the greenbacks into parity with gold for the first time since 1861. That helped ease the public's deep-seated suspicion of paper currencies. The greenback was now genuinely "good as gold," and people were ready to accept paper and metal equally.

But at the same time, the price of silver had fallen, and bimetallists felt that reinstating it would cause inflation and lead to better times.

They got their way. The Bland-Allison Act of 1878 passed over the veto of President Hayes. This legislation required the Treasury to purchase millions of dollars' worth of silver bullion each month and coin it into silver dollars, which were restored as a legal tender, except when gold was specified by law or private contract.

The next fifteen years were the most bullish ever for silver. Those in the "Free Silver" movement—mainly in the western frontier states—wanted the unlimited coinage of silver in response to the growing complaints of the farmers and miners that made up the bulk of their populations. Farmers were buried by debts that could not be paid off due to deflation, and they wanted inflation, which would allow them to pay their debts with cheaper dollars. Mining companies were sitting on a glut of supply from western mines, driving the price below the point at which the silver could be profitably extracted. They hoped that increased government demand would bail them out.

Free Silver advocates didn't get all they wanted. But they were able to push governmental silver purchases higher, via a requirement that the Treasury buy 4.5 million ounces of silver per month—paying for them with a special issue of Treasury Notes that could be redeemed for gold. There were plenty of customers for whom gold was still king. Over the next three years, $132 million in gold was withdrawn from the Treasury. That proved to be too much, too fast.

The Treasury's depleted gold reserves led to the Panic of 1893 and caused widespread public fear that the gold standard might be abandoned. In response, President Cleveland called a special session of Congress, and silver purchase was repealed in the autumn of that year.

Silver's price fell like a stone, from $1.16 per ounce in 1890 to $0.60 in December of 1894. On November 1, 1895, US mints halted production of silver coins once again, and the government closed the Carson City Mint. Banks discouraged the use of silver dollars.

Bimetallism was done for, but proponents were not going down without a fight. Their hero was William Jennings Bryan, a fiery populist from Nebraska dedicated to his state's Free Silver farmers. He won the Democratic nomination for president in 1896, largely because of the bimetal advocacy that reached its pinnacle in his electrifying speech to his party's national convention. It culminated in his famous cry that *"you shall not crucify mankind upon a cross of gold!"*

In part, Bryan lost to William McKinley because of the discovery of the cyanide process by which gold could be extracted from low-grade ore. This increased the world gold supply and caused the inflation that free coinage of silver was supposed to bring.

Bimetallists' final defeat came in 1900, with the Gold Standard Act's passage, which established gold by law as the only standard for redeeming paper money and ended the bimetallism that had allowed the exchange of silver for gold. It also set the value of gold at $20.67/ounce—where it had stood since 1834—by government decree. And it effectively limits inflation by preventing the Treasury from printing too much money and running out of gold. Bryan ran for president again and lost again. The United States was firmly committed to a policy of sound and gold-backed money.

Until it wasn't.

THE FED

By the late nineteenth century, times were good. Really good. There was universal money that fostered commerce. *Gold*. Both the European governments and the US guaranteed that they would redeem any amount of their paper money for its gold value. With all these diverse currencies' values firmly tied to physical metal, transactions no longer had to be conducted with heavy bullion or coins. Paper would do just fine.

True, there were risks. For example, gold prices and currency values fell every time miners found large new gold deposits and introduced fresh bullion into the system. On average, annual gold production growth rates were slightly less than the global economy's growth rate. In general, the system functioned pretty well, to the benefit of everyone. International trade exploded.

Then two things happened: the Federal Reserve and World War I.

Mistrust of a central bank had bubbled below American society's surface and its politics, from the founding of the republic on into the twentieth century. The two national banks that had been tried both failed to gain any traction among the people. In fact, most citizens still subscribed to the proscription against centralized money control that had been put forth in no uncertain terms by James Madison when he wrote:

"History records that the money changers have used every form of abuse, intrigue, deceit, and violent means possible to maintain their control over governments by controlling money and its issuance."

In 1900, worldwide, there were eighteen central national banks, mostly in Europe. The Bank of England (established in 1694) was the oldest and most powerful. It's impossible to overstate the BoE's importance. It controlled the money supply of Great Britain, which stood astride the world as a mighty empire upon which the sun never set.

The pound sterling ruled. So strong was the British currency that its relationship to gold hadn't changed since 1717, when Sir Isaac Newton, as master of the UK Mint, set the gold price at £3.17s. 10d. per troy ounce. It was an astounding inflation-free period. And the exchange rate between England and the US was $4.86 in dollars for one pound sterling.

Within two short decades, all of that would change forever.

In the US, the gold standard seemed secure in 1910. But, behind the scenes, powerful forces were gathering to make some changes—dramatic changes.

In November of that year, there was an important meeting on Jekyll Island, off Georgia's coast. It was an appropriate site.

Mega-banker J. P. Morgan, a member of the exclusive Jekyll Island Club, arranged for the group to use an organization described in a 1904 magazine article as "the richest, the most exclusive, the most inaccessible" club in the world.

That meeting turned out to be the most important in all of America's monetary history. It would have far-reaching consequences for the next hundred years, and beyond.

Coming together on Jekyll Island were six men: Senator Nelson Aldrich and his private secretary, Arthur Shelton; Congressman A. Piatt Andrew; JPMorgan banker Henry Davison; National Citibank president Frank Vanderlip; and German-born, New York City investment banker Paul Warburg. A seventh member of the group—it's not believed he attended, though his presence would have been felt—was Benjamin Strong, vice president of the Bankers Trust Company and the future founding chief executive officer of the Federal Reserve Bank of New York.

Utmost secrecy was the watchword. If anyone had gotten wind of it and bothered to ask, the official reason for the gathering was that the men were engaged in a duck hunt. But the Jekyll Island group was actually conferring to develop an audacious plan that was monumental in scope: the restructuring of the entire banking system of the United States.

The participants believed that American banking, and the country's monetary policy, suffered from serious problems that had to be addressed. Immediately at issue was the Panic of 1907. But, to these men, that was just the latest symptom of a broken system. Panics—runs on banks where the institution can't raise enough cash to meet sudden depositors' demands—were destabilizing but not lethal. They were also not uncommon. They had disrupted economic activity in the United States regularly during the nineteenth century, occurring on average every fifteen years.

Panics forced financial institutions to shut their doors, leaving long and deep recessions in their wake. The solution to a panic is *liquidity*, but thousands of American banks exist around the country, each holding large, required reserves of cash. During a crisis, those funds were frozen, with no national authority able to move them around to alleviate the situation.

At the same time, some of the big-city banks' excess reserves were loaned out to brokers who in turn lent them to investors speculating in the equity markets, using the stock purchases as collateral. This system made bank reserves additionally immobile when needed and/or left them tied up in volatile equity markets, leading to overall financial instability.

The reformers felt that a strong central bank was the solution to the problem of periodic panics. It would also address another perceived roadblock to American economic growth: gold. The gold standard meant an inelastic supply of currency in the United States. That supply was unable to expand or contract in response to changes in the market, which in turn caused interest rates to vary substantially and often unpredictably from one month to the next. The inelastic supply of currency and limited supplies of gold also contributed to long and painful deflations.

However, a strong dollar was one of the positive results of a deflationary environment. It surprises most people to learn that the US dollar was actually worth more in 1913 than in 1800. There had been *net negative inflation* (of about -20 percent) for a century!

Inflationist economists hated this. They still regarded the lack of currency inflation as a retardant to economic growth. They fully believed that through the magic of their monetary genius, they could prevent inflation from ever turning into hyperinflation, even though history argued strongly that no one is clever enough to do that forever.

The financial reformers had been waiting a long time to gain the upper hand, and they were about to have their day.

The Jekyll Islanders developed a plan that served as the basic foundation for becoming the Federal Reserve System. Their efforts didn't bear fruit right away, but they persisted, and in 1913 President Wilson signed the Federal Reserve Act into law (and, at the end of his life, called it his greatest regret, which was a pretty high bar). The Act closely resembled the draft proposal drawn up on Jekyll Island in Georgia in 1910. While promising to bring stability to the banking system, it also created an entity that handed almost unlimited financial power to a few people at the top.

The Fed's history has spawned shelves of books in and of itself, and there's no reason to go into that in detail here. Suffice it to say that it became the American central bank for which people like Washington, Jefferson, Madison, and later Andrew Jackson had warned us. (Or, as Henry Ford once put it: *It is well enough that people of our nation do not understand our banking and monetary system, for if they did, I believe there would be a revolution before morning.*)

But, since the Fed is a mystery to so many citizens, a few words of introduction are in order.

The Federal Reserve is neither federal nor a reserve. Actually, it is not even a single entity. It's a consortium of twelve private banks located around the country. A seven-person board of governors, appointed by the president, directs national monetary policy through periodic meetings of its Federal Open Market Committee (FOMC). The Fed's headquarters is the Eccles Building—a massive marble structure, designed in the Stripped Classicism style, that squats on Constitution Avenue in the heart of DC. That building arguably hosts the most powerful people in the world outside of the White House.

You see, the Fed creates money. Most Americans don't know this; they think the federal government creates money through the Treasury Department. But it doesn't. All the Treasury does is distribute the money it collects in taxes to the recipients designated in the federal budget.

When the Treasury runs short on money, i.e., it runs a deficit (which it has done every year since the Clinton administration, and for most years before that), it has to borrow. It does this through the issuance of bonds, which, in the best of times, are snapped up by American citizens and foreign countries seeking dollar-denominated debt that provides an attractive yield. But government's lender of last resort is the Federal Reserve. The Fed can conjure up money at will, whatever amount desired, and loan it to the Treasury Department, which then spends it into the economy.

The Fed can also provide money to member banks, at highly favorable interest rates, in return for IOUs that go onto the Fed's balance sheet next to the government bonds. And the banks can then put 90 percent of this newly created fiat money into circulation, based on the principle of fractional reserve banking (explained below).

Making this currency harder or easier to get determines the breadth of the money supply. It's a very delicate balancing act. As national productivity increases, you want enough money out there to allow the natural laws of economic supply and demand to function as they would in an ideal world. Not too little, not too much.

Okay, how does this all work?

In theory (and, for the most part, in practice), the Fed exists for several reasons. At the outset, it was responsible for establishing Federal Reserve Notes' convertibility into gold, with the initial reserve holding set at 40 percent. Of course, that function is long gone. But what remains adds up to extraordinary power:

First, it controls *the Fed funds rate*. This is the interest rate at which depository institutions lend reserve balances to other depository institutions overnight on an uncollateralized basis. It's what people mean when they say that the Fed has raised or lowered "interest rates" because other interest rates follow this one up and down. This gives the Fed some modest control over inflation. If inflation is deemed too high, the Fed raises the funds rate, tamping down demand for more money to cool the economy. And *vice versa* if deflation sets in and the economy needs a low-interest-rate boost.

This has enormous consequences. Recall the basic functions and characteristics of money that I outlined in Chapter 4. Here's another to add to the list:

- Money is a commodity.

That's right. Think of it like any other commodity; money itself has a price as it moves around in an economy. That price is interest rates. In a free market, interest rates would vary according to the laws of supply and demand. You could borrow or lend money at whatever price the market would bear.

But when a consortium of banks like the Federal Reserve has a great deal of control over the price of money, interest rates are artificially set according to those banks' decisions. To be fair, the Fed sometimes makes those decisions for the public good, but, as you would suspect, they also make plenty of them that favor themselves. In either case, though, distortions arise. No free market would ever support centrally dictated zero interest rates such as we have now. The profit motive is the essence of capitalism, and zero interest rates play havoc with that.

Second, the Fed has direct control over the money supply, which it must have to take an active role in fulfilling its stated role: to maintain both GDP growth and unemployment at what it considers optimum levels. In the best of times, it can facilitate GDP growth at a sustainable rate and help keep unemployment low.

But yes, there's a trade-off. This also means it can funnel newly created money to its favored recipients, who get first crack at spending it before inflation whittles away at its value as it snakes through the economy.

Of course, the banks that are borrowers love it. They get to luxuriate in what is essentially free money and indulge their worst impulses to pursue outsized profits, i.e., they can engage in risky behaviors that result in horrible misallocations of capital, which leads to violent reactions to the detriment of the rest of society and is exactly what we've seen in 2008 and again in 2020.

This isn't baked in the cake. If we lived in a world of responsible, civic-minded people who cared about ordinary Americans, these things wouldn't happen. And if a frog had wings, he wouldn't bump his ass so much.

Third, as noted, it can lend its created currency units to the federal government—through the purchase of bonds—which uses them to pay its bills. Under a gold standard, the Fed was limited in how much currency it could create because at least 40 percent of it had to be backed with gold. Conversely, when the gold standard goes away, it can create as much currency as it wants out of thin air. And Washington can run up trillion-dollar deficits until, well, we don't yet know until when. But it's some time out there in the future. When the great experiment that is Modern Monetary Theory (MMT) breaks down. Maybe.

Fourth, the Fed can use created money to buy government bonds and some species of private debt. It used this power quite a bit during the 2008-09 financial crisis when it took a lot of toxic assets off of banks' hands and squirreled them away on its balance sheet. By law, it is only supposed to carry US Treasuries and *mortgage-backed securities* (MBS) on that sheet. But in response to the 2020 crisis, it has been allowed to buy other forms of corporate debt as well (including so-called junk bonds). It is as yet prohibited from buying corporate securities—although some observers believe that's exactly what it's already doing behind the scenes through the shadowy Plunge Protection Team. If not, the day may not be far off. And that's ominous. Under capitalism, the government is not supposed to take ownership of private enterprises. But if the Fed were to acquire large blocks of a company's stock, it would become a part, or even a majority, owner of that company, which smacks of socialism.

Finally, the Fed is charged with maintaining the financial system's core liquidity as the lender of last resort. As noted earlier, bank depositors demand their money back during financial panics, liquidity dries up, and banks can fail. The Fed is there, in part, to ensure that this doesn't happen. It can head off a panic by making loans that re-capitalize struggling financial institutions. This was a key argument made by proponents of a strong central bank. Once the Fed was in place, they claimed, panics would become a thing of the past.

This was one of the institution's most important selling points. Without a Fed, you get nineteenth-century America, an era basically of financial Darwinism. A hundred years of overall relative stability were punctuated by many severe and painful financial ups and downs. Successes and failures were not only the norm, but they could happen on a large scale.

The system worked. Not perfectly. But it worked because the gold or bimetallic standard tended to curb excesses.

Now fast-forward to today. Not only is the gold standard gone, but the financial system is a pretty shaky house of cards. Currency units have no underpinning. If something went wrong in one corner of the system—as it did in subprime housing in '08—the whole edifice could come tumbling down.

In its most important role, the Fed is there to prevent that, and MMT is now its chosen tool. If it hadn't intervened in '08 or '20, then the system would have frozen up. Liquidity would have evaporated. Finance would have descended into chaos, and we would have been transformed into the kind of survival-of-the-fittest society no one wants to experience. History is unequivocal about what happens when monetary systems collapse. It ranges from horrible to unspeakable.

That said, there's plenty of blame to go around. And it's fair to place a big chunk of that blame on the Fed—as its critics incessantly do—for creating the conditions for disaster in the first place. Its easy-money policy permitted monster financial houses to make gargantuan decisions with no regard to whether or not they were acting with any kind of wisdom. They did it over and over again because it doesn't matter.

Why? Because the Fed *must* ensure that the system remains liquid. The alternative is too ugly to contemplate. But the flip side of that mandate is that the Fed feels compelled to bail out banks when they screw up. Make a boatload of poor business decisions? You're covered—so long as you're deemed too big to fail. If ever there was an illustration of the saying, *damned if you do, damned if you don't*, this is it.

But to return to 1913.

As noted earlier, what the big bankers most wanted was to get rid of the gold standard, which they viewed as an unacceptable drag on capitalism and prosperity. It constrained government spending and economic growth and—hardly incidentally—banking profits. (In fact, many cynics believe that Jekyll Islander Paul Warburg helped direct the new United States monetary system to benefit mostly one person, himself. And he has been suitably vilified over the years. The comic strip "Little Orphan Annie," which debuted in 1924, features a character named Daddy Warbucks, who was more than loosely based on Paul Warburg. Warburg eventually became so rich and powerful he could pick up the phone and give orders to the president.)

Little did Warburg and his fellow anti-gold bankers suspect that two catastrophic world events were about to make accomplishing their goal a whole lot easier.

First, seven months after the creation of the Fed, World War I broke out.

WAR ONCE AGAIN

The international gold standard that had prevailed since the 1870s crumbled with the onset of war, which once again proved impossible to finance through taxation. (*Have I mentioned this before?*) The early combatants—England, France, Germany—were quick to resort to paper currency inflation after their gold flooded out to purchase needed goods. The primary beneficiary being the USA, which sold supplies to the allies before entering the conflict itself, near the end. From 1913 to 1920, US gold stocks went from 2,293 to 3,679 metric tons, increasing more than 60 percent.

To paraphrase Randolph Bourne, war can be the health of the state—provided you stay on the sidelines and don't fight it.

Eventually, though, America joined in both the war and in the profligate currency inflation. In 1914 the US national debt was $2.9 billion...but by 1919, it was $27.4 billion (a 945 percent increase in five years if you're keeping score). Still, the country got off easy compared to other combatants. WWI marked the beginning of the end of the British Empire; it stoked the Russian Revolution; it laid waste to France; and, via the Treaty of Versailles, it impoverished Germany to such an extent that that country, desperate for strong leadership, wound up with Hitler.

The human toll is difficult to imagine. It's estimated that total military deaths added up to around 800,000 for Britain, 1.4 million for France, around 2 million for Germany, and over 2 million for Russia.

After the war, the US emerged as the only, basically undamaged country among the major powers. It reinstituted a modified gold standard in 1919, and there was enthusiasm among some of the European nations to follow suit, especially in the UK. At the same time, though, British politicians fretted about the dollar's growing attractiveness—which had maintained dollar-to-gold convertibility—and of dollar-denominated assets. (Britons were slow to accept that their glorious Empire was fading away, soon to be gone forever.)

After all, while Britain and France struggled to rebuild in a deflationary environment and Germany descended into hyperinflation, America was booming. Its economy continued gaining in strength, vaulting the country to the top spot in the world for the first time. The Roaring Twenties had been ignited, and they burned with a brief but brilliant flame.

The dollar was effectively floating against the other currencies, which were no longer convertible into dollars. (The US eagerly accepted gold and had accumulated the majority of the world's supply.) In the early to mid-1920s, exchange rates fluctuated wildly, with most currencies experiencing a substantial devaluation vs. the almighty dollar. America had the gold and—sorry, Great Britain—its currency had replaced the pound sterling as king.

For all practical purposes, the dollar was rapidly evolving into the reserve currency of the world.

That wouldn't officially happen until 1945 because, as it turned out, there would be some rather consequential glitches along the way, most significantly the Great Depression and World War II.

But during the relative calm between 1919 and 1931, things of great significance were transpiring in the gold realm, much to the short-term benefit of the US but to the detriment of the rest of the world. Eventually including America.

GOLD STERILIZATION

This is how former Fed Chair Ben S. Bernanke—a self-proclaimed expert on the Depression—puts it:.

> "...during the period in which the United States was on the gold standard, gold flows into and out of the United States were completely sterilized, and thus allowed to have no effect on the US monetary base."

It's important to understand the dynamics and the effect of gold sterilization fully, how it caused global monetary chaos (setting the stage for the Depression), and the parallels it has in the modern world.

So, what is Dr. Bernanke talking about?

In the years following the end of WWI, the US had been receiving excess gold inflows from its trading partners in the rest of the world. Under international agreement, the US was supposed to expand its currency supply to match the incoming gold, which would help correct trade imbalances. But it would also cause domestic inflation and dilute the strength of the dollar.

And that would slow the economy and rein in the burgeoning boom of the '20s.

This was intolerable to the bankers at the fledgling Federal Reserve, who saw an opportunity to flex their newly acquired muscles in their godlike role as inflation preventer. But what to do? Simple. The Fed just locked the excess gold away in Fort Knox. *Poof*, it was sterilized. For accounting purposes, it no longer existed.

Unethical, but pretty nifty.

This allowed the postwar American economic boom to continue expanding into a bubble by keeping US-manufactured goods cheap and encouraging exports. The burgeoning exports caused even more gold inflows, which the Fed would lock away, keeping our exports cheap, and so on, and so on.

But, in essence, the Fed was cheating. It cheated the world monetary system all through the '20s to keep them roaring. And it kept cheating into 1931 when the country—along with everyone else—was already beginning to be ravaged by a crippling deflation.

You see, sterilizing gold inflows wasn't just conveniently anti-inflationary in the US (during a time when the raging American economy should have created increasing inflation). Still, it was hugely *de*flationary for the rest of the world.

Since the outbreak of WWI, the US gold stock had grown from just over $1.5 billion to almost $5 billion—a staggering amount in those days. Now, there's only so much gold in the world, right? So, with so much of it disappearing into the sterile American black hole, it meant that, even with the new additions from mining, the rest of the world had to continuously adjust to an ever-dwindling supply of gold.

From here, I need to reprise my discussion of *fractional reserve banking* and international banking agreements. Fair warning: It does not involve simple math. But please bear with me and think this through. It's all a prequel to where we are today.

Currency reserves, or central bank reserves, are the asset (in the old days, gold) that the central bank (the Federal Reserve, in the US) uses to back the fiat currency it issues. Under a 40 percent reserve requirement (which originally meant gold), the Fed could print $50 worth of fiat currency for each $20 worth of gold in its vaults. Okay? The value of the currency reserve has been increased by a factor of 2½.

Not terrible... But it doesn't stop there. The $50 the Fed just printed is called "high-powered money," because it can itself be multiplied again and again through the second phase of fractional reserve when it enters the commercial banking system. Normally, commercial banks operate under a 10 percent reserve, i.e., those fifty high-powered dollars must be kept on hand against the possibility that depositors want to take their money out. But the bank can loan out nine times that amount in dollars that have no real existence outside of entries on a balance sheet. This is how—*abracadabra!*—$50 can grow to $500, all based on a mere $20 worth of gold in the vault.

If you or I tried this, I think you know what it'd be called: *fraud*. But back to the 1920s.

When a country settled an international transaction in gold, it was supposed to contract its money supply, not just by an amount equivalent to the gold paid out but by the inverse of the currency reserve ratio. Under a 40 percent reserve, a $20 payment to a foreign country in gold required $50 of currency to be pulled out of circulation. Moreover, if the banks were using that money to create loans. Bank assets must also be contracted by the inverse of the fractional reserve ratio, so now a $20 gold payment would cause the money supply in that country to contract by $500 theoretically.

None of this is easy to envision. If you follow it, however, then you can see how highly deflationary gold outflows were.

For everyone else, that is. Because the US wasn't playing by the rules, it was cheating.

Gold just kept flowing into the country, and then it would disappear into the Federal Reserve's vault. The Fed was sucking up gold from around the world like a giant vacuum cleaner, contracting the entire world's money supply while not decreasing the supply of dollars like it had agreed to do. Mission accomplished: the mandated domestic deflation was avoided and the inflationary economic boom was prolonged.

This could not end well. And it didn't. The fallout was the Great Depression, a direct result of the Federal Reserve's machinations.

But first, back over there across the Pond...

In 1925, the UK was grappling with deciding whether or not to return to the gold standard. Winston Churchill, Chancellor of the Exchequer at the time, was the decider. John Maynard Keynes—the economist responsible for most of the founding principles from which MMT evolved—was a trusted advisor. Keynes warned that the British pound would be overvalued if Britain returned to a gold standard at the prewar parity. Churchill ignored him and went ahead anyway, putting his country on a *gold exchange standard*. (A gold exchange standard differs from a strict gold standard in that the reserve country does not agree to exchange gold for currency with the general public, only with other central banks.)

Whenever a government attempts to dictate prices in a free market society, it creates an opportunity because free markets will always overwhelm the government dictates and win. Such was the case with the British pound and gold.

Under both the gold standard and the gold exchange standard, exchange rates are fixed or pegged, whereby a country's central bank stands ready to buy or sell any quantity of gold at a fixed price denominated in that country's currency. But prices within a country are set by the free market's discovery of the currency's quantity and velocity in that country.

That created a disconnect in Great Britain. Because it had printed so much currency during WWI, prices were far higher than the prewar exchange rate could tolerate for a proper balance of trade.

Britain's imports were too cheap, and her exports were too expensive. The resulting trade imbalance meant that Britain was buying more than it was selling to the rest of the world. When she bought from the rest of the world, she paid in gold. This was the source of much of the gold flowing into the vaults of the Federal Reserve.

Britain was at a serious crisis point by 1931. With the supply of gold diminishing more rapidly than the supply of currency, the fraud of fractional central banking, artificial currency pegs, and gold sterilization—all were in danger of being exposed. Because when a central bank runs out of gold but still has lots of currency (claim checks for gold) in circulation, it can no longer sell unlimited quantities of gold to maintain the peg or exchange rate.

Thus, before it runs out of gold, it must either devalue its currency or leave the gold standard. Otherwise, the emperor will be stripped of his clothes, and the true insolvency of that country will be laid bare for all to see.

Churchill never had to face the consequences of going on the gold exchange standard. But his successor as Chancellor of the Exchequer, Philip Snowden, did. What Churchill bequeathed the luckless Snowden was a triple whammy. He had to confront the debt and damage hangover from WWI, the diminishment of the Empire's status in the world, and a steep rise in the status of the US dollar. But more than that, he was also presented with a terrible challenge to the strength of his country's money.

With no real choice, Snowden did what he had to do.

In the words of economist/historian Murray Rothbard, on September 21, 1931, Great Britain, "the government that induced Europe to go onto the treacherous shoals of the gold bullion and gold exchange standard during the 1920s, that inducted the United States government to inflate through foreign investment, that tried to establish sterling as the world's premier currency, surrendered and went off the gold standard without a fight... throwing the world into monetary chaos, and disrupting world markets."

Snowden resigned a month later and denounced capitalism as unethical and to champion the establishment of a British socialist utopia.

Didn't happen. But other European nations soon followed Britain's lead with regard to gold. As a result, governments, businesses, and private investors from around the world began to fear that the US might join the flight from the gold standard.

Suddenly, there was a panicked dash for old-fashioned cash. Everyone was trying to convert their dollar-denominated assets (investments) into dollars and convert those dollars into gold. Within the US, banks were running out of gold coins, and at the same time, tremendous outflows of gold began to leave the Federal Reserve's vaults, destined for far-off lands. But the Federal Reserve determined to put a stop to that.

The Fed reacted vigorously to stem the crisis. Less than three weeks after Britain threw in the towel, the Reserve Bank of New York raised its rediscount rate to 2.5 percent and a week later, to 3.5 percent, the sharpest rise within so brief a period in the whole history of the system, then or since.

The move stopped the gold drain, but it also intensified internal financial difficulties and was accompanied by a spectacular increase in bank failures and runs on banks. In October of 1931 alone, 522 commercial banks with $471 million in deposits closed their doors. In the six months from August 1931 through January 1932, 1,860 banks with $1,449 million in deposits were suspended.

The Fed was willing to sacrifice all those banks with all those deposits and further clamp the brakes on the economy due to the higher cost of money.

Why? The Fed had plenty of gold to meet the demand. It had been sterilizing gold inflows for more than a decade. It had tons and tons of "excess" gold that it could have handed out like Santa Claus without having to contract the money supply one iota. So why?

Shamefully, the Fed was willing to plunge the country further into depression—a depression whose alarm bell had rung with the stock market crash of October 1929, and that was rapidly going from agonizing to unbearable—simply to protect their precious gold.

As bank failures increased and the Fed refused to budge, the US economy went into free fall. From March of 1931 to mid-1932, wholesale prices fell at an annual rate of 14 percent, income at a rate of 31 percent, and production at 32 percent. Price declines can be sweet for a while, but they lose their appeal when your income is contracting more than twice as fast. Conversely, people long for inflation provided that their incomes are keeping pace.

As 1932 dragged on, the whole country could see the effects of a deflationary depression, even if most people couldn't put a name to it. Nearly everyone was desperate for leadership that could pull the economy out of the seemingly bottomless hole in which it had fallen.

Enter their "savior."

FDR

As the Depression progressively deepened, President Hoover got the heave-ho from voters, and Franklin Roosevelt was elected in 1932.

Now, any deep discussion of the Depression and FDR's response to it is way beyond this work's scope. Many whole books have been written debating the subject. For our narrower purposes, what matters is FDR's attack on gold.

He didn't wait long. On April 5, 1933, just a month after his inaugural address, Roosevelt took the nation off the gold standard.

What he did was declare a National Emergency and issue *Executive Order 1602*, by which:

- all gold coins, gold bullion, and gold certificates (over $100) were to be turned in to the Federal Reserve banks by May 1
- those who had special gold coin collections or needed the gold for industrial or professional use were exempted
- as gold coins, gold bullion, or gold certificates were turned in, each ounce was valued at $20.67, and the American people

would receive Federal Reserve notes redeemable in silver at that exchange rate

- violation of the order was punishable by fines up to $10,000 (the equivalent of nearly $200,000 today) or up to ten years in prison, or both

However, Roosevelt said that gold "is essential only for the payment of international trade balances," and foreign parties' convertibility was preserved. Thus, like Churchill before him, FDR was going to try the very same type of gold exchange standard that had just spectacularly failed across the Pond.

A day later, FDR closed the banks in response to a run on the gold reserves at the Federal Reserve Bank of New York. By the time banks reopened on March 13, they had turned in all their gold to the Federal Reserve. Neither they nor any private citizen could any longer redeem dollars for gold, and no one but the government could export gold.

What did Roosevelt hope to accomplish? Let's give him the benefit of the doubt and assume that he had the country's best interests at heart. So, he wanted ultimately to end the Depression and get America moving forward again. When he was campaigning, he believed that balancing the budget was important, that it would create confidence in consumers, business, and the markets, thereby encouraging investment and economic expansion. But after he became president, he radically shifted gears and came to believe, like Keynes, that inflation was the cure, i.e., extra money injected into the economy would get it going.

Big-time inflation is not possible under the gold standard, so it had to go. Thus, on January 30, 1934, the Gold Reserve Act ratified Executive Order 1602 into law. It forbade the private ownership of gold, except for jewelry and coin collections. It prohibited the private export of gold. It removed gold as legal tender and halted domestic convertibility. It allowed the government to pay its debts in dollars, not gold, and authorized the president to establish the dollar's gold value by proclamation. Obligingly, FDR unilaterally proclaimed an increase in the price of gold from $20.67 per ounce to $35 per ounce.

FDR justified this move by saying (a bit disingenuously) that, "since there was not enough gold to pay all holders of gold obligations...the Government should in the interest of justice allow none to be paid in gold."

Be that as it may, this was the net result: Those who had turned in their gold in good faith were out of luck. The silver dollar certificates they received had been devalued by 70 percent. Or, to put it another way, FDR succeeded in inflating the money supply by that amount. This gave him an infusion of resources to finance his visionary government programs that were designed to put people back to work.

Importantly, all of these shenanigans applied only to Americans. Under the gold exchange standard, foreigners could still settle debts in gold and freely swap gold for dollars and vice versa. That would continue to be the case for another thirty-seven years.

One consequence was that foreigners stampeded into US currency, which was already pretty desirable and had suddenly become even more so. They were only too happy to exchange their gold for dollars at this more-favorable rate. In addition, American gold miners were highly incentivized to produce more of the metal and deposit it with the government. For these reasons, the country's gold reserves swelled, and that underpinning made the dollar stronger. Even so, the US continued to struggle economically, for reasons economists have debated ever since and which are beyond the scope of this book.

But I do have to add that staying on the gold exchange standard far longer than anyone else was a major factor in establishing the dollar's global strength, which it has maintained from FDR straight through to today's world of MMT.

TRICKY DICK

Next came the last great global conflict, World War II.

Now it may seem perverse to just skim over the most devastating conflict ever fought, one which was truly worldwide for the first time. But what came *after* the war was more important in monetary history.

Here's what you need to know: As if I haven't emphasized this enough, wars are expensive, and they cannot be financed with tax receipts only. Participant nations always have to go into debt. For the US, that meant deficit spending ran the federal debt up to a 1945 peak of 112 percent of GDP.

Amazingly, at least to modern eyes, the nation speedily paid down its debt after the war. Partly this was due to fiscal conservatism, but it was largely the result of the economic boom that commenced with the return to the workplace of millions of GIs in addition to the millions of newly working women who remained employed. The GI Bill spread higher education far wider than it had ever been before, and that led to a better-educated workforce capable of continual technological breakthroughs.

The economy hummed; pent-up demand for goods and services that had been stifled by forced wartime rationing exploded; the middle class grew like gangbusters. By the mid-'50s, the debt had been halved from its peak, and from 1968 to '84, it remained below 40 percent of GDP. After that, it rose steadily for fifteen years, dipped with the 2000 recession, and then took off for the moon.

Deficit spending during the war had necessarily been so high that no one dreamed it would ever be approached in peacetime. The year 1945 would endure as the all-time apogee, everyone thought.

But then, no one anticipated MMT. For the first time since the war, federal debt eclipsed 100 percent of GDP in 2013. After noodling around for the next six years, it then began an assault in earnest on the WWII peak of 121 percent—and blasted right past it. As of the beginning of 4Q20, federal debt stood at 138 percent of GDP—and is headed inexorably higher.

As with World War I, America emerged from WWII with its infrastructure pretty well intact, while the European combatants had leveled much of each other's countries. The US was the world's leading power, so there was no surprise over the pivotal Bretton Woods agreement.

Anticipating the coming Allied victory, representatives from the US and forty-three other countries met in Bretton Woods, New Hampshire, in July of 1944. They gathered together to determine how postwar commercial and financial relations would work.

The agreement they reached established a gold exchange standard whereby each signatory nation's currency had a fixed parity to the dollar, which itself was pegged to, and could be exchanged for, gold at $35 per ounce. The American dollar was thereby formally anointed to the position it really already held: the world's reserve currency.

That worked fine—for a while. Other countries were taking in a lot of dollars in international trade, the US was paying down the bulk of its war-incurred debt, the domestic economy was strong, and the buck was solid.

The primary circulating paper money was "silver certificates," which stated that the note's face value was "on deposit in the Treasury" of the USA. They could be redeemed for that metal at the owner's discretion. Also circulating were Federal Reserve notes—which simply promised to pay face value "to the bearer on demand." These were redeemable, too. So, for all practical purposes, the US was on a silver standard, at least domestically.

But even that eroded over time. By 1964, all silver had been removed from dimes and quarters. The silver content of half dollars was first reduced by more than 50 percent and then eliminated. Physical silver dollars still circulated and were commonly used in commerce, but no new ones were minted after 1935. (It had been quite the long run, hadn't it? From 1794 to 1935, nearly *900 million* silver dollars were coined.)

In June of 1968, President Lyndon Johnson finally bowed to the inevitable, proclaiming that henceforth all US currency—Federal Reserve Notes and silver certificates alike—were merely fiat money. They were legal tender but could not be redeemed for anything.

However, the gold exchange standard put into place by FDR remained in effect. Dollars could still be swapped for gold in the international marketplace. Washington felt it important to preserve the appearance that its paper money was "backed" by a considerable gold stash at Fort Knox. That made the country look stronger—and propped up the dollar—since the US was the last major nation to have preserved full convertibility (even though it would never have had enough actual gold to redeem all the paper dollars floating around the world).

Maintaining such a fiction was easy enough to do while the dollar was strong. But in the 1960s, the problem with the United States dollar was that it had been so strong, so good, for so long.

Internationally, everyone used the dollar as their reserve because the dollar was actually a warehouse receipt valued on that piece of paper for a certain amount of gold, and everybody needed that.

Well, the French—and particularly their president, Charles de Gaulle—knew full well that the US government didn't have remotely enough gold to back the paper dollars it was issuing.

So, de Gaulle called the American bluff, more or less. He said, "Okay, this is what this receipt says. It says if I turn these in, I'm going to get an ounce of gold for each thirty-five of them." Then the French started sending their dollars back to the United States and draining its gold reserves. It all came to a head at the start of the '70s.

And it wasn't just the French. As the longstanding Bretton Woods agreement began to collapse, other nations (like Britain and Germany) began to wonder if a cash-strapped and debt-crazed United States was in any kind of financial shape to be leading the global economy.

The gold drain (and declining confidence in the buck) unnerved the new US president, Richard Nixon, who worried what would happen to the American economy if there were a full-out run on gold. He was no econ savant, so he turned to his best counselors at the time. They were advising him that there was no way out; he had to renege on that promise of convertibility.

It was, in essence, a default on the nation's obligations. Humiliating.

But on August 15, 1971, Nixon capitulated, saying simply, "We are no longer honoring the dollar based upon the gold standard." Nixon canceled gold convertibility for everyone, not just France. The event is commonly referred to as "closing the gold window," and it resulted in a steep decline in the value of the dollar on world markets.

True, the rest of the world had gone off the gold exchange standard decades earlier—Canada and Britain in 1931, France in 1936. But gold still ruled because the American dollar, the world's reserve currency, was pegged to it. The year 1971 marked the beginning of the end of the gold standard, even in the minimal way it was still practiced in the US.

The dollar itself was quickly and officially devalued, with a repricing of gold from $35/ounce to $38/ounce in 1972, and then to $42.23/ounce in '73. That was possible for the government to do because it was still in control. Private ownership of gold remained forbidden to American citizens so that no free market could develop, and gold was prevented from discovering its true value based on consumer sentiment and the laws of supply and demand.

In March of '73, Congress made it official, declaring that the American dollar was no longer backed by anything except the government's full faith and credit. It was still "legal tender," but it would be allowed to float untethered to anything. Simultaneously, most of the other major countries adopted a floating exchange-rate system for their currencies.

The most momentous effect of this policy change was that it opened the dollar-printing floodgates. No longer constrained in any way by a physical backing, the government was free to issue new "money" to its heart's content, by the trillions of units.

It was the final triumph of the inflationists. Or, as Nixon aptly put it: "We're all Keynesians now."

Washington kept its firm grip on the gold price for just a little while longer.

But the final nail was hammered into the gold standard's coffin on January 1, 1975, when President Ford ended the government's price-fixing monopoly and permitted American citizens once again to purchase and own gold. That created today's gold market, where the metal is like any other commodity. An ounce is worth precisely whatever someone is willing to sell it for and someone else is willing to pay for it.

It turns out it was a lot more than $42.23. From that point at the beginning of '75, gold soared to a high of $850 in January of 1980. One way of stating that is to say that gold had been undervalued by over 1,900 percent. Another point of view is that the US dollar had been similarly overvalued.

THE PETRODOLLAR

As the gold standard was in its death throes, the Nixon administration had another major worry: In the absence of convertibility, how could the dollar hold onto its status as the reserve currency of the world? After all, American hegemony depended on a strong (and somewhat artificial) global demand for the US dollar. Maintaining that demand was vital if the US continued propping up its "welfare and warfare" state, addicted to ever-increasing deficit spending. A dollar that tumbled off of the top of the heap would be devastating to the American economy.

Nixon was determined to prevent that from happening. But what to do? He hunkered down with his secretary of state—Henry Kissinger, who was dedicated to the doctrine of American exceptionalism—and together, they hatched a bold plan.

At the time, the world oil supply was largely controlled by the Organization of Petroleum Exporting Countries (OPEC), a confederation headed up by its leading producer, Saudi Arabia. So off Kissinger went to meet up with the Saudi sheiks.

It was an unlikely pairing, the Middle Eastern Muslim oligarchs and the American Jew who had fled Hitler's Germany. But somehow, it worked. Over the next couple of years, a series of meetings culminated in a June 1974 agreement between the US and Saudi Arabia. By the terms of the accord, the Saudis would get:

1. **American military protection for their oil fields.** This was the big key since Sunni Muslim Saudi Arabia was no match, militarily, for powerful neighbors like Shi'ite-majority Iran and Iraq—two nations that might conceivably covet Saudi oil enough to invade. (True, Saddam Hussein's minority Sunnis ruled over the Shi'ites in Iraq and was about to go to war with Iran, but the Saudis couldn't count on the status quo forever.)
2. The US also agreed to provide the Saudis, *in perpetuity*, with all the sophisticated weaponry they might need to modernize and continually upgrade their military.
3. The US guaranteed to restrain any attacks from neighboring Israel.

That was a godsend. And all the Americans wanted in return?

1. The Saudis must agree to price all of their oil sales **in US dollars only**.
2. The Saudis would invest their surplus oil proceeds **in US debt securities**.

Really?

The sheiks thought it was the best deal ever. The Americans were offering to throw a protective umbrella over the country, hold its many enemies at bay, preserve the monarchic dictatorship, and ensure the Saudi economy's stability—which flourished in that desolate kingdom of sand only because its vast underground oil reserves were the world's largest—and all Saudi Arabia had to do was perpetuate a system of international trade that was already pretty much in place.

Thus, was born the *petrodollar*. It was a boon to the Saudis and turned out to be a game-changer for the US. Within a year, the rest of OPEC had followed suit, and the US dollar once again solidified its post-WWII status as the global reserve currency.

The Nixon/Kissinger solution was quite the accomplishment, brilliant yet breathtakingly simple:

The world ran on oil—not only the developed world but also those dirt-poor nations that were just beginning to emerge from eons of poverty and needed energy to fuel growth. Everyone wanted the new gold, which was black instead of yellow. To get it, every country had to raise the dollars needed to buy it. They would—in many cases quite literally—do *anything* they had to do. Since the US had maintained an iron control over the energy market, this meant a soaring demand for the greenback, which has never waned. It also ensured that the goods flooding into the US were priced as favorably as possible to keep those precious dollars flowing to the exporter. In one fell swoop, America's lofty standard of living was preserved for decades to come.

Everything was coming up roses, with only a single negative side effect. As Americans gorged themselves on cheap imports, the domestic manufacturing sector took it on the chin.

But that's another story.

TODAY

The 1980 maximum gold price, inflation-adjusted, has never been seen again. (It would come to about $2,660 in 2020 dollars.) But without the restraint on government spending that's imposed by a gold standard, the Fed has cranked out currency far above demand. This means serious inflation, aka the erosion of the dollar. What cost $1 in 1971 now costs $6.37. That's cumulative inflation of 537 percent; or, looked at the opposite way, the dollar has lost 85 percent of its 1971 purchasing power.

This is one of the goodies the Fed—exercising its mandate to promote "moderate," controlled inflation—has blessed us with. At the same time, Fed members have exhibited a truly mind-boggling inability to comprehend the basics of what is going on in the economy. Here are just a couple of recent examples:

In July 2007, Ben Bernanke was the chairman of the Federal Reserve's Open Market Committee, aka *the people who make the most important monetary decisions in the country*. This is what Dr. Bernanke said at the time: "Overall, the US economy seems likely to expand at a moderate pace over the second half of 2007, with growth then strengthening a bit in 2008."

Then, in early 2008, when everything was coming apart at the seams, Bernanke assured us that "The Federal Reserve is not currently forecasting a recession" and that the federal housing agencies Fannie Mae and Freddie Mac "would make it through the storm."

Within months, Fannie Mae and Freddie Mac had collapsed, the economy had fallen into the harshest downturn since the Great Depression, and the entire financial system was so close to seizing up entirely that only the infusion of hundreds of billions in federal loan money was able to stave off a catastrophe. It bought some time.

But now, twelve years later, in 2020, at the end of this long and winding road, we have come to MMT.

The Fed and the Treasury Department have responded to the latest disaster—the coronavirus crisis and the accompanying recession—in the only way they seem to know: throw ungodly amounts of money at it. Beyond that, they have crushed interest rates down to near zero in defiance of what a free market would do. (They are even considering *negative interest rates*, which would be an unmitigated disaster, as I explained in Chapter 3.)

So, what happens in the aftermath of the creation of so many *trillions* of new currency units?

Well, we don't know. We just don't know.

We know that the notion that a comparable amount of gold should back paper currency was tried in every major country and prevailed for hundreds of years. It worked. It facilitated free trade and a long arc of prosperity unique in the human experience. All but the most diehard gold-bug economists now agree that the gold standard being dead is a good thing, that having a hard-backed currency would stifle progress in the modern world. They're probably right, but it doesn't matter. As I've been saying all along, MMT is the designated solution to all monetary problems—and it isn't going anywhere.

In other words, as I stated in Chapter 5, the gold standard isn't coming back any time soon.

Nevertheless, the US government continues to maintain a gold reserve of over 8,000 metric tons—about 256 million troy ounces—worth about $500 billion. China and Russia have been growing their own reserves by leaps and bounds in recent years. Perhaps—as with the personal gold that I encourage everyone to own—governments still see the metal as the ultimate hedge against current and future inflation.

However, as our current problems shake out, we are likely in for a roller coaster ride over the next couple of decades. Multitudes see a future as bleak as that envisioned by economist and constitutional law expert Dr. Edwin Vieira Jr. Dr. Vieira has issued a warning of the dire consequences of continuing down this path. He writes:

"So, the question is not 'Will the present domestic and international monetary and banking systems split apart at their seams?' but whether, in the course of their inevitable unraveling, they will drag this whole country—the real America, the America, which was once worth the price of admission, the America which used to be a beacon of hope for the entire world—down with them."

I acknowledge the dangers, Dr. Vieira, but I have a very different vision, the one that I've laid out in this book, which sees an unprecedented increase in world prosperity, spurred on by the Rise of America.

As you can see from this Appendix, the history of money in the US—as with every country, really—has lots of twists and turns, of ideas tried and abandoned, of shifting public sentiments.

Expect the same with MMT.

Nobody knows how this experiment will end; we'll have to wait and see. But of this, I'm sure: the nations that will prosper will be the ones that do not depend on others for credit, critical elements, and energy—led by America.

APPENDIX II

THE MATHEMATICAL DERIVATION OF GBOES

IF YOU DON'T KNOW CALCULUS, YOU CAN SKIP THIS SEC-tion. I've summarized my conclusions in plain text in Chapter 6. But I include the calculations for all my math nerd friends!

So, green energy production and reserves are calculated in megawatts (MW).

Since the megawatt hour is a unit of energy, and BOEs are based on energy, we just need to do a little unit conversion to transform megawatts into GBOEs (green barrels of oil equivalents).

For example, let's say we have a geothermal power plant. Geothermal energy production works by using steam from the earth to make turbines spin.

We have to assume that our geothermal power plant operates at a specific capacity (for this exercise, let's use 100 percent capacity), 365 days a year, twenty-four hours a day. Then we can take a megawatt year and convert it into kilowatt hours.

Here's how the math works out:

$$1 \text{ MW} \times \text{year} \times \frac{1000\text{kW}}{1\text{MW}} \times \frac{365 \text{ days}}{\text{year}} \times \frac{24 \text{ hours}}{\text{day}} = 8{,}760{,}000\text{kWh}$$

- Our megawatt year of green power is now 8.76 million kilowatt hours (kWh). Now we convert kilowatt hours into megajoules using the defined ratio:

$$8{,}760{,}000\text{kWh} \times \frac{3.6\text{MJ}}{1\text{kWh}} = 31{,}536{,}000\text{MJ}$$

- Now we can convert to green BOEs, using the definition of a BOE as 6.12×10^3 MJ.

$$31{,}536{,}000\text{MJ} \times \frac{1 \text{ BOE}}{6.12 \times 10^3 \text{ MJ}} = 5{,}154 \text{ BOE}$$

- All cleaned up, the conversion goes like this:

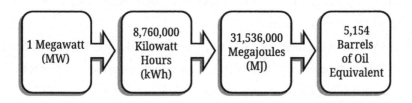

- Now we know that one megawatt of green power produced over one year is equivalent to 5,154 barrels of oil per year—or fourteen barrels of oil per day.

With that equation in mind, let's crunch some numbers on overall well potential.

To model the production from a geothermal well, we use a harmonic decline. In the equation below, P represents the well productivity, G represents initial geothermal well productivity, and Di represents the constant harmonic decline.

$$P = \frac{P_0^G}{1 + D_i t}$$

We took three realistic decline rates and modeled the one-hundred-year production from a geothermal well that started at 175 MW, or 901,950 GBOE per year. If we want to do the same for a wind or solar farm, we can just replace the MW number.

This is the key part of Katusa's GBOE production. We need to make the production comparable on an apples-to-apples basis. To do this, we have to bring in some calculus. To calculate the cumulative production over the first T_1 years, we use an integral:

Cumulative BOE production over T_2 years =

$$\int_0^{T_2} P_0^0 e^{-\delta t} dt = \frac{P_0^0}{\delta} - \frac{P_0^0 e^{-\delta T_2}}{\delta}$$

Now: how would a comparable oil well look?

The question we have to ask ourselves is this: What initial production rate would an oil well need if it were going to produce the same cumulative number of BOEs over its much-shorter lifespan?

To calculate that, we need to model the production from an oil well. The equation below does just that, with initial oil well productivity and the exponential decline rate—which we set at 14 percent because of the average conventional oil well decline rate.

$$P = P_o^O e^{-\delta t}$$

Again, to calculate cumulative production over the first T_2 years, we use an integral:

Cumulative GBOE production over T_1 years =

$$\int_0^{T_1} \frac{P_o^G}{1+D_i t}\, dt = \frac{P_o^G}{D_i} \ln(1 + D_i T_1)$$

This is done so the "oil patch" executives and investors can figure out how much oil a well would have to gush *initially* to produce the same number of BOEs over its lifespan as a geothermal well (or any solar or wind farm) can produce over its much longer lifespan.

These lifespans vary, so we chose three representative values for each kind of well. For the oil wells, we looked at lifespans of ten, fifteen, and twenty years. For the geothermal wells, we chose twenty, fifty, and one hundred years.

Now we set our cumulative production equations equal to each other, insert decline rates (1.75 percent for the harmonic geothermal decline and 14 percent for the exponential oil decline), and run through our well lifespans (T_1 = 20, 50, and 100 and T_2 = 10, 15, and 20).

But before any of that can happen, we need investors to wake up to the fact that green energy is economic in the present energy matrix.

The math I've presented is completely sound and correct.

- The math that allows natural gas to be included on the financial books as BOE (barrels of oil equivalent)
- It also allows for green energy produced from a solar, wind, or geothermal field to be included.

As noted in Chapter 6, once the concept of GBOEs is widely adopted—which it will be—then expressing a company's green energy holdings in conventional terms becomes possible. And an investor then has a relatively easy way to determine just how valuable that company's green projects are compared with its fossil fuel ventures.

APPENDIX III

THE INTERNATIONAL
URANIUM MARKET

THE REALITIES OF THE GLOBAL URANIUM MARKETPLACE are complicated, especially from the US point of view. I didn't want to get sidetracked with all the ins and outs in Chapter 6. But they do bear on the Rise of America. So, for those interested, I'll spell it out in detail here.

As noted in Chapter 6, American uranium production is moribund. It could be started up again, but mining is not profitable at the current price of $30/pound (something more like $45–$50/pound is needed for ISR projects and closer to $60/pound for conventional mining). And even when US mines were producing, the bulk of the country's uranium needs (over 90 percent) still had to be filled by imports.

This has meant doing business with Russia and their allies from the former Soviet Union (FSU).

THE RUSSIAN-AMERICAN CONNECTION

In 1993, the two countries signed a twenty-year agreement popularly known as the "Megatons to Megawatts" program. Under the terms of the deal, Russia would down-blend 500 metric tonnes of high-enriched uranium (HEU)—enough to build 20,000 nuclear warheads—and convert the material to low-enriched uranium (LEU) that would be sold to the US to be used as fuel by American nuclear power plants. (HEU is weapons-grade uranium; LEU can't be used for bombs.)

That agreement came on the heels of the 1991 signing of the Soviet-US Strategic Arms Reduction Treaty (START I), which mandated a reduction of the two countries' nuclear weapons stockpiles by approximately 5,000 warheads apiece. That deal had a nice feel-good quality to it, but it was really just a commercial deal. The US got a steady supply of relatively cheap uranium. Russia—which was in dire economic straits amid the chaos from the breakup of the Soviet Union—got a projected $12 billion in a coveted hard currency.

Megatons to Megawatts ended, as planned, in December of 2013. But another program was running concurrently. In 1992 the US Department of Commerce signed the *Russian Suspension Agreement* (RSA) with the Russian Federation's Ministry for Atomic Energy, the predecessor to today's ROSATOM. This agreement suspended an anti-dumping investigation against Russia in exchange for a quota limit on Russian uranium imports.

Despite these two programs having worked out well, Washington is always wary about anything to do with Russia. It almost goes without saying that uranium is considered a resource vital to national security. Next to its military, one could argue that the American energy sector is the nation's most important. Without it, hospitals aren't powered, airports don't work, and defense systems are inoperable. Within the system, uranium energy is baseload power. It's a crucial contributor to keeping the lights on.

Given uranium's critical role in energy production, the US government has—with an understandable sense of precaution—determined that the country shouldn't become too heavily dependent on supply from an adversary that might not have America's best interests at heart. Like...well, Russia. Diversification was long ago deemed to be very important to national security.

Thus, under the RSA, the importation of Russian uranium into the US was limited to 20 percent of the country's yearly supply needs. The RSA has been amended as market and geopolitical conditions changed, with the latest version having been agreed upon in October 2020, covering the next twenty years.

The stated goal is to protect America's energy and national security interests and limit Russia's ability to manipulate America's uranium markets while reducing Russian uranium imports.

Under the new twenty-year amended agreement, Russian uranium enrichment imports are limited to an average of approximately 17 percent over the next twenty years and would be no higher than 15 percent starting in 2028. Limits for allowable Russian uranium concentrate imports contained in enriched uranium were set at an even lower level (7 percent of US demand through 2040).

THE CURRENT SUPPLY CHAIN

Now, where does today's uranium come from? Well, among the important producers are Namibia (largely controlled by China), Australia, Niger, Russia, and Canada. But the top dog, by far, is Kazakhstan, part of the former Soviet Union. To the uranium market, Kazakhstan is like Saudi Arabia, Russia, and all OPEC are to the oil market, all rolled into one. The Kazakh state-run operation, Kazatomprom, is the largest, lowest cost uranium miner in the world. It produces over 40 percent of primary global uranium.

Kazakhstan uses a mining process called in-situ recovery (ISR), which is the cheapest way to get uranium out of the ground. In turn, this is one of the reasons why Kazakh uranium is cheap, especially when coupled with the economic benefits of its state sponsorship.

Once the Kazakh ISR miners extract uranium, in their case using low-Ph acid solutions, it must become concentrated, converted, and enriched before it can be put to use in nuclear fuel applications. Raw uranium ore is almost all U_{238}. That's inert. Only about 0.7 percent is U_{235}, which is the fissile isotope of the element necessary for the sustainable nuclear reactions that heat and boil water in a power plant. So, first of all, the stable compound U_3O_8 is extracted from the ore (this is the "yellowcake" of popular parlance). It is then converted to a uranium hexafluoride gas, which is the feedstock for centrifuges in the enrichment process. This UF6 gas is spun through high-speed centrifuges that separate the U_{235} from the heavier U_{238} until the desired concentration is reached. Finally, the enriched gas is converted into the uranium dioxide that can be pelletized and placed in nuclear fuel assemblies. The LEU needed for most currently operating reactors is 4–5 percent U_{235}. (For bombs, you need super-refined HEU, which is about 90 percent U_{235}.)

A QUICK PRIMER ON ISR

ISR is the cheapest way to produce uranium because it does not involve the blasting, digging, hauling, and crushing of rock inherent in conventional open-pit or underground mines/mills.

ISR technology pumps sodium-bicarbonate (the equivalent of soda water) into porous rock that holds elevated uranium concentrations. The process oxidizes the uranium into a solution (washing it from the grains of sand), which is then pumped to the surface for ion-exchange recovery and processing into yellowcake. It is effectively a reversal of the natural processes that deposited the uranium in the first place. Accordingly, an ISR operation is more like a water-processing facility than a mine.

Here's the important point: Since Kazakhstan doesn't have enrichment facilities, it sends much of its uranium to, or through, Russia, which has the largest enrichment capacity on the planet. From there, the uranium finds its way to markets around the world, including the US, although sometimes in a rather circuitous fashion, as we shall see.

The official US Department of Energy analysis of US imports holds that 50 percent comes from pro-American nations: 20 percent from Australia; about 26 percent from Canada; and about 4 percent from other "somewhat friendlies." Of the second 50 percent, Russia supplies a maximum (under the RSA) of 20 percent, and the remaining 30 percent is from the FSU states of Kazakhstan and Uzbekistan, along with Chinese-aligned Namibia. Moreover, Russia directly controls a bulk of Kazakh production through Uranium One.

So, while the US limits annual Russian uranium imports to a fifth of the foreign total, half emanate from the Russian sphere of influence, after which most is funneled through Russian enrichment.

This is a situation that makes the US government uneasy, to

say the least. You can see why it gained the attention of the White House and Congress. Considering that half of imports come from countries who would be anti-American if push came to shove, Washington unsurprisingly sees this as a clear and present danger.

Remember that the domestic industry, while holding great potential, is uneconomical at current prices—and even in an emergency shortage, companies would need six to eighteen months to bring their mines back online. There's no master switch you can flip. Moreover, at best, US mines could produce only 10–15 million pounds per year from existing mines. Any more than that would require new mines, which require new permits, and the permitting process is a lengthy one.

Adding to US nervousness is the fact that that import number may, in fact, be understated.

THE URANIUM GAME

It's a matter of simple economics. Recall that Canada accounts for more than a quarter of US imports. But Cameco, the primary Canadian producer, had to shut down one of its major mines, McArthur River, in 2018, for economic reasons, despite its very low cost of production. It remains closed. Another major mine, Cigar Lake, was shut for six months in 2020.

This dramatically cut back its production, but Cameco still has to fulfill its contracts with global utilities, forcing it to secure uranium from non-Canadian sources. Not only did this resolve its inventory issues, but it represented a nice arbitrage opportunity for the company. By shutting in its North American production and sourcing from the market, it more rapidly draws down excess global supplies, while crystallizing a margin between the utility contract price and their purchase price.

Further complicating things is that Uranium One, formerly a Canadian miner and one of the world's largest, became a subsidiary of Russia's state-owned Rosatom in 2010 (its controlling interest is now 100 percent). Uranium One is in charge of Russian mining interests outside of Russia, which includes control of Russia's Kazakhstan interests and 20 percent of US uranium capacity in Wyoming as well. Within the Rosatom family, Uranium One is now controlled by Tenex, which markets Russia's enrichment supplies to global utilities. Tenex's supply of natural uranium comes from domestic mines in Siberia and Kazakh imports from Uranium One.

The Uranium One deal provoked a furor in the conservative media/political sphere, which alleged that the Democrats had sold out American interests in return for bribes paid to the Clinton Foundation. While some assert that the attempted cover-up of these "sins" were the genesis of the Clinton campaign's Russian collusion allegations to take down Trump, the Uranium One controversy has subsided without any criminal charges being filed to date.

But the network of Russian/US uranium interests remains hopelessly entangled. Even more so because there's another big player in the field, Centrus Energy. It is now fighting Tenex over quotas for LEU imports, and it plans to deploy a US-based, commercial-scale enrichment facility over the long term as market conditions recover. It's an American company, but it gets its uranium from, you guessed it, FSU (ultimately, Russian) sources. Without US government grants, Centrus's goal of supplying HALEU (High Assay Low Enriched Uranium, which is below weapons-grade enrichment but higher than current commercial enrichment levels) just won't happen. Currently, Centrus is a broker of enrichment services from the Russians, hence the fight over quota access with Tenex.

(See, I warned you this was going to get complicated. But there's more to come.)

With American vulnerability to its "enemies" now pretty fully exposed, several responses were initiated. One was the pressure on the Commerce Department from the US Congress and White House, to negotiate a more favorable version of the RSA that I mentioned earlier. Another was Section 232, which more famously resulted in the Trump administration imposing tariffs on foreign steel and aluminum imports.

This is a section of the Trade Expansion Act of 1962. It authorizes the Commerce Department to conduct investigations to determine the effect of imports on the national security. Investigations may be initiated based on an application from an interested party, a request from the head of any department or agency or may be self-initiated by the secretary of commerce.

In January 2018, two US domestic uranium mining and milling companies petitioned Commerce to investigate whether uranium imports from foreign state-owned enterprises pose a threat to national security. The department concluded that they did. But President Trump surprisingly didn't concur with the conclusion under the strict terms of the 232 investigation. While he chose not to order an imposition of quotas on imports, he acknowledged there was a national security issue with respect to uranium mining. As a result, he established the Nuclear Fuel Working Group (NFWG), under the Department of Energy, to "examine the current state of domestic nuclear fuel production to reinvigorate the entire nuclear fuel supply chain." In retrospect, this approach is proving to be more helpful to the industry and perhaps less likely to be undone by future administrations.

What's going on behind the scenes is this: domestic uranium producers need a higher price so that they can reopen closed mines and begin producing at a price that makes economic sense. In order to get what they wanted, they tried playing the America First/national security card with President Trump, whom they expected to be sympathetic.

The domestic miners did get sympathy for their cause, as the national security implications of America's overreliance on foreign supplies of critical minerals has become a broadly accepted, even bipartisan, concern. Then, why did it not translate into more concrete trade (tariff/quota) restrictions? Because there is an equally powerful counter-lobby, the nuclear utilities. They have long-term contracts with Russia's Tenex, which guarantee them low prices that Tenex itself has pushed down with undisciplined supply. The quota argument to Washington is that increased fuel costs from trade restrictions would impose additional financial burdens, potentially causing the premature shutdown of economically marginal nuclear power plants. So, the utilities would have preferred the RSA not be extended at all. This puts them directly at odds with the American producers.

Honestly, the utilities are being a bit disingenuous here. The fact is that say a $20 per pound price hike means little to them because once a reactor is up and running, the price of uranium makes up less than 5 percent of the operating costs—unlike natural gas, where fuel accounts for approximately 75 percent of the final generated electricity cost.

However, it could backfire on the utilities if this infatuation with cheap (perhaps dumped?) uranium destroys the viability and diversity of their uranium supply options going forward. As it stands, for much of 2020, the industry saw no production from Canadian and US mines as a result of the depressed market price. Perhaps more alarming, the economic incentives needed to develop the next generation of new uranium mines needed (globally) to meet rising demand and depleting resources will simply not be there in time. Such a supply shock could be further accelerated given current geopolitical conditions, with such a high concentration of supply in Russian hands or under their influence. Events in the Baltic, Mediterranean, and the Persian Gulf all come into play, not to mention Chinese ambitions in the South China Sea. Not exactly a time to be without reliable domestic supplies when 20 percent of America's electricity needs a secure uranium supply and 100 percent of US Naval Nuclear Propulsion requirements need US-origin uranium.

There is also the work of the NFWG to take into account. After over two years of deliberations, in April 2020, the interagency group released a report containing the recommendations the president asked for. The NFWG advocates for several actions starting in 2020, with continued implementation over ten years. An urgent measure, it states, is the expansion of US uranium reserves, which would have the effect of revitalizing the domestic industry and rectifying market distortion by state-owned entities. The president's proposed budget for fiscal year 2021 supported the plan, requesting $150 million per year for ten years to establish a strategic uranium reserve (similar to petroleum) that is stocked with domestically mined uranium and American conversion services. US Senate appropriators have included the strategic uranium reserve in their draft FY 2021 funding bills (@ the full $150 million—split between Energy/Water and Defense). The NFWG report also suggests considering the development and deployment of US uranium enrichment capacity, improving the competitiveness of US uranium and nuclear fuel/reactor suppliers. The Department of Energy has already announced significant funding in the form of grants and backstop guarantees for multiple small modular and advanced reactor designs.

Such funding spurs demand across the nuclear fuel cycle. Further, Russia has "aggressively" targeted the US market and "weaponized its energy supply as an instrument of coercion," the report concludes, and it promotes a reduced reliance on Russian uranium imports and a more competitive American nuclear industry at home and abroad. The latter is an important tool in American leadership in regions where China and Russia have already made significant inroads.

As you can plainly see, there are an awful lot of crosscurrents at work in this industry. At this point, the latest RSA amendment appears to be a reasonable compromise as far as Russian imports go. An increased Russian quota in the first three years is painful for US interests and seems counterintuitive to national security, but it doesn't disrupt US utilities' already-contracted supplies at a time in which they are facing their own economic challenges. However, beyond that, the allowed Russian imports drop substantially, especially in terms of the uranium component. I understand that this has already caused US utilities to begin thinking more strategically in terms of domestic uranium in their future supply portfolios. With regards to the Strategic Uranium Reserve, it appears to have strong, bipartisan support, as evidenced by its inclusion in the draft Senate FY 2021 appropriations bills. This very meaningful stimulus, targeted so specifically toward a near-term revitalization of the US uranium industry, will be welcomed by producers with advanced-stage and production-ready assets.

In line with that, my projection is for low prices to prevail for the next few years before trending higher again. Over 50 million pounds of uranium can be mined economically at a price as low as $20 per pound and another 50 million pounds that are economical at $35/pound.

But back to Kazakhstan. The movie *Borat* has portrayed the nation as a backward place for Americans. But the Kazakhs are actually quite a savvy folk. They are well aware that their control of 40 percent of world uranium production gives them a lot of clout. For years, they have indulged in a practice that I call *Cut 2 Kill*. The Uzbeks have also been playing along.

I picked up the phrase when reading about the way John D. Rockefeller operated in the late nineteenth and early twentieth centuries. As he grew to dominate the oil business through vertical integration, he was able to drive competitors out of the market by underpricing them. He could afford to lose money on the one hand if he knew he'd make it back on another. Cut prices to kill your opponents.

Likewise, with Kazakhstan and, to a lesser degree, Uzbekistan. They can depress prices any time they want by pushing more uranium into the market, and they've used that leverage in the past, in order to successfully cripple American producers.

Moreover, they are well aware of their F/X advantage. It goes hand in hand with *Cut 2 Kill*, and they exploit it. They pay for their mining operations in the local currency, the *tenge*, each of which is worth only a fraction of one US cent. This allows them to mine uranium on the ultra-cheap. But when they sell it, they do so in US dollars, greatly increasing their profit margins.

Despite all of the intersecting forces that have kept the uranium price down, I still believe that there will likely be a near-term bump for a couple of reasons.

IRAN

For one thing, there have been the impacts of Trump's Iran sanctions.

I don't think the market has quite figured out the implications of these. Sanctions are way more powerful than bullets, let's get that straight right away. And if Trump's Iran sanctions are continued, that will have ripple effects in the next few years that nobody is talking about. For example, it's not just sanctions against Iran. By definition, the sanctions mean that any company that does business with Iran—from selling computers to buying oil—can't work or do business with or in the USA.

That's a way bigger stimulus for the uranium market than Section 232 would ever be. Why? Because Iran is one of Russia's largest export markets for reactors, technology, and fuel, and the FSUs have also been known to supply uranium to the Iranians. So, Russia may be forced to choose; either dump Iran or dump America. Can't have both. And if China acts as an intermediary—that means, if you work with China—China gets slapped also in Trump's Iran sanctions (if the existing sanctions remain). Will Putin dump Iran? Not bloody likely! But perhaps in a post-Putin Russia, Iran could become vulnerable.

(A lot naturally depends on whether the incoming Biden administration maintains Trump's Iran sanctions, or reinstates the Obama-era deal, or does something else entirely. We have to wait and see.)

The irony in all of this is that the Ad Hoc Utilities Group (led by Exelon) actively lobbied against further sanctions on Iran (the largest state sponsor of terror) because of American overreliance on Russian nuclear fuel supplies. If the Iran sanctions hit Russia's Rosatom, the Utilities Group would be cut off from those supplies overnight. Exactly what the Nuclear Fuel Working Group report warned against.

This actually works to the benefit of both Russians and Kazakhs because you will see a pop in uranium's price if that happens.

And the other thing is: coronavirus.

THE VIRUS'S IMPACT

What effect is the pandemic having on global uranium production?

Numerous operations from Southern Africa to Saskatchewan were forced to take the worker health and safety precaution of shutting down uranium operations to prevent the spread of COVID-19.

For example, when the pandemic first hit, Kazakhstan shut down its biggest cities and declared a national emergency. Many of the state-owned uranium sites are in remote regions. Workers live in close quarters. It was in everyone's best interest that no one got sick or impacted their families and burdened rural hospitals.

Kazakhstan originally reduced uranium production in its twelve largest uranium ISR mines by 17.5 percent, which is about 11 million pounds of uranium (if annualized) gone offline. That's a big chunk of output.

Another major hit to global production was Cameco and Orano's early decisions to shut the Cigar Lake Mine and McClean Lake Mill. Coupled with the earlier economic decision to suspend McArthur River, Cameco was entirely without uranium production for much of the year. Now that mines in Kazakhstan and Canada have begun to open back up, we expect the total reduction impact on 2020 global output to reach about 20 million pounds. Any resurgence of the virus with additional lockdowns could extend the impact further, of course.

The thing is the virus has had ripple effects. It has caused shutdowns in mining itself and disruption in the chain that supplies drilling equipment, casings, chemicals, and the like.

Let's take a closer look:

One real benefit of having visited operations in Kazakhstan more than fifteen years ago is that I have seen what the bottlenecks were. It was never the uranium, but rather:

- Sulfuric acid
- Drilling and wellfield construction

Neither has been an issue in Kazakhstan since 2006. That was when Cigar Lake was delayed, and the price of uranium took off.

SULFURIC ACID

Sulfuric acid is important; it's used to break down and extract uranium from the raw ore. But there is no shortage of sulfuric acid globally. The two largest producers of sulfuric acid in the world are China (50 percent of global production) and the United States (25 percent). There may be short-term delivery and reagent issues in Kazakhstan. However, I do not see any long-term impact from short-term delivery issues.

DRILLING AND WELL INSTALLATIONS

During my site visit, I noticed it was the same driller at all the various projects. One company, VolkovGeology, does over 90 percent of the drilling in Kazakhstan.

For much of 2020, there were no drilling/wellfield installations at any of the producing ISR mines in Kazakhstan. For ISR projects, each new production zone needs new wells for injection and for retrieving the solution pregnant with uranium. So, a lot of wells need to be continuously drilled, cased, and completed at the operating mine to continue production.

Though the virus minimally impacted Kazakh uranium production in the first half of 2020, the lagging effect is significantly reducing output in Q3 and Q4. But the big knock-on effect of the virus is the well drilling, casing, and completion delays for 2021 production.

What does this all mean for Kazakhstan?

The virus has impacted 2020 uranium production; however, the real wild card is what the impact will be for 2021 uranium production in Kazakhstan—and, by extension, for the world since Kazakhstan is the major global supplier. Let me elaborate...

There is roughly a six- to nine-month lag between drilling and completing a uranium ISR well and the well reaching commercial production. So, downtime in drilling affects future quarters' production, rather than today's or next week's.

There is a significant difference between bringing on a conventional rock-moving mine versus an ISR project. In an ISR project, after you get back to drilling and injecting the sulfuric acid solution into the deposit, it takes up to three months for the reservoir to build up again and allow for the solution to become impregnated with the uranium to make it ready to be pulled up and for production to resume.

But the Kazakhs are as resourceful as they come. Once they can start drilling, casing, and completing the wells, there will be no shortage of drill rigs or workers to get production caught up for 2022. Having said that, they have reconfirmed the 20 percent economic-driven reductions to licensed capacity to continue through at least 2022.

The big question right now is the possible pinch in 2021 production. I've been watching potential supply chain issues in sulfuric acid and well casings, but thus far, I do not see any long-term issues.

Cameco has bought about 26 million pounds throughout 2020 to cover its contract book and COVID-19 production reductions and add to its inventory levels for delivery commitments. With an annual contract book of about 36 million pounds. and production from Cigar Lake at about 18 million pounds, it looks like it will need to buy another 18 million pounds in the market to meet its sales contracts in 2021, assuming McArthur remains shut. The Kazakhs have also been recent buyers in the spot market with their reduced production rates. These activities will eat through some of the above-ground inventories and help accelerate the fundamental rebalancing.

To sum up, I believe global 2020 production will be lower by approximately 20 million pounds than previously expected due to the forced COVID-19 shutdowns. It still remains to be seen, however, how quickly these mines ramp back up. Regardless, the annual gap between production and consumption has grown to over 60 million pounds in 2020. Global production for 2021 is expected to be at about 135 million pounds, leaving a gap of 44 million pounds in 2021 compared to utility demand. However, this could be a larger deficit if production cannot resume to early-2020 levels. The magnitude of these gaps is unstainable, with inventories and other secondary supplies a limited, finite resource. Coupled with strong growth in new reactor construction, this bodes well for a rising uranium market that has only recently begun to emerge from a profound nine-year bear market.

As I have predicted, the recovery in uranium prices has been painfully slow due to the drawdown of excess secondary supplies, made worse by previous overproduction, and there will probably be a relatively sharp near-term bump up for all of the reasons elaborated above. The spot price in 2020 already saw a welcome 25 percent increase early in the year but has traded sideways or slightly down since June 2020. The longer these conditions remain, the higher the probability of volatile recovery, so we will continue to closely watch these fundamentals.

However, this all plays out, the reality is that the Rise of America must be partly fueled by nuclear power. Unquestionably. Which means a source for the raw material, uranium, must be secured. And that means the country will do whatever it takes to secure it. Whomever is in the White House, there has been a growing realization that a lower, or even no-carbon-energy future cannot be achieved without a significant contribution from, and growth of, nuclear power.

APPENDIX IV

HOW TO PROFIT DURING
THE RISE OF AMERICA

AS YOU KNOW BY NOW, *THE RISE OF AMERICA* IS NOT A book of investment advice. Nevertheless, in my twenty-year career in the natural resource sector, I have learned a thing or two worth sharing. So now—for those readers who are active investors, and especially those attracted to natural resources—let me turn to some of the specifics of my investment philosophy and strategies.

To begin with, of course I know that COVID-19 has thrown a monkey wrench into every market. Neither I nor anyone else can predict all of the consequences of the virus (nor of the violence exploding in the streets), especially in the near term. But it's important to keep in mind that *we've entered a* changed *world, not a completely* new *one.*

- I believe that long term, this too shall pass.
- I believe that the future of money and finance are clear, as I explained earlier.

- I believe that neither the US dollar nor the markets are going bust.
- I believe that China will not rule the world any time soon.
- I believe there are great days ahead and that we will witness the Rise of America, for reasons I introduced at the outset and summed up in Chapter 8.

Okay. To be a successful investor or speculator, you must govern yourself according to a set of rules. And there is no better core principle than the one made famous by Warren Buffett, history's most successful investor. I made it the cornerstone of my own investing career:

Rule No. 1: Never lose money.

Rule No. 2: Never, ever ignore Rule No. 1.

This can be said another way. Cut your losses quickly. If the reason you invested in a company changes, it's time to sell your stock and move on. When you succeed in cyclical sectors such as mining or energy, it's critical to remember to reduce your risk by taking your principal investment off the table and let the balance of a successful speculation ride out.

And above everything else, only invest in the best management teams within the sector.

Many investors and speculators forget how to put these rules into practice. They get sucked up in the latest euphoria, especially if they're inside of their first boom cycle. There are common mistakes that new investors make over and over again, causing them to miss out on big gains and suffer catastrophic losses.

One of the most important themes of this Appendix is how

to adhere to Buffet's Rule and avoid those mistakes—especially within my personal domain, the natural resource sector. I chose to specialize in this market because it offers investing rewards, if you're careful and disciplined, that frequently and dramatically exceed those to be found anywhere else.

You too can make money here. But you have to follow some guiding principles. Though I'll be talking about the resource sector, those principles are generally adaptable to most small-cap markets.

What follows is a distillation of all the resource market knowledge I've acquired over my twenty years in the business—as a successful analyst, project financier, developer, and hedge fund manager who always has his own skin in the game. I started with nothing and worked my way up the sector's ladder of success. If I could do it, so can you. Hopefully, sharing my knowledge will help you achieve your goals.

This is a real nuts-and-bolts section, so let's get right to it.

KATUSA'S KEYS

Investing in the resource sector has huge potential rewards.

But I won't sugarcoat it—there are also huge risks.

Many resource companies simply aren't worth the paper their shares are printed on. They might have incompetent managers, low-quality (or nonexistent) assets, questionable accounting (yes, there are plenty of crooks in the biz), or all three. They aren't worth your time or your money. Knowledgeable and invested management teams are absolutely critical for a successful project. In mining, more so than in any other business, it all comes down to the people.

So, some resource firms are useless; others are great investments that can multiply your money manyfold. But how do separate one from the other?

Again, I'm not in the sugarcoating business.

It isn't easy.

If it were easy, everyone would do it, and then where would we be? There'd never be any good buys left to find. On the other hand, it isn't brain surgery, either. Anyone can do it **IF** they're willing to put in the work.

There are no shortcuts. Period. You have to become intimately familiar with the sector. You must: understand the terminology and how the technology works—specifically the geology and metallurgy of the specific ore bodies, study the history, track the trends, and identify the important people involved and their previous track records along with their specific skill sets that allow them to tackle the tasks at hand. If you want to get really good, you have to make site visits and know what you're looking at.

This is how I do it. I conduct a deep analysis of six critical factors in order to create a model that uncovers the likely winners. If you want to proceed on your own, this is where you should start. Practice evaluating resource companies using this list until you begin to see what distinguishes the wheat from the chaff. When you can do that, you'll be able to look at potential investments with a more professional eye. And you'll amp up the probability of investment success.

I do want to make something very clear: I do not do all of this alone. Because of the size of my fund and investments, I have built an incredible team of experienced analysts, engineers, and geologists to help me fully address all the different points listed below. Ultimately, I make the final call, but I don't want to pretend I'm all-knowing. I started out as a lone speculator and investor, applying my investment ideas to the resource sector, and the success I had led me to become one of the largest financiers in the field. It's an incredibly daunting task, to be sure, but one that can be tackled. My overriding maxim has been never to rush into an investment. Investigate before you invest, do not invest, and then investigate.

I call my six factors for successful investment **Katusa's Keys**. They should become yours. Here they are:

1. People
2. Projects
3. Financial Structure
4. Promotion
5. Catalysts
6. Price

1. PEOPLE

I start here because this key is *by far* the most important.

Let's say you have a major business decision. You have a chance to buy an ownership stake in a local business, and you have to choose between two potential partners.

One is young and single. He wears a Rolex, drives a Porsche, dates the most beautiful women, and attends all the best parties. He's considered a real up-and-comer. But his business track record is spotty as yet, and several of your closest associates don't trust him.

The other guy is middle-aged, a family man, and has been doing business in town for thirty years. Everyone you know raves about his integrity and business acumen—he's been serially successful. He drives an old pickup truck.

Who would you rather partner with?

To me, the answer is a no-brainer. I'll take the older, steadier guy every time.

Now you might think this little exercise is irrelevant to our purpose here. But it isn't. Because you and I face this kind of decision every time we consider investing our hard-earned money in a public company. What we do can mean the difference between making multiples on an investment or losing money.

While making the conservative choice in the scenario above may seem obvious, a similar kind of logic can fly out the window when people buy stocks. All too often, they choose the reckless highflyer of the moment over the stodgy, old dude who's been around the block a few times.

Remember, when you buy shares of a public company, you are buying shares of a real business. You become one of the owners of that business. As an owner, you are buying a claim on the company's assets and future cash flows. The managers of that business essentially become your partners.

Unfortunately, if you're like most investors (myself included, believe me), you've "partnered" with some people who were either unproven, dishonest, incompetent, or all three. There are boatloads of folks out there—from project developers to promoters to the financial "talking heads" on TV—trying to sell you one story or another. All of those stories are "good" ones. They're all "sure things." As trusting humans, we always love a good story. It's just so easy to get caught up in them, and before you know it, you're investing in something without a clue as to how solid your partners are.

And, by the same token, we will too often pass on a story that seems boring, with little to no short-term "flash," even though it might offer a higher probability of long-term gains.

As an example, when you think of boring vs. flashy, remember one of the success stories of the 49ers. Thousands of prospectors flocked to California in the mid-nineteenth century, looking to make their fortune in gold. Most went broke. But a savvy few made their own fortunes a different and less risky way: by ignoring the lure of the high-risk/high-reward world of actual mining (and it's backbreaking work) and instead, selling miners the things they needed, like picks and shovels and durable clothing. Among them was an innovator named Levi Strauss.

You may not be able to identify the next Levi Strauss, but the point is, you should treat your money with respect, which means partnering with proven winners as much as you can. Success breeds success. Winners tend to keep on winning. That's why, for me, the single most important factor when analyzing a business is the people running it. It's even more important than the quality of a mineral deposit or the company's financial position.

Great management teams will eventually develop their pipeline to acquire great projects and optimize the profits for shareholders. Average management teams will take the best projects and screw them up. That's just the way it goes. Only invest in great people. Not nice people. Not people who *think* they can do it. Not the well-intentioned but incompetent. Remember: Investing and speculating is hard, and you must lock in gains when you have them—the best in the business do so regularly; so should you. It is the harsh world of resource development, and anything and everything that can go wrong will. Above all, you need a committed and capable management team that has more at stake than you do for the best chance at making the venture a success.

Another benefit to siding with proven winners is that they tend to attract the right shareholders. So, you need to investigate and find out who the major shareholders are.

Why would this matter? In many cases, a major shareholder may have ulterior motives different from other shareholders' best interests. It could be a corporate raider looking to break up the company and go after the cash for a short-term gain, which would distract the existing management team from executing their business plan. There can also be cases where a major shareholder's own issues will result in significant selling at an inopportune time—such as when the company may need to raise capital for continued funding of the project—something that can significantly raise the cost of capital and thus cause dilution for all shareholders.

Finding out the names of the large shareholders requires very little effort. It's public information. You will find not only the name of the shareholder but also the cost basis for his purchases. With some further research, you can often get a good sense of that particular large shareholder's specific intention.

When you're looking for someone to invest with, you also want them to have "skin in the game," i.e., be serious shareholders in their own enterprise. Importantly, you will also want to know what the cost basis of their investment was. If they just started the venture and the cost basis of their shares is already ten times less than what is being made available to you, you will most likely want to pass on that investment or speculation. This is most true for newer companies and not relevant if the management team has made the company successful a decade or two ago. Regardless, it's good to know their cost basis and whether management is selling or buying stock and at what prices.

(This is a good tipoff: Corporate officers may sell shares of their stock for any number of personal reasons that you can't know, but they buy at current market prices for only one—they're confident in the company's future to the extent that they want to have even more of their own skin in the game. A very good sign. Conversely, it's generally a pretty bad sign if all the execs are dumping massive numbers of their own shares at the same time. They probably know something you don't.)

All of this information is free and publicly available. You just have to put some effort into digging it up.

To make the point, consider this: Have you ever invested in a company run by executives who owned little or no company stock? Have you purchased a mutual fund or an ETF that held companies whose managers owned little or no stock?

Chances are very good that you have. You may own some of those companies right now.

Don't worry. You're not alone.

Investing in a company whose managers have no skin in the game is one of the world's most common investment mistakes. We've all made it at one time or another. They don't teach you this critical bit of wisdom in high school, college, or business school. But once you think about it, it becomes obvious.

With ownership comes a respect and care for expenses, assets, and cash flows that have no substitute. It will turn a salaried manager who thinks nothing of spending $3,000 on a nice office chair into a guy who will sit on a used chair in order to save a few bucks. It will turn a conventional "nine to five" employee into a guy who will happily work Friday night instead of heading for the nearest pub.

Essentially, you want a management team that spends the company's money like it's their own savings fund, not someone else's. This is why, if you can, go to the office of the company and see what they spend money on. The culture of the business can often be seen just from the entrance lobby of the company. If it's a small startup, call the company, drop in and see how accessible the management team is. In my experience, the best management teams run the lowest-cost G&A (general and administrative) expenses and squeeze dollars out of nickels.

Ownership transforms a reckless CEO who plays fast and loose with shareholder capital into a watchful, prudent shareholder advocate. It turns a CFO who uses aggressive, very questionable accounting into a Boy Scout.

Picture the most hardworking business owners you've known. I'll bet they treated equipment with respect. They used supplies carefully. They took pride in their company. They got to work early. If they saw a piece of trash on the floor, they picked it up.

This is why, when I start analyzing a potential investment or talk to managers about placing money with them, my first question is always, "How much stock do you own?" And if the answer is "not much" or "zero," my analysis is finished.

I don't bother with people who have no skin in the game. Neither should you.

2. PROJECTS

Once I'm satisfied that I'm investing with the right people, I'm ready to move on to projects.

My area of special expertise is resource companies. Whether I'm buying into a company with existing production, a company developing a single asset, or a company exploring for deposits, what I always want is to invest in high-quality projects that have the potential to attract the attention of majors who will buy them out. Plus, I only invest in projects with production costs in the lowest-cost quartile of the industry. The resource sector is so cyclical that eventually, the price of a commodity during a bear market will reach the lowest-cost quartile of production.

I do not spend any time or energy on evaluating small projects. Small projects lead to small profits but still have the high-risk nature of big profitable projects.

This is where I really do my due diligence, which consists of answering a series of four critical questions. Most of them are common sense and shouldn't need to be stated, but it doesn't hurt to compile the list and follow it.

First up...

Is the resource deposit and economics as management claims it to be?

Sadly, the history of the resource industry is replete with stories of companies that overstated their assets. It's not always management's fault, but rather the third-party engineers the company uses to compile the data to create the economics for the project. I want to invest in companies where the deposit size is as advertised, and the geology is such that the metallurgical recovery will occur as stated.

Suppose you do not know how to verify a company's claims by completing your own intensive review of the posted geologic data. In that case, next best is to do a "people" check on the engineering firm that is completing the preliminary economic assessment (PEA), prefeasibility study (PFS), or the bankable feasibility study (BFS). Each one requires more data and money than the previous study, and ultimately the BFS is what is used to raise the capital needed by management to build the project.

Management teams must hire a third-party engineering firm to study the project and provide the results that are used to attract capital from investors. These reports are crucial, and so much of the investment decisions are based upon them. But should they be? I want to focus some energy on them.

Here is a quick trick I came up with years ago. These studies can be 300-plus pages in length and very time-consuming to go through properly. But with little effort, you can research the engineering firm being used by the company to see if they are a top-tier firm or a slapstick operation. Not all engineering firms are equal.

Moreover, we have to keep in mind that these firms are employed by the company and use the company's data. As the computer nerds say: garbage in, garbage out.

But let's assume that the company we are interested in is a top-tier engineering firm. That is not enough due diligence for us to just stop there.

During a bear market, money is tight and is usually only available to the best management teams. Thus, only the best engineering firms and geologists are employed. But it's very rare that investors enter a sector during the bear market; they much prefer bull markets.

During a bull market, more money is raised, and more reports are needed to attract additional capital. Engineering firms get busy, and even the best firms expand and hire more engineers and geologists. Why? It's increased business for their owners, and they also want to make more money.

But there is a key factor here that I want to emphasize. Every engineer and geologist working on the report of the specific company must sign off. And the name of the individual preparer, say, for example, the metallurgist engineer, is what you want to focus on. Is their track record successful or full of botched engineering reports in previous cycles and company reports?

Pareto's Law—20 percent of those involved produce 80 percent of the worthwhile results—is in full force in technical reports. You will find that the characters of the individuals, both good and bad, follow them in their career. If the technical data that a specific metallurgist worked on for previous companies was a failure and the recovery was in fact 30 percent lower in the actual real-world operation, then their report was suspect. You must pause and research further. And you will likely see a pattern there. It's rare to find just one botched technical report. You have to follow past technical reports' conclusions and then see what the actual operations yielded. That is critical to determining the person's current skill set. The past is prologue.

You will also find that the engineers or geologists with spotty track records will have hopped around from firm to firm and from bull market to bull market, meaning that they get laid off during the bear markets because their own firms didn't want to keep them around during the lean years.

And yes, companies have been known to fake the data, but it's rare with today's strict requirements and guidelines such as 43-101 reports. Usually, what you see is what you get. Which means, of course, that you have to know your geology. But this is a quick "hack" that can give you a warning sign about the quality of the people working on the technical report at hand.

Next...

How big is the resource?

Obviously, we want to find companies with large, high-quality, tier-one resources that will be attractive acquisitions for large producers. Those are the deposits that get bought out by the big companies at significant premiums. Always ask yourself, will this project attract a big company's interest? A tier-one gold deposit, for example, contains over 5 million ounces and can produce at least 500,000 ounces or more per year for a minimum of ten years. Those are the types of projects that move the needle for a major gold producer. A tier-two deposit, one that will move the needle for a mid-tier gold miner, is a project that can produce at least 200,000 ounces or more for ten years or more. Below that, I'm generally not interested.

Then...

Where is the resource located?

Countries like the US, Canada, and Australia have laws that make resource extraction an attractive business and protect companies that engage in extraction. Not all provinces and states in these nations are mining-friendly. But some countries in South America, Asia, and Africa, on the other hand, are totally *un*friendly; they have recent histories of confiscating resource projects. Personally, I like to focus my investment research on resource-friendly jurisdictions, preferably ones with a +SWAP Line bonus and tend to avoid places that don't pass the AK-47 test that I wrote about in Chapter 5.

And finally...

How much will it cost to bring the resource to production?

Infrastructure is crucial to mining success. If a resource is located near highways or railways and an electric power source, the cost to extract and transport the output is relatively low.

But if the resource is in a remote area where infrastructure must be built from scratch, it can cost billions of dollars to develop. Some terrific deposits can actually be worthless because they require too much infrastructure investment to justify development.

Again, this is where the track record of the people who are working on the technical report is critical. After twenty years in the business, I have never seen the actual preliminary feasibility study (PFS) have a lower total capital cost to build the project than the first technical report, called a preliminary economic assessment (PEA). I've also never seen the next report—a bankable feasibility study—have a lower overall capital cost to build the project than the previous PFS.

The point I am trying to make is that the earlier the stage a project is in, the more optimistic the economics tend to look. We all prefer to walk on the sunny side. But resource extraction is an incredibly high-cost and complicated venture. Mother Nature does not yield her bounty easily. Thus, you want to increase your chances of success by sticking to projects in jurisdictions where there is a rule of law, infrastructure in place, increasingly realistic assessments, and simple geology (meaning: avoid complicated metallurgy).

3. FINANCIAL STRUCTURE

Debt is a killer in the resource sector because the business is so cyclical. Projects that are financed using aggressive commodity price projections rarely work in the long run. Also, companies with just one project will have a higher cost of capital (i.e., will have to pay higher interest rates) than companies with many projects in process.

I want to see companies with low or minimal debt and plenty of cash to fund their operations. If they don't have that, they are likely to dilute shareholders by issuing more shares.

I'll have more to say on dilution in a moment. But management's ability to raise capital—and what the cost of that capital is—is key. Net present value (NPV) is the significant number. NPV is the difference between the present value of cash inflows and the present value of cash outflows over a period of time. For example, many technical reports are based on the NPV at a 5 percent discount rate, where the actual cost of capital is north of 12 percent. That significantly changes the economic potential of the project. That is why understanding the true cost of capital is key in successful resource development.

4. PROMOTION

Even the best assets in the world need promotion by strong management teams.

If a company has great potential, the rest of the world needs to know about it. If the world doesn't know about it, there won't be anybody around to buy shares and drive up the company's value.

I want to make sure management has a plan to "spread the word" with institutional investors and financial publishers. This will create the interest in a stock that is needed to push the share price higher.

5. CATALYSTS

What is it about the company that will drive up the price?

If the catalyst is just higher commodity prices, pass on that company. Finding significant discounted value that will be realized upon achieving specific events is how one creates significant wealth in the resource sector. Higher prices help, but all those benefits will disappear when commodity prices turn against you (and remember, it's a cyclical business, and they are volatile).

So, is the company working on a big discovery? Is it furthering the development of a high-quality asset? Is the price of its resource poised to move higher because of an X factor that few people know about?

Make sure you know exactly what the timeline of events (and risks) are to the catalyst timeline of your investment or speculation. An indicator of management failing is if those catalysts aren't achieved on time or on budget.

6. PRICE

It's said that "price is what you pay, value is what you get." This is especially true in the natural resource market. You can find a company with great people and great projects, but if you pay too much for your ownership stake, you can still lose a lot of money.

This whole idea comes down to treating your investments like you treat almost anything else you buy. You should focus on finding great values and not paying stupid prices.

Too frequently, naïve investors get excited about a company's story, and they just buy the stock. They don't pay any attention to the price they're paying or the value they're getting for their investment dollar.

Don't be a sucker and overpay. Make sure you get good value for your investment dollar. Hunt for bargains. What you're searching for are companies that are undervalued by the market at the moment, i.e., is the price per share less than the NAV (net asset value) per share? This would be computed, say, for a gold miner, based on expectations of ounces of production at a given gold price per ounce. You can find companies, especially in a down market, that sell for half or a third of their NAV. They're not common (junior miners tend more often to be *over*valued), but they're out there.

Of course, a company could be selling for less than NAV and still not be undervalued. So, you have to do the rest of the research. But if you find one that also checks off the five other criteria on this list, then you've got a bargain that will likely pay off big as either:

1. production begins and the price rises toward a fair reflection of NAV or
2. the company is bought out, for a premium, by one of the majors.

FURTHER CRITERIA

There are 700 producing gold mines in the world, along with countless others in varying stages of development—1,357 mining companies are listed in Canada alone. If you want to invest, efficient use of your time is critical.

Generally speaking, it's very rare that a project is a real green field discovery. Most projects have been owned and worked by a previous management team at some point in the past. With that comes a lot of data with the money spent on the project to advance the asset (read: *OPM*-other people's money). Having access to the historical data is crucial to understanding the potential future success of the project.

I want to identify single producing projects that:

- are not already owned by majors
- are located in +SWAP Line Nations
- and have the potential to produce at least 100,000 ounces per year

I then eliminate these:

- low-grade projects
- projects that expect to have short mine lives (less than eight years, with no exploration potential to increase the mine life)
- high-cost mines (ones with cash costs of more than $800 per ounce I avoid, as a general rule, since if cash costs are $800, all-in sustaining costs are ~$1,200 per ounce)

In addition to my above strategies, I then use the following quick filters to establish if further due diligence is warranted on projects that have passed through the above filters:

- **Payback Period:** If a project looks like the capital expenditure will be paid back within three years, I put it at the top of my list of projects to focus on. Anything under five years is rare and should be further studied.
- **Lowest Cost Quartile:** If a project appears to have low all in sustaining costs (AISC) and is within the lowest-cost quartile within its sector, further consideration is warranted
- **Long-Life Projects:** As I've mentioned many times now, the resource sector is very cyclical, thus you will want exposure to projects that have a long life (twenty-plus years), which gives the owner strong cash flow during bull markets and the ability to stay operating during bear markets.
- **NPV to Capital Expenditures (Cap Ex) Ratio:** This is a great metric to compare a specific opportunity to its market peers. If done properly, and the same realistic discount rate with an accurate cap ex for all projects is applied, this will quickly determine how the present opportunity fares against other opportunities in the marketplace. The average for quality preproduction stage projects in the gold sector is about 1.5. Anything above 3.0 ratio of NPV to cap ex deserves further research.

- **Price to Net Asset Value (NAV):** As a general rule of thumb, if the NAV is correctly calculated, a price below 0.4 for an advanced tier-one or tier-two asset with permits in place will work out well for investors if given enough time. Producing companies generally get over 1.0 price/NAV and streaming and royalty companies even get valued above a price/NAV of 2 (people are paying for future growth). I prefer to get future growth for free as value investors in the resource sector look for deals and buying well below NAV is value hunting if the above metrics are met. In the depths of a bear market, producing assets trade below 1.0 NAV. In bull markets, nonproducing assets can trade above 1.0 NAV. That means they are trading above what they are worth. Unless there is a tangible reason, that is a good reason to sell because the project is more than fully valued.
- **Grade Is King, Size Is Queen:** Small, low-grade projects are to be avoided. High- grade and big projects are what you want. Most projects are somewhere in between.
- **Simple Metallurgy:** Avoid complicated metallurgy. Simple metallurgy usually results in lower cost and more effective recovery rates. Complicated metallurgy results in higher costs and lower recovery.
- **Nature of Deposit:** Will the mining be open pit or underground? Obviously, underground needs much higher grades. But if open pit and two-thirds of the deposit is within the top one-third of the resource, that is promising. For underground, make sure you understand the rock stability and the further complications required for underground mining vs. open pit.
- **Management's Track Record with Dilution:** When equity or debt raises happen, are they value added or just dilution? What is the real cost of capital for the project being financed?

These are just a handful of the quick metrics I use to determine if a project warrants further study time. Understanding how to determine what projects deserve your time quickly and avoiding deep dives on projects that aren't going to work, is important for efficiency.

After I've done the above, the real digging begins. I must have a positive answer to these questions:

- Who would the project be a good fit for in terms of a major seeking acquisitions?
- Does mining the deposit require a unique skill set which discourages many potential suitors?
- Are there any potential synergies with mines operating nearby?
- Is there some low-hanging fruit to be plucked which creates additional value for the buyer?

Obviously, I can't always find what I'm after. Sometimes I come across a project that meets my criteria, but the price isn't right. That is where patience is required. The sector is so cyclical, there will inevitably be an opportunity to enter if you are prepared (having the analysis and cash) when the market sells off.

This has gotten me a reputation—and some criticism—for being overly cautious, and I don't mind that one bit. I will wait as long as I have to until something irresistible shows up on my screen. I have a system of evaluation, and I stick to it religiously, without ever taking shortcuts. This is the *Way of the Alligator* (see below), which is the way to success.

I'll be the first to admit that I've missed my share of great profit opportunities. But if you've tracked my career, then you know that my procedure has identified many more winners than losers. And I'm able to place very large bets on the outcome because I know I'm backing a good company and that the entry price is right and there will be a liquidity event (exit) to profit on.

PORTFOLIO MANAGEMENT

As I've been stressing, there are many elements that go into becoming a successful market investor. And one of the most important is: ***avoid catastrophic losses.***

This is a truth that should be entirely self-evident. It reflects what is perhaps the greatest difference between investors who prosper and those who always struggle and lose money in the market. Yet, all too often, it is honored only in the breach.

Careful portfolio management is crucial. I can't emphasize this enough. What follows are the ways in which I manage my own.

INVESTMENT VERSUS SPECULATION

This is a hugely important difference to keep in mind.

An investment can be a speculation, but a speculation can never be an investment.

Please never forget that. Let me explain:

By definition, an investment should have an operating asset, free cash flow, and a dividend.

In contrast, a speculation is based on a catalyst (or set of catalysts) that will take the share price higher. It is a burning match. It's successful if the catalyst happens before the match burns your fingers and you are forced to let go.

An investment can have a speculation angle to it, i.e., there may be a catalyst you know is coming, but your real assessment of its value is based on the investment fundamentals of the business's underlying profitable assets. The catalyst is a bonus.

An investment uses fundamental value analysis so that an investor can study and calculate the right entry point.

POSITION SIZING

After deciding if the opportunity is a speculation or an investment, the next decision is to put the amount of capital into the opportunity.

I will share my own rules here. Never invest more than 10 percent of your resource portfolio in any one investment. Never invest more than 5 percent of your resource portfolio in any one speculation.

Position sizing is what blows up most speculators and investors and is absolutely key to achieving long-term success in the resource sector.

Many people think of position size in terms of how many shares they own of a particular stock. But it's much, much smarter to think of it in terms of what percentage of your total capital is in a particular stock, bond, fund, or commodity.

For example, if you have $100,000 at your disposal for your resource portfolio and buy $2,000 worth of stock in a company, your position size would be 2 percent of your resource fund capital. And so on.

With regard to position size, what you must always do is protect yourself from a "catastrophic loss." This is the type of loss that erases a big chunk of your investment account. It's the kind that destroys retirement accounts...and even blows up marriages. I'm talking about a loss that leads to a $250,000 account plummeting to $100,000 or $50,000 in value.

The most common cause of catastrophic losses is going "too big" on risky positions. This occurs when an investor takes a much larger position size than he should. He'll find a stock he's really, really excited about. He'll be lured—either by a promoter or his own misfiring brain—into thinking he's onto a "sure thing." In his mind, he'll start spending all the profits he's going to make. So, he lays down a huge bet. He'll place 30 percent, 40 percent, 50 percent, or more of his account in that one idea. He'll go for broke.

It's a market law: *there is no sure thing.* You ignore that at your peril. If this poor guy's position doesn't work out, he can easily suffer a 50 percent hit to his asset base. In some cases, he can suffer a devastating 100 percent loss of capital. (Like those unfortunate Enron employees who put all of their retirement money into the company's stock and then lost everything when Enron proved to be crooked and went bankrupt.)

Those people made horrible position sizing mistakes by risking everything on just one stock.

Remember the cruelty of the math here: if you take a 75 percent loss, then what you have left must quadruple just to get you back to break-even—and 75 percent losses are a lot more common than quadruples.

The obvious damage from a catastrophic loss is the financial hit. For the average person who's handed a 75 percent haircut, it'll take many long years to make that money back, if ever. But the less obvious damage is even worse than losing money. It's the mental trauma. People who suffer that kind of loss consider themselves failures. They see years of working and saving flushed down the toilet. They're unlikely to save, much less invest again. Many never recover. They may have PTSD, develop substance-abuse problems, even attempt suicide.

Do not be one of them. Do what the pros do.

Generally speaking, most top investors in the resource sector will never allot more than 5–10 percent of their account to a single position. Some professionals I know won't put more than 3 percent into one position. My personal limit is 10 percent for investments and 5 percent of investable capital into a speculation.

In addition, I never buy my whole desired allocation at one time; rather, I pursue a tranche allocation approach.

TRANCHES

No matter how much I fall in love with a new acquisition, I always buy in *tranches*. A tranche is merely the allotment in a particular stock-buying trade, and the term is applied when the buyer intends to accumulate a given position over time. This means following a simple rule: **Never buy your intended position in a stock all at once.**

I've met many, many successful traders and fund managers all over the world. And you know what? I've yet to meet anyone (or any software algorithm) that has mastered a stock purchase's timing perfectly, at least not consistently. So, take as much of the risk out of the timing element as you can by buying up to your desired position in tranches. Make volatility work for you, not against you.

Remember this: **always use limit orders, never place market orders.** No exceptions. If you don't already know, algorithms love a market order because it allows them to manipulate the price in their favor (to your detriment). You'll end up paying more than you should. (And vice versa on the sell side.) Decide on the price you're willing to pay and stick to it with a limit order. If that's below the current ask price, put in a "good 'til canceled" order and let the market come to you.

Now, if, say, you have $5,000 to invest (from your 10 percent allocation to one company, as noted above), then split that up into tranches. A good rule of thumb is four equal 25 percent positions (so in this case, four positions of $1,250 each), although I'll sometimes use three equal tranches. The goal is to accumulate your position over time.

You place the order for your first tranche at what you consider the ideal entry point. If you're really excited about the stock, you can buy your first two tranches at once. Then sit back and wait for Mr. Market to give you a sale and buy more of the stock at cheaper prices. This way, if the stock rises, you're along for the ride. If it goes down, you can scoop up shares for a discount.

You can also buy a second tranche at a higher price than the first if you become convinced that a reasonable entry point has moved higher for some genuine reason. Just don't do it if you become infatuated with a stock's *momentum*, a sharp rise based on nothing. The share price in a resource company often goes up only based on the fact that a large fund is trying to take a position in the open market, not based on the fundamentals. That is a bad thing to base your tranche buying on because most times, the share price will come back down after that large fund is done buying. Be smart and control your emotions. Don't get greedy.

Be especially poised to act in times of high volatility.

I'll share a specific real-life event.

On March 15, 2020, just as the US Fed chairman called an emergency press briefing, I could see that a sell-off was in the cards. So, I called my team on a Sunday, and we burned the midnight oil to put together a "hit list" of stocks I planned on buying at specific prices. These were stocks my team and I have been following for years, but I had not bought them because I wanted to wait for a significant market sell-off to start my tranche purchases. I sent out the same report to my subscribers that night. In that alert, we featured five terrific companies that I wanted to own and at what price. The following two weeks, these companies were trading at fire-sale prices. The market got spooked over the following weeks, and it was an incredible buying opportunity that we used to buy large positions of the companies in our report. This was a real-time example of using volatility as your friend.

My tranche prices were very aggressive on the downside. In some cases, we put in limit orders 20–30 percent below the prices I was already comfortable getting. But in times of chaos, even multibillion-dollar, tier-one companies can swing wildly. When the dust settled, I had picked up two of my five favored companies on the cheap and almost hit on a third. Yes, it meant I didn't get filled on all five, but that didn't matter. We made an incredible amount of money on the two we did hit on, and we had ample capital left to deploy if the market continued to get worse.

Buying in tranches means you'll miss out on some profits if your selected stock takes off and never looks back. But look at it this way: You're still profiting. Plus, you also can fill second and third tranches on the down days that inevitably pop up with no change in the company's fundamentals if you want to. Or you can just enjoy the ride.

I learned this rule through hard experience. It works. I now do tranche buying with every position I own. Not only do I buy in tranches to build a position, but I sell in tranches, too. This is especially critical if you have a large stock block to dispose of and don't want to spook the market (and drive the price down) by selling all shares on the same day. Once you become accustomed to buying and selling in tranches, the worries about timing your entry and exit perfectly will not weigh so heavily on your mind.

Another word of caution: Do not be like so many newcomers to an investment newsletter or service. Newbies get overly excited, which immediately causes the emotions to take hold and investing discipline to be lost. I can assure you that many of my own new subscribers, who tend to be pretty sophisticated, lost out on opportunities to make money by putting all their cash into the first company they saw recommended. If that stock fell, the investor would panic and then sell out. Feeling dejected, the investor throws in the towel, cancels the subscription, and misses out on many, many more opportunities to profit in the future.

This is the worst kind of novice mistake and buying in tranches protects against it. It is something all the investing legends do and something I do personally and with my funds. Again, without exception. You have to allow time for a company's story to mature and for the cost averaging of your position to work its magic.

Patience, my friend, patience...

THE KATUSA FREE RIDE

When you have a profit, risk mitigation is key to protecting your downside and leaving the opportunity of huge upside available to you. Remember, you don't just buy in tranches, but you must also sell in tranches.

The most efficient strategy (and the one I use) is the **Katusa Free Ride Formula**.

In building net worth, you need to turn paper gains into realized profits. Your online brokerage account numbers don't equate to new BMWs or mortgage payments until you click that *Sell* button. You want to recoup your original investment, removing all risk from the trade, and leave the rest to ride. The Katusa Free Ride Formula tells you how.

It's simple math. Just divide your original entry price by the current selling price and multiply that by your original number of shares. The result is the number of shares you need to sell.

Do that, and you'll greatly increase your peace of mind.

To be sure, skilled investors vary their position size depending on the particular investment. For example, when buying a blue-chip stock that has increased its dividend payment for thirty consecutive years, a position size of up to 10 percent can make sense. (But not more. Remember that even the big guys sometimes go bust. Think Enron or Worldcomm.)

However, when dealing with more volatile vehicles like junior resource stocks, position sizes should be smaller. These companies are volatile; some will be moonshots; others will sink to the bottom of the ocean. So, first, decide how much of your portfolio you feel comfortable investing in them. This should be money that you can afford to lose without it affecting your lifestyle. Around 10 percent might be all that a prudent person wants to risk.

Then, never allocate more than 10 percent of your junior resource portfolio to any one investment stock, and never more than 5 percent to any single speculation stock. This will keep your risks at an acceptable level.

Unfortunately, many investors will plunk down three, five, or ten times as much as they should. That's a recipe for disaster if the company they own suffers a large unforeseen decline.

These declines happen with much greater frequency than most folks realize. No matter how promising a company sounds, its fortunes can always turn south. Smart position sizing will keep the damage caused to an acceptable minimum.

Now for sure, I can get as excited about a company's prospects as anyone. I love analyzing balance sheets and visiting projects. I love taking a stake in a small company whose excellence is not yet recognized and watch it achieve success.

But as I've said many times before, I'm very conservative. This is especially important in markets where stocks are low-volume, high-volatility—which describes junior mining companies to a *T*.

STRESS

As important as position sizing is, and it's very important, so is the next rule: **If an investment causes you to stress to the point you can't sleep—sell.**

At the very least, if you are overly distracted by any of your positions, and it causes stress, discomfort, or you're losing sleep, then sell enough stock to alleviate the pain.

Life is too short to worry about a stock position. Enjoy the present and have fun. If your stress level is high continuously and is becoming more and more intolerable, then you have to do some quiet reflection. It may be that:

1. you're overinvested, in which case lighten up, or
2. speculating in these markets just isn't for you.

If it's the latter, that's okay. Get out. Spend more time doing the things you love. You will not only get more pleasure out of your life, but you may also be more successful as you gain self-awareness and discover what works for you.

If you're mortgaging the house, spending your kids' tuition, jeopardizing your car payments, or even just plundering the vacation fund, then you're playing with fire. Follow my earlier rule: Only speculate with money that won't change your lifestyle if you lose 100 percent of it.

DON'T EXPECT THE IMPOSSIBLE

It's completely unrealistic to expect that every investment you make is going to pay off. And that's especially true with the juniors.

But if you construct this segment of your portfolio properly—with no more than 10 percent in any one of these volatile stocks—and you select your holdings as carefully as you can, then you should have overall success.

Let's say you have a basket of nine individual stocks. Over time, three may go nowhere. Three more may nosedive or even go bankrupt. But the other three will make you enough money that you won't care what happens to the rest.

This is typical of equities' performances in this area. Do not be dismayed by the losers. The winners will always win bigger than the losers lose. Ride the winners according to the Free Ride formula detailed above. You'll be very happy with the results.

BOOM, BUST, AND ECHO

I don't care what kind of market we're in because if you stick to my principles, you can make money in any market type. I've done it. You can do the same. But to succeed, you're going to have to look at markets in a different way than you're accustomed.

UNDERSTANDING CYCLES

How so? Well, everyone knows about the "business cycle." Booms are succeeded by Busts, which yield new Booms. That's always the focus for analysts. Equities (and the businesses that underlie them) traverse an endless series of peaks and valleys. A stock rises on the back of strong company results and plummets when things turn sour. Or investors simply tire of a stock, come to see it as overbought, and a selloff results. Sectors, and indeed whole markets, follow the same pattern.

There is a general sense of euphoria during a Boom, a feeling that the market will continue notching new highs forever. Of course, it can't. There will inevitably come a Bust, after which gloom sets in, and investors begin to fret that it's never going to turn around. And they are just as wrong.

I've not only studied markets intensively for many years now but have become one of the largest financiers in the resource sector over the last decade. Eventually, I was driven to conclude that the traditional way of analyzing cyclical sectors is badly flawed. There is more to a cycle than just Boom and Bust, bull and bear. There is also a sideways market that always appears somewhere between the last Bust and the next Boom. It is neither. Yet, it's an integral part of the process, with unique and definable features.

It's the third, most critical part of every cycle, and it has never been properly described before, which is why I coined the term *Boom, Bust, & Echo* for resource markets.

UNDERSTANDING THE ECHO

During this period, the market is in what seems like a dead zone. The mainstream shuns it. Yet what's actually happening is entirely normal, an integral part of all business cycles' natural evolutionary process.

Understanding how it works can make the difference between succeeding and failing in the markets.

As I've tried to explain the concept to friends of mine in the investment business, and at investment conferences where I have been the keynote speaker, I've gotten the distinct feeling that my words are just bouncing off and returning to me, as if I were shouting into a lifeless desert canyon. So, I decided to turn that feeling into my own catchword for this particular phase of the market cycle that I've identified. I call it the *Echo*.

It is neither Boom nor Bust, but it precedes or follows them as surely as falling leaves mark the end of summer and the onset of winter. In my opinion, it's the most important aspect of the business cycle, yet it's the one that gets the least amount of attention.

It is, somewhat counterintuitively, a space in which fortunes are made.

The Echo has never been properly described before now. It always follows a Bust and prefigures a coming Boom. Heretofore, it's been ignored because while it's happening, market sentiment is so negative that no one wants to get involved. Professional analysts and individual investors alike stay away until there are clear signs that another Boom is fully underway, and it seems "safe" to jump back in. And fund managers whose funds have been sapped by redemptions simply don't have the available cash, even if they would like to buck the prevailing sentiment.

This is a shame because the Echo has specific characteristics all its own. They are unique and, more importantly, predictable.

The fact is that profit opportunities abound at this time. Enormous wealth is created during the Echo, more so than during either of the other market phases. The savviest, most successful investors already know this and deploy their financial resources accordingly.

Now, you can, too.

But you can't optimize your prospects without knowing where you are in the Echo part of the cycle.

The good news is that's a skill that can be learned.

As you know, my background is intensively in natural

resources investing. Which doesn't mean I only go around with a hard hat on, shining my miner's light on everything I see (though traipsing through underground mines can be fun!).

Still, I'm always aware of what's happening elsewhere in the financial world. And natural resources may not be the ideal crucible in which to test out a new economic concept. Why? Because it's the most volatile sector in the world. Things happen so fast and run to such extremes that it can be difficult to see trends and cycles unfold in real time. But maybe that's why my concept evolved here. My observation of Boom, Bust, & Echo at work in natural resources has allowed me to create a structural template to lay over any market, sector, or particular company. That template works everywhere and everywhen.

For example, even though my area of expertise is natural resources, the tech sector will allow me to illustrate what I'm talking about more easily. For one thing, people are more conversant with tech than mining. Plus, you're undoubtedly (and perhaps painfully) aware of the dot-com Boom of the late 1990s that ended in a Bust of truly colossal proportions. It took the axe to every company short on viability, vaporized countless billions of dollars, and wrecked the NASDAQ Index for years to come. It was such a bloodletting that it caused many tech investors to swear off of the sector forever.

Examine any NASDAQ graph for the past twenty-five years and you can see, plainly revealed, a classic Boom/Bust scenario. Though the Index had been in a steady uptrend since 1980, it really went ballistic in late 1998, rocketing upward in a nearly unbroken vertical line from 2,377 to its peak of 7,167 in early 2000—a 200 percent jump in just over two years. The subsequent Bust, playing out over the next eighteen months, took it all the way back to 1,677, a haircut of more than 75 percent.

Between the Bust and the beginning of a new Boom in 2009, no one wanted any part of the NASDAQ. For six and a half years, it traded sideways. It was so rangebound that its value was almost exactly the same in February of 2009 as it was in September of '02.

As of the time of this writing, the Index is up about 600 percent from early '09. I'm not going to speculate on where we are in the NASDAQ cycle, nor how long the current boom will last, nor how bad the Bust will be when it comes. What interests me is the period between the lows of '03 and '09.

That's the Echo. You can find it at the center of any market's Boom/Bust cycle.

Now, if you were a tech investor, and you wanted to *buy low/ sell high*, you obviously didn't want to jump into the NASDAQ right at the Y2K moment, propitious as that may have seemed. That would've been a disaster, as the Boom was just hitting its all-time peak.

Yet it's equally true that you didn't want to jump in at the very bottom of the Bust in late 2002, even if you had future-vision glasses and had known you were looking at the ultimate low.

It might have seemed like a solid entry point, but it wasn't. Your investment would have been flat for the next six and a half years. So simply buying low is only a part of the story. *When* you buy low is much more important.

To maximize your success, you'd have wanted to invest in the NASDAQ as the Echo was about to run its course, in late 2008 or early 2009. If you could have done that, you'd have caught the Boom train just as it was about to leave the station. And you'd be sitting on a fortune today.

But to make something like that happen, you have to carefully study your market and apply to it your understanding of the

Boom/Bust/Echo cycle. They don't teach that in econ classes. Instead, they teach straight lines to fit the data into their models. That might suffice for Booms and Busts, but it doesn't work with the Echo, which is nonlinear. It vibrates and moves around.

You need the ability to determine where in the cycle you are at any given moment. And you don't have to perfectly time the market—Booms, Busts, & Echoes all last for years. Any time during the late stages of an Echo is a good time to buy in.

That ideal moment is easy to spot with the kind of retrospective analysis a historical graph gives you. It doesn't take a stock market savant to see it. But the present tense is more challenging. Nobody can call a market turn in real-time; if someone suddenly developed that ability, the rest of the herd would quickly follow, and that mass movement of money would itself distort the market in unforeseeable ways.

What *is* possible, however, is always to know approximately where you are in the Echo. If that's part of your toolkit, you can invest accordingly, holding back during its early and middle phases and deploying your capital when you determine that the end of the Echo is nearby or that it has recently passed.

Such times are when the foundations of fortunes are laid. Just ask the happy tech investors who had the nerve to pile in, in 2009.

And let me really stress one thing right here: Investing using the Echo is not a get-rich-quick scheme. Quite the opposite. The key ingredient is something that most people—especially foolish investors who follow the herd in and out of markets—don't have nearly enough of: *patience.*

Just as you have to be patient while awaiting the Echo's end, you have to be equally patient during the life of the subsequent Boom and let your profits multiply.

CHARACTERISTICS OF THE ECHO

Now, let me briefly introduce some of the Echo's basic characteristics, using the familiar Boom/Bust/Echo in the tech sector to illustrate. Then I will relate a detailed real-life example of how I applied all of the above analysis into a very successful investment in the resource sector.

To profit from Echo investing, you have to grasp why this phase of the cycle exists, what happens during it, and how it signals that it is ending.

Both Booms and Busts exhibit sharp peaks when you look at them on a graph. The market turns on a dime and heads in the opposite direction. It will routinely continue in that direction for years, but there is always a starkly evident turning point, albeit only in retrospect. (If we could call a market's absolute top or bottom in real time, we'd be genuine prophets, but no one can do that.)

The Echo is different. There are no distinct peaks or bottoms that you can point to after the fact. It emerges in the wake of a Bust and serves as a kind of quiet time, with no dramatic moves one way or the other. The market, which has just seen massive ups and downs, needs a lull to regain its senses.

That doesn't mean nothing is happening within an industry. On the contrary, it can be a time of great activity. A hell of a lot will be happening below the surface, out of sight for the most part. For the simple reason that no one is watching.

Here are a few of the important markers that *always* appear during any Echo period:

- **Consolidation**—this occurs both within businesses, as they streamline and implement greater efficiencies, and between them, as the strong eat the weak. M&A will occur at zero premiums during the Echo. Big-premium M&A is usually a sign of a bull market top.

- **The liquidation of bad debt**—many companies will take on excess debt during the euphoria of a Boom and get squeezed during the Bust. In the Echo, those who can afford to pay down their ill-advised debt will do so; those who can't pay it down will not make it.
- **Recapitalization**—those who have maintained solid balance sheets and merit refinancing will get it and will also be able to float new shares if they need to.
- **Increasing market share**—on the part of those who are healthy enough and visionary enough to do it.
- **Defining the fittest**—the best of the best, those who not only survived the financial Bust debacle but are strategically poised to catch the next Boom.

It's also the time during which informed investors can swoop in and take advantage of highly attractive buying conditions. As the old finance truism has it, *the cure for low prices is low prices* (i.e., the market is self-correcting; a fall of prices to unreasonably low levels will inevitably trigger a rise), During an Echo, the seeds of the next Boom are slowly germinating. But no one notices, and the stock of even the strongest companies goes on sale in the bargain basement.

All of the above happened in tech during the first decade of this century.

A CLASSIC ECHO IN THE NASDAQ

That Echo followed a market crash for the ages. It should have been one that was almost impossible not to see coming. Instead, in the late '90s, everyone with a pulse believed that the internet would be a game-changer and every budding entrepreneur wanted a share of the loot. The Boom in internet business creation was naturally accompanied by a Boom in the stock market's tech sector, as investors who didn't know a bit from a byte clamored to get in on the action.

Sure, the promise of commerce in cyberspace was hovering right there on the horizon. The problem was, though, one critical key ingredient was missing. There was no infrastructure in place to deliver the kind of service people wanted. All we had at first was existing phone lines. That left users with only one alternative—dial-up—and it was expensive; inconvenient, in that it tied up the phone or forced getting a second line; and slooooow. The nascent internet was one that could not support many startup businesses. Yet it was so cheap to turn an idea into an internet presence that thousands of millionaire wannabes jumped right in. And millions of naïve investors treated every wobbly little startup as the next coming of Walmart.

Hardly anyone bothered to notice that there was a serious mismatch between customer demands and provider capabilities, and by the latter part of 2000, the whole thing toppled over. Telecoms failed to meet revenue projections. Stocks crashed. Seed money dried up. Debts became unserviceable. The smaller companies went bankrupt by the hundreds; the better companies merely survived, tightening their belts as their market caps nosedived.

The great tech crash of 2000–'01 was an extreme example, but it was a classic Bust in all respects. A great deal of malinvestment had to be unwound. It happened quickly, as it always does on the downside. In general, the Bust phase is about half as long as the Boom that preceded it. This was no exception. There were a couple of "dead cat bounces" along the way, as you might expect. The tech market declined until the Bust's bottom was reached about two years after the Boom's final peak.

As noted, tech then went into a six-and-a-half-year Echo. But while the market went dead flat, what was bubbling beneath the surface would eventually launch the next Boom—a spectacular one, as it has turned out. Specifically, these were the years during which the barriers to cybercommerce came crashing down, and the internet came of age. Because of broadband.

The requisite cable technology for bringing broadband to the masses had existed for some time. It was there in the '90s. But the billions upon billions of dollars needed to build out the information pipeline was a crushing weight upon a neophyte industry still struggling to attain simple profitability.

For a while, the obstacles made it look like the internet might turn out to be history's most overhyped technology. Nobel Prize economists such as Paul Krugman made statements like, "By 2005 or so, it will become clear that the internet's impact on the economy has been no greater than fax machines." The market was full of naysayers.

It wasn't like people weren't working to address the problem. But with debt overburdens, unreasonable expectations, and plummeting valuations, companies began missing analysts' guidance. Market gurus turned against the sector. Everyone was selling. Shorting ballooned, ratcheting up the pressure. Companies that tried to raise more money found themselves fighting against sentiment. Credit dried up. The once "exciting" cutting-edge technology sector became a place littered with significant investment losses and tragic stories.

Unfortunately for companies that had spent a lot of money trying to bring speedy internet to the multitudes, their investment had to be written down. And once write-downs of that magnitude begin, many companies enter a death spiral that I call the "great unwind." Accounting rules—such as GAAP (generally accepted accounting principles) and IFRS (international financial reporting standard)—usually require mark-to-market valuations of assets. You're not allowed to hide the losers or continue to carry overpriced purchases on your books at artificially inflated valuations. Or, at least, not until the Fed steps in to take them off your hands.

As the value of those assets craters, so does the book value of the company. Which in turn leads to increased write-downs and liquidations. In addition, companies with debt have something called debt covenants—specific financial ratios required by lenders to be maintained. As the book value decreased with such write-downs, many debt covenants were breached. When debt covenants are breached, the company is in violation of the debt, and further selloffs must occur to pay the debt holders. In many cases, the shareholders (since equity comes after debt holders in the company's ownership structure) were left with nothing after the debt was settled.

And so on, ever downward, amplifying the effect. That is if a company carries a $500 million market cap and its book value drops by 50 percent, which doesn't mean it'll level off at a $250 million market cap. Depending on how negative investors turn, the market cap—and stock price—could crash by 75 percent more or even go to zero (which happened to many a neophyte tech company during the Bust).

As the great unwind intensifies and companies scramble to stay afloat, management teams and boards of directors inevitably catch all of the blame. Often, they resign or are replaced, and one of the first things the new guys tend to do is try to stabilize balance sheets. Leading to more write-downs, more liquidations, and further stock-price declines.

The early 2000s were years of contrast for the internet. On the one hand, there was ongoing financial turmoil in the sector, with huge shakeups due to the conditions outlined above. Corporate stocks, especially those of the startups, got hammered. On the other hand, the major players were pouring cash into broadband, which exploded in availability and usage. As the internet finally began delivering the quality and speed people wanted, new users signed up as fast as they could. Between 2000 and 2001, for example, smack in the middle of the Bust, residential high-speed internet access subscriptions spiked by 50 percent. And that, as we now know, was just the beginning.

As time passed, all of the investment in broadband technology began paying off. The hardware didn't go anywhere. Fiber optic cables were laid, satellite links were established. This was all very desirable stuff. So, while surface interest in the sector dried up, the frantic activity behind the scenes was undiminished.

The massive write-downs that had to happen because of over-leveraging meant that the unsound companies perished. Their tangible assets disappeared into bankruptcy or were auctioned off by the banks to their savvier, better cashed-up competitors for pennies on the dollar (provided that those assets still had value—which they usually did to someone).

Many of the companies that went belly up had incredible assets and technologies that future companies harvested. Canada's largest tech company during that time was called Nortel. Without getting into all of the details, Nortel was an investment disaster for Canadians, and its parts were harvested (some say hacked) by one of China's largest tech companies, Huawei. My point is, not all the investment money was wasted, and many technologies weren't applicable until the hardware caught up many years later, as was the case with Nortel.

It was a period of what I call the "lonely trades," when companies sorted themselves out. Some prospered or at least held the line (even if their share prices declined). The stronger management teams understood that the key was to find ways to grow market share prudently without blowing up their cap structure. This meant avoiding excessive risks and lethal levels of debt while consolidating and repositioning their companies to seize the opportunities within a new, rapidly evolving environment.

Great opportunities are always there during an Echo. But although things may look quiet, there is always great volatility, too. Companies struggle to maintain their grip on a good balance sheet. Fail to do that, and you're toast. And by the way, many companies caught up in turmoil try to fight their way out of a hole through mergers or acquisitions. Very risky. It won't work if it means assuming too much additional debt; that decreases not increases, cap structure and sets up a potential "value trap." Plus, it can also mean taking on a business someone else has already failed at and which may be outside your real area of expertise—a recipe for disaster.

Think of it in terms of food: In a Boom, it's easy for all to feast; in a Bust, many starve, but all have to reduce their calorie consumption; in an Echo, one man's poison is another man's banquet.

As the weak hands were shaken out after the tech crash, the surviving healthy companies had top-quality assets they'd acquired on the cheap and they could continue building out the internet on the back of clean balance sheets. Plus, the cost of the underlying tech had also come down. Result: broadband became not only widely available but much more affordable as well. Every year, access to the internet became not only cheaper but faster and more data rich. This was a boon not only for users but also for increasingly complex retail businesses like Amazon and financial innovators like PayPal. The infrastructure's capabilities were finally catching up with these companies' visionary business plans.

I've used the technology cycle as my example because it's one that we're all familiar with and where the catalysts of Boom/Bust/Echo are starkly visible. It's also instructive of the basic general characteristics of an Echo—where, after a Bust, the uncompetitive are culled out, and malinvestments are written off. Only then can a sector consolidate itself and slowly prepare for the next leg up. I've seen the exact same things play out in every market, including my own specialty, natural resources.

SPOTTING THE ECHO

You want to capitalize on the Echo. Its late stages are where savvy investors go into an unloved sector and do the kind of buying that will provide life-changing profits as the next Boom takes off. But how do you recognize where we are in the cycle?

Well, you have to familiarize yourself with your chosen market. And I mean, in detail. Get to know its history. Learn the factors that tend to drive it upward or downward. Pay attention to the characteristics I bullet-listed above. Remember that Booms feature frantic business activity with a positive slant as if the good times will never end. Busts are equally frantic to the downside, as investors jam the exits while businesses scramble to stay afloat and often fail. Echos are the opposite of both of these. They're periods of very quiet activity, consolidations, and risk-aversion.

One good sign of a turning point is a change of capital inflows. That is, how much money are companies in the sector raising?

Businesses' ability to raise money is critical to the functioning of our economic system. It may happen privately, through venture capital providers, to fund startups and early-stage companies. Or it may happen publicly, for more mature companies, through an IPO on the NYSE or NASDAQ. But happen it must. Without seed money, it's a world of no innovation, no new companies, no progress.

Capital inflows track Boom, Bust, & Echo cycles very closely and following them can be very helpful in determining where you are at a given moment. As with stock prices, investments tend to rise during good times, dry up during a crash and stay more or less flat in between.

During a Boom, money is pouring into the sector. Then it drops off a cliff in the Bust. During the Echo, capital inflows will be rangebound. If they've been flat for years, then start to turn up, it's a signal that the next Boom is just around the corner.

Take my tech sector example. When it was booming, the amount of money raised went up almost vertically. After it peaked, it dropped off about equally dramatically. But if you looked at the activity on a graph, you'd notice this: there tends to be a subtle offset in correlation among the three.

The final peak on the NASDAQ was reached in early 2000, and the collapse began. But companies continued to raise substantial money into the beginning of 2001. It wasn't until then that capital inflow dried up and plunged to its 2003 low. On the other end, the Echo ended in the spring of 2009 (after the worst of the global financial crisis), as capital started flowing increasingly, quarter over quarter.

This is to say that the cycle of money-raising trails that of the stock market. Money continues to flow into the sector after stock investors have already panicked and started heading for shelter, and it doesn't come back as soon. On the front end, this seems to suggest that those financially backing new businesses remain optimistic longer than those who are just trading stocks. But it may simply reflect that a significant number of IPOs continue to happen after the obvious downturn because of prearranged financings. Or both.

On the back end, it's less complicated. Financiers are more reluctant to re-commit, and they wait longer.

In between, during the Echo, there will likely be some minor ups and downs in the flow of capital. Distinguishing those from real, sustained market shifts is key. It requires careful study.

Another indicator is the relationship of debt to market trends. As previously noted, the Echo is a period in which a lot of the bad debt taken on during the Boom is liquidated. But debt also is crucial to fueling market cycles—no available money, no new sharp up moves for the market. Access to debt drives Booms, while Busts are triggered when too many companies' debt burdens become insupportable.

The cycle stagnates during the Echo. Everyone is living in fear. Businesses are afraid to expand; banks are reluctant to lend. It's a self-perpetuating dilemma.

Following this is simple. You just track the accumulation of debt in a sector and compare it to its overall market cap. When debt and market cap begin rising in tandem—especially after years of being flat—then it's probably the late stages of an Echo.

And always remember that it's foolish to try to time markets. You don't have to be exact; you just have to position yourself on the right side of a developing trend.

CASE STUDY OF REAL INVESTMENT: ALTERRA POWER

President Obama had just won the election. Tens of billions of government stimulus and hundreds of billions of dollars of market funds were looking to cash in on the green energy dream.

Valuations were lofty and priced to perfection. That meant that the enterprise value of the green energy companies with "concepts" (not even permits or operating plants) were fully valued and needed to build their green energy projects on time and budget with 100 percent power output as promised.

There truly was a euphoria from bankers to investors; everyone felt good about the potential. Everyone forgot one critical item: economic project reality.

Alterra Power Corp. was one of the most exciting new startup green energy companies. More importantly, its chairman and largest investor was Ross Beaty. Ross Beaty is a legend in the mining world and has returned somewhere in the order of 8,000 percent returns to his early investors in mining. Alterra Power was his first foray into the energy patch.

In September of 2009, at a large investment conference in Denver, I moderated a panel that included Ross Beaty and other billionaires involved in the green energy sector.

The audience was eating up what the billionaires were pitching. Until one investor asked the audience what my opinion was, as the only mathematician in the group.

I stated quite openly that the whole green energy sector was priced to perfection and that these companies were nowhere near capable of delivering what they were trying to accomplish. I said I expected anywhere from a 50–75 percent correction. Then I'd figure out how to play it.

I was mocked for my comments. Alterra was over $20 per share at that time.

By late 2014, Alterra was working toward delivering everything it said it would do, and the stock was selling for about $3 per share.

The share price was down 85 percent from the Denver investment conference, yet the company was now operating and executing its business plan.

What happened? The traditional Boom, Bust, & Echo happened.

Billions of dollars of capital were lost as projects just didn't work as planned. The whole green sector imploded by 2013, and there was a massive investor turnover. The sector went from a Boom (2008–2010) to a Bust from (2011–2013) to an Echo (2014–2017).

In late 2014, I called up Ross Beaty and asked him out for a coffee, and he agreed. (Recall what I said about the best management teams making themselves accessible—and Ross is one of the best of the best.) I brought many pages of calculations to our meeting. A planned thirty-minute coffee went on for over two and a half hours. I had done my homework in a way Ross had never seen before.

The valuation metrics I mentioned above were screaming that Alterra was dirt cheap. After Ross's own position in the company, I became one of the largest shareholders of Alterra. Everywhere I went, I was pounding the table on Alterra as a valuation proposition. I was on the front page of Canada's largest newspaper talking about how this was the easiest double in the Canadian energy patch with very little risk.

Yet, nobody cared. Everyone just assumed because so much money was lost in green energy that it was uneconomic. The reduced cost of solar panels and wind farms was ignored. The business was doing better than at any point in its history, yet it was at its cheapest valuation ever.

An Echo looks like this. It's a lonely trade, but it's how big money is made in the resource sector.

THE LIQUIDITY ISSUE

During a bull market, liquidity is not an issue. Ideally, you want to build your positions during the Echo phase of the market, and liquidity is a big issue in the Echo.

If you invest in mining stocks—or any micro-caps, really—there is one thing you have to be aware of: liquidity.

Liquidity is the dollar volume a company trades on a publicly listed company. Many junior miners, for example, trade less than $250,000 a day in volume. That's peanuts for a publicly listed company.

On that type of volume, even a single moderately sized buy order of $100k or $200k would send the share price up 20 percent in a day. Or collapse the price if it was a sell order.

By the same token, if a lot of new shares hit the market, all at once, they're apt to have a sizable effect. This happens all the time with companies—mostly smaller ones—that are forced to do financings but would rather issue shares than taking on debt.

There was over $4 billion in equity financing in the junior mining sector in the first eight months of 2020, and most of those shares have been restricted. This means that investors were not allowed to sell until a given amount of time had passed. But for many of those shares, the waiting period ended in the fall, and they came free trading. That meant a lot of selling pressure, especially among shareholders sitting on a significant gain.

When a situation like that comes along, a major question you have to ask is: *Who will absorb those shares once holders are free to sell?*

If a company has low average liquidity, the answer to the question may be that buyers will be scarce, which means a drop in share price.

This sort of situation cuts two ways. If you're a shareholder with doubts about the company's long-term prospects (a position you should take great pains to avoid), then you may want to cut your potential losses by getting out before the free trading moment arrives. Or you may want to lock in profits at the current price level. But if you're a shareholder convinced of the company's potential, then a price drop, when and if it arrives, is a good point to pick up additional shares. And, if you don't own shares but have been eyeing the company for a while, any price decline would mark an ideal moment to buy your first tranche.

The absolute best way to build a position in a very illiquid market without running the share price higher is via corporate financings such as private placements (PPs).

PRIVATE PLACEMENTS AND KATUSA WARRANTS

In the world of professional investors, we understand that one of the best ways to make money is through private placements (PPs).

These are kind of a mystery to the average investor who never gets to participate in one. But what they are is simple. A company seeking financing announces a private placement or an equity financing where investors get to purchase shares in the company.

Ordinary investors don't get in on this action for one of several reasons: they may never even hear about them; they're not invited to participate; they don't have a specialty broker (discount brokers don't handle PPs, or they're not "accredited").

There are many ways of becoming an accredited investor, but for an individual, it generally means that you must have a net worth greater than $1 million, excluding the value of your primary residence, or your income must have been at least $200,000 per year (for the past two years), with a reasonable expectation of the same or increased income level for the current year.

The regulations were no doubt put in place with the best intentions to keep naïve investors who don't know what they're doing away from high-level deals like this. Some are risky, for sure, because there's no safety net.

On the other hand, plenty of investors who aren't millionaires yet are sophisticated enough to enter a PP with clear eyes. Thus, the authorities are now reconsidering the necessity for the regs, and we will probably see changes (or their elimination) in the near future.

Over the last decade, I have become one of the largest financiers of private placements in the resource sector. They are a great way to make serious money if you pick, structure, and choose wisely.

But what I really want when I consider investing in one is: I want to see listed, long-life warrants. Warren Buffett rarely talks about it publicly, but he is a big believer and taker of warrants in his financings. He got incredible warrants from GoldmanSachs during the global financial crisis, for instance.

A warrant comes as part of the unit during financing. It enables the holder to purchase its stock at a specific price before a specific expiration date. Think of a warrant as a kicker that can double your fun.

Let's say a financier via a private placement is offering one share for $1, and it comes with a listed full warrant for five years that can be exercised at $1.50. You buy 10,000 shares and receive 10,000 warrants. In this case, let's say the stock is now trading at $2 per share, and you can sell your shares for a quick $10,000 profit. But you can also hold onto your warrants and exercise them at any point in the following five years. Let's say the company really takes off and doubles again. Your warrant allows you to buy 10,000 shares at $1.50, which you can turn around and sell for $40,000. You pocket an additional $25,000 in profit. Nice, huh?

Here's the kind of deal that I live for: During the Echo phase of a cycle, a private placement comes up with a company I really like (for all the reasons we have discussed earlier in this Appendix). I want their shares, but I also want a full warrant that's exercisable for five years. And I want what's become known in the trade as the **Katusa Warrant**.

My friend, legendary resource investor Rick Rule, gave it that nickname in 2015, and it's stuck ever since. A Katusa Warrant simply means that I insist on one that will be listed and fully tradable once the company goes public.

Listed warrants have an advantage over non-listed warrants in the natural resource space. Because these companies' stocks are usually sub-$500 million, companies, large funds, and ETFs are prohibited by their own rules from trading in them. But they are not prohibited from trading warrants. Warrants are just an option, like a put or a call option. The big funds are allowed to buy these companies' listed warrants, but not the actual shares. Strange, but true. And when these big boys get interested in a warrant, it can have a very positive influence not only on the warrant price but also on the underlying shares' price.

THE WAY OF THE ALLIGATOR

In 1980, a geologist named Walter Alvarez and his father, the Nobel-Prize-winning scientist Luis Walter Alvarez came out with an outrageous revision of dinosaurs' natural history.

At the time, most of the scientific community firmly believed that dinosaurs went slowly extinct over a long period of time. But in what is now known as the "Alvarez hypothesis," the father/son team disagreed. They claimed dinosaurs went extinct due to the sudden effects of a large asteroid that collided with the earth and released over a billion times the atomic bombs' energy dropped on Hiroshima and Nagasaki. The impact caused huge tidal waves, earthquakes with a magnitude of ten or eleven, and massive, continent-wide fires.

The cataclysmic collision threw up a dust cloud that blocked sunlight, creating an "impact winter" that prevented photosynthesis for several years, killing off plants and herbivores, along with their predators. That was most of the planet's species, including all of the dinosaurs.

Years of studying the evidence, plus the discovery of a massive impact crater off the coast of the Yucatan peninsula in Mexico, put the debate to rest. The Alvarez hypothesis is now fully accepted. About 66 million years ago, that asteroid—estimated to have been six to ten miles in diameter (almost twice the size of Mount Everest)—caused the greatest extinction event in the planet's history. It's estimated that 75 percent or more of all species failed to survive.

Only a few, very-adaptable species made it through. You can probably guess one of them: the cockroach. Small creatures whose food chains were based on detritus (dead particulate organic material) or insect life—probably including our tiny, furry, distant human ancestors—would also have had a reasonable shot at making it. And "crocodilians" are members of this elite survivor club as well. This is the order of predatory reptiles that includes the alligator and the crocodile.

That's right: alligators survived what the dinosaurs couldn't.

Over sixty million years later, they're still going strong, essentially unchanged in all that time.

There are various theories as to why alligators have survived and thrived for so long. They're cold-blooded, which means they don't have to eat very often. They live in fresh and not saltwater, which seems to have increased their chances. They have incredible immune systems.

Plus, one major thing alligators had, and continue to have in their favor, is their brilliant and highly efficient hunting strategy. Alligators are "ambush predators," as opposed to "pursuit predators." They don't spend their days chasing gazelles or monkeys. They don't expend lots of energy sprinting after the catch.

Instead, alligators take a patient "sit and wait" approach to hunting. They spend long periods doing nothing but waiting in the water for the perfect time to strike at obvious opportunities. When unsuspecting prey approaches the water, alligators spring forward with awesome speed and force.

The alligator's ambush hunting strategy allows it to get huge returns on the energy invested in the hunt. It has helped the alligator become one of the most resilient, most successful species in the history of the planet.

I know you're not here for nature lessons. I'm telling you all this because I believe it reveals one of the great secrets for achieving investment success. Let me explain.

When we're kids, we're taught that we'll achieve success if we work hard and stay busy.

More hard work in the gym means performing better at sports. Working hard on your studies means getting into the right schools. Working long hours means getting ahead in business.

Don't get me wrong; hard work has its rewards. It's a necessary prerequisite to getting what you want in life. But at some point, hard work and especially its corollary, "staying busy," are actually detriments to investors. Staying busy typically translates into losing money instead of making money.

Most people who have earned enough money to invest have the natural urge to continue to "do something" and "stay busy." That's how we got the money in the first place, the reasoning goes.

But unless you're a skilled, lightning-fast day trader, the market does not reward frequent activity. In fact, it penalizes it.

The urge to "do something" leads you to be impatient and less selective with your investments. It forces you into mediocre opportunities. Said another way, your investments' quality typically moves inversely to your number of investments.

For investors who look to steadily increase their wealth by holding positions for months and years, an excess of activity is a killer. The market simply does not serve up truly great opportunities every day. Sometimes, we only get two or three per year.

For too many investors, having a large cash balance in an investment account feels like having a wad of cash in a casino. You don't want to let it burn a hole in your pocket. Why let it sit there and do nothing when you can "play" with the money? Why not at least take a shot at something new?

This amateur thinking is tragically flawed. It seals its own fate. It is why casinos earn billions of dollars in profit at the expense of impatient, probability-ignorant gamblers.

Sitting on cash can be very frustrating, I know. But if you have no investment capital when the great opportunities do arrive, then they're of no value to you. Doing nothing, staying patient, and waiting for the next no-brainer to show up is the right move. Then you're fully prepared to snap your jaws shut around it.

That's the Way of the Alligator.

All of this said...

Here's the thing:

My fundamental strategy is never to lose sight of what is truly important for achieving long-term investment success. And that is making sure I'm not exposing myself to catastrophic losses.

I didn't build a highly successful investment career on the back of classroom learning. Yes, my background in math has helped me—a lot. But most of the wisdom above came via the school of hard knocks, and I pass it along in the hope that you, too, will benefit from the insights I've been fortunate to gain over the past twenty years.

Successful investing is a marathon. It's not a sprint. Building long-term wealth for your family comes down to regularly making intelligent decisions that provide a good balance between capital growth and capital safety. It takes discipline. It takes market knowledge. It does not result from rolling the dice and "going big" on a single stock.

But most important of all, I have learned: do not lose sight of what matters.

WHAT TRULY MATTERS

In late May of 2012, at the age of thirty-three, I had incredible chest pains. I was rushed to the emergency room and ended up having quadruple bypass surgery.

And I learned that Discipline = Success in all aspects of life. Not just investing.

I've traveled to over a hundred countries, including hundreds of site trips, hotels, and flights.

Along the way, I actually lost track of what mattered in life. Early in my career, I started out with a financial goal in mind.

I hit that number sooner than I planned, so I went and wrote a new number—not basing it on any real logic, but mainly to see whether or not I could achieve it.

I was more than willing to put in the hard work, long hours, and personal sacrifice, and I quickly found the journey more enjoyable than the destination.

I hit my revised goal and kept rolling. Then the global financial crisis of late 2008 hit full force. I, alongside my subscribers, watched as our portfolios got crushed.

After that dreadful year, the resource sector came roaring back from 2009–2011, which were great years for the portfolio. But everything changed for me the day I was rushed into emergency heart surgery.

I share this story only because there is what I consider to be an important lesson or two in it.

LESSON 1: LISTEN TO YOUR BODY.

My career is based on being on the road, analyzing, and looking for the next big score. But when I started having chest pains combined with an odd tingling running down my left arm and pain in my jaw and teeth, I knew something was wrong.

I rushed to the hospital emergency room.

LESSON 2: IF THE FIRST ANSWER TO YOUR QUESTION DOESN'T SOUND RIGHT (OR LOGICAL), ASK FOR A SECOND OR THIRD OPINION UNTIL YOU ARE SATISFIED.

Call this the "Gut Confirmation Bias."

After I explained my condition, a nurse assured me I just had anxiety, and she advised me to go home and take the prescribed anxiety medication. Based on my age and physical condition, she was certain that, at worst, I'd had a panic attack.

Panic attack?

Anxiety?

My gut told me that wasn't it.

I *knew* it had to be something else. I requested to see a doctor and undergo more tests. The staff doctor didn't feel it was anything more than anxiety, and again I got the advice just to go home.

But I knew something was wrong.

I refused to leave the hospital until I saw a cardiologist. It makes sense, right? I believed I was having heart pains; I didn't want to listen to a nurse or a GP about having anxiety.

My amazing wife stood by me the whole time in full support, and that made a world of difference. I am a blessed individual.

Now, this is where the story gets interesting.

When I finally got to see a cardiologist, he (again) said I was suffering from anxiety and that I should go home and rest.

I requested an angiogram, and he finally, reluctantly, agreed to run some tests if I promised to leave right after.

By that time, I had invested forty hours in the whole ordeal. And the pain wasn't any better.

Five minutes into the angiogram, the cardiologist screamed for a nurse to get the surgeon immediately. I asked him what was going on. That was when he said to me: "*I am sorry. You need emergency triple bypass open-heart surgery* **right now**."

It was the first time that my life literally flashed before my eyes, and I realized I'd been wrong all these years.

During this ordeal, not once did I think about my money and business success.

All I could think of were things I hadn't done with my wife and loved ones.

I started to think about all the things I now realized I wanted to do. I thought to myself, *If I only get one more chance, I will change what I have done up to this point.*

As I was being wheeled into surgery, one of the nurses recognized me. During the surgery prep, she and the surgeons started asking me questions about their portfolios' stocks.

I didn't mind actually—the absurdity of it all kept my mind off what was about to happen to me and what might happen.

Maybe that's what they had in mind.

Then my last thought as the gas hit me was, *"One more chance, and I'll..."*

The situation inside my chest cavity was worse than what the angiogram had indicated: I needed a quadruple instead of a triple bypass.

The cardiologist who performed my surgery told my wife and me that he couldn't believe my heart was still ticking. I wouldn't have lasted another week before a massive heart attack would have taken me out due to all the blockages in my major arteries, he said.

The main reason I write about this personal experience is to reinforce the idea that you know yourself and your body better than anyone else—even doctors.

If you aren't getting answers, you feel are right or the service you require, don't be passive and just accept it. Request a second opinion. Go somewhere else. This applies not just to health but to all aspects of life.

Persistence often does pay off.

LESSON 3: RE-EVALUATE YOUR GOALS.

The third point of this story is goal setting.

What I neglected to do when I wrote down my financial goals was to include all my other goals in life—my health goals, exercise goals, charity goals, personal goals, and family goals, among others. Don't forget about what really matters in life: a balanced portfolio of family and friends. And hell, I will also include work and money because I love what I do, and all of these are important to me.

LESSON 4: CUT TIES WITH THE ANCHORS.

If any stock in your portfolio is causing you stress and dragging you down, you either own too much and should sell some or all of it, or speculation, and this style of investing isn't for you. There is nothing wrong with trying investing and, after giving it a fair try, admitting it's not for you. I believe the most prudent and successful way to succeed in speculating/investing in the cyclical resource sector is the way I am personally trying to go about it. The same can be said about cutting ties with negative, jealous people who gossip about others. They are no different than a crappy stock in your portfolio; get rid of it and focus on the good things.

Discipline = Success in resource markets and all aspects of life.

APPENDIX V

PAPER GOLD

GOLD IS TRADED IN PHYSICAL FORM—THE BUYING AND selling of coins and bars—and also in the much larger paper market.

You can participate in either, but personally, I'd never encourage speculating in the paper market. It's way too unpredictable. It's artificial. It's been speculated that the paper market is rigged. And you'd be playing against people with considerably more money, lower cost of capital, and way more market savvy than you have. They control the market, and they have a vested interest in seeing that they win, and you lose. You can try it if that's your inclination, and if you feel like you're particularly good at predicting the future but be aware of the risks.

On the flip side, I actively encourage you to invest in physical gold. Its price trend is favorable—for the reasons covered in Chapter 5—and that trend will remain in place for the foreseeable future. Gold is among the best investment you can make as a long-term, buy-and-hold asset.

That said, if you're an active investor, it's important that you at least understand the paper market—and its relationship to the trading of actual physical metal at the personal level—because that's where the ups and downs in gold's price originate in paper. For those readers with full knowledge of the COMEX, you can skip this part. For the rest of you, a brief primer:

The "paper" market consists of contracts to buy or sell gold on the Commodities Exchange, or COMEX, a part of the CME Group. (I say "paper" because that is the conventional term for the market, though we know that all modern contracts are merely electronic.) Each contract is for 100 ounces of gold. It carries a price and a settlement date.

As these contracts trade, the *spot price* of gold responds. *Spot* is the price at which the big traders are trading, and it's the current "price of gold" reported in the online tracking sites and newspapers. Technically, spot is the price set twice a day by the London Bullion Market—through a process more complicated than I need to go into here—but the price of the near-month futures contract on the COMEX tends to move in lockstep, and that's the price you'll generally see quoted as spot. (However, the spread between the two prices sometimes diverges enough to create arbitrage opportunities, a subject I'll touch on again later.)

On the COMEX, if there are more sellers of contracts than buyers, the spot price drops, and vice versa. However, the important thing here is to understand that this is *not* the price of gold you'll be charged in your local coin shop. I'll explain why in a moment.

You, or anyone, can buy physical gold on the COMEX. There are many hoops to jump through, the entry price is high, and taking delivery is a hassle, but it's not impossibly difficult. A committed individual can do it. Mostly, though, the buyers and sellers of physical gold on the COMEX use the exchange as an instrument for the purpose of hedging. Large jewelry companies, mints, and gold mining companies all hedge using the COMEX to shore up their balance sheets. Their bankers require some to do so; others do it to eliminate any volatility in price swings to their business cash flows.

So, even though what happens on the COMEX directly affects what you pay for gold in the here and now, it is first and foremost a *futures* market.

Examples: Let's say you're a miner who will be delivering a large quantity of gold to market six months hence. You're worried that gold's in a downtrend and that in six months, you will have lost a lot of your profit. So, you SELL six-month contracts at today's price (called *selling short*) to be assured you'll make the money you need to make. At settlement, you deliver the gold to the contracts' buyer. (You also take the risk that the price goes higher in the interim and that you miss out on the appreciation. But you probably sleep better at night.)

Or: Suppose you are a major jeweler who knows he will need a certain amount of gold in six months—but is afraid the price will be much higher at that time. So, you BUY enough contracts to ensure that you get what you need at a price you're willing to pay (called *going long*). At settlement, the seller of the contracts delivers your gold to you.

That kind of buying and selling of physical gold does take place on the COMEX. But it's the exception. For the most part, this is not a "real" market in tangible goods. It's a casino whose participants are interested in only one thing: laying bets against other players, with the goal of making paper profits.

Thus 99 percent of all contracts result in no physical gold ever changing hands. A speculator who thinks gold will be more expensive by the settlement date buys a long contract, sells it before settlement, and pockets the difference. If he thinks the gold price is headed lower, he sells a short contract and later buys it back. Or in either case, if the trade has gone against him, but he's still optimistic, maybe he rolls the contract over to the next month. Most trades are put on and closed in very short amounts of time.

It can get complicated, with rollovers and margins and hedge trades and whatnot, but there's no need to dig any deeper here. Those are the basics.

CME Group reports that the equivalent of 27 million ounces of gold trade on an average day. If a thirty-one-day contract month has twenty-two trading days, then that means nearly 600 million ounces of gold should be changing hands each month. As noted, they're not. Only a small fraction of that amount represents physical gold on the move. Considering that the world's physical annual gold production is slightly north of 100 million ounces, you can see how much larger the "paper" gold market is from the actual physical gold market.

What this means:

If you, as an individual investor, want to buy one contract—100 ounces of gold—on the COMEX and are willing to follow the requisite conditions, you're welcome to do it. But you are micro-scopically small potatoes. Your buy order, with the intention of taking delivery, will not affect the price one iota. You don't matter in the grand scheme of things.

The way the price moves depends on the behavior of the really big players. The whole market is relatively small. So, let's say you have the wherewithal (i.e., you're a big bank) to sell short 10 million ounces. That pushes the price down substantially. Other big players see a falling price and start closing out their own long positions; or, increasingly, large funds employ computer algorithms that *automatically* enter a sell order when a target price is breached. These sells drive the price even lower. It's a cascade effect. When the price hits the original seller's target, he buys back his contracts and pockets a tidy profit.

That kind of movement happens most often on the sell side. But it can happen on the buy side as well. Someone placing a massive buy order can convince others that a big up move is underway, persuading them to jump on the bandwagon because of FOMO (a nice modern acronym that describes much market behavior as driven by "fear of missing out," or FOMO). Again, the original buyer profits by selling out at a target price.

A lot of such movements take place within a single trading day. Computer algos have gotten so good that they can generate profits over very short periods in a way that is essentially risk-free for the major players.

Note: It's particularly risk-free if the player can engage in mischievous behavior such as front-running the market. Suppose a major bank has large clients who have set stop-loss limits on their gold investments. The bank will know where those limits are and can capitalize by deliberately triggering a client's stop-loss sales through its market manipulation. Front-running is technically illegal, though difficult to prove.

Nevertheless, price rigging in the paper gold market has been well-documented. Some of the largest banks that finance both the gold mining companies' debt and equities are involved in such schemes—and prosecuted. For example, Deutsche Bank copped to doing it a couple of years back and turned over a trove of relevant documents as part of its settlement. These included transcripts of voice recordings that featured traders cheerily conspiring to cheat their own clients and other market participants.

That document dump led the Department of Justice (DOJ) to charge six JPMorgan traders with crimes, and Bank of America also got caught up in the net and paid fines. This has led to a larger DOJ investigation into JPMorgan, the bank itself rather than specific employees, which may lead to the bank being charged under RICO statutes—meaning that it would be considered an ongoing criminal enterprise.

Such is the "legitimacy" of the futures market, and it's one reason why I believe that average investors should not fool around in it.

None of these shenanigans is likely to be a part of your own investment strategy, I trust.

However, I go into them by explaining why there can be such a disparity between the spot price of gold and the retail price of a coin. Spot is determined by the supply and demand for *contracts* in the paper world; retail is determined by the supply and demand for *physical metal* in the real world. The difference is the *premium* over spot that a retail seller demands.

The dealer whom you patronize doesn't give a damn about the paper market. He only cares how badly his customers want their physical metal vs. how much he can get his hands on to meet demand. When people are clamoring for coins when supply is short, the dealer will increase the premium, and the difference between retail and spot will grow—regardless of what the paper market is doing. Conversely, a supply glut means lower premiums, whether or not spot is rising.

My point is this: If you are an investor in physical gold—as I hope you are—don't bother worrying about what's happening in the spot market. It's not an accurate mirror of the physical market. Do not be dismayed at a sharp drop in the spot price; do not be irrationally exuberant at a steep rise. Either of those things could encourage you to try to play the paper gold market by latching onto the moment's trend. That's a good recipe for losing your shirt. Remember how powerful your competitors are. They'd be only too happy to take your money. As far as physical gold goes, just buy it, and hold onto it, and you will be amply rewarded.

Gold has maintained its value as the most-coveted physical asset for thousands of years. It's the ultimate form of wealth preservation. It strengthens with any dilution of a national currency (inflation) and in times of uncertainty. The long-term trend in a free market is always up, and the price you'll pay to own a coin (or receive when you sell one) will rise in response to many factors, but especially to increases in the money supply. Ultimately, the gyrations of the paper market are inconsequential.

Let me add one last note here. You will also see gold ETFs (like GLD) defined as a "paper gold" market. These are quite different from the paper on the COMEX. Basically, they're like shares of stock you buy in an equity market, each of which purports to be backed by a specific amount of physical gold held in a vault someplace. They have their place—mainly as a less risky way to play rising gold prices if that's your thing—but they are no substitute for the real deal, and I don't like them for several reasons. An ounce of physical gold in your personal possession will still be an ounce next year. A paper ounce's value will be degraded because of management fees. Plus, you can't trade that paper for actual metal. Plus, you are placing your trust in a company whose accounting procedures are, to put it as nicely as I can, not entirely transparent.

May the winds of profitable investment be always at your back.

THE FORBIDDEN CHAPTER

CONGRATS FOR MAKING IT THIS FAR. TO GET ACCESS TO the final chapter that the publishers thought was too controversial to print, please scan the QR code below and enjoy what you read. You will find it nowhere else.

Marin Katusa

Made in the USA
Las Vegas, NV
07 June 2021